T0347086

Journal of Education for Students Placed At Risk

First published by Lawrence Erlbaum Associates, Inc., Publishers
10 Industrial Avenue
Mahwah, New Jersey 07430

Transferred to digital printing 2010 by Routledge

Routledge

270 Madison Avenue
New York, NY 10016

2 Park Square, Milton Park
Abingdon, Oxon OX14 4RN, UK

Guest Editors' Introduction: Research on Direct Instruction in Reading

Martha Abele Mac Iver

Center for Social Organization of Schools
Johns Hopkins University

Elizabeth Kemper

Department of Education
North Carolina State University

This special issue of the *Journal of Education for Students Placed At Risk* (*JESPAR*) is devoted to recent studies of the Direct Instruction (DI) reading program and was inspired by several presentations on DI at the Fort Worth Reading Symposium, sponsored by the Fort Worth Independent School District in August 2000. As a result of that conference, a dialog began with many of the authors whose research is presented in this volume. Popularized by recent media reports, including the PBS documentary "The Battle of City Springs," as well as articles in *Education Week* (Manzo, 1998; Viadero, 1999), the *National Review* (Nadler, 1998), and *Policy Review* (Palmaffy, 1998), DI has enjoyed renewed prominence over the past several years. DI as a whole-school reform initiative grew out of the earlier reading instruction research of Sigfried Engelmann and his associates, who developed the Direct Instruction System for Teaching Arithmetic and Reading (DISTAR) program more than 30 years ago. Numerous experiments focused on how students learn most effectively shaped the many technical details of the program, which requires teachers to follow carefully scripted lessons in a specific sequence. Kameenui, Simmons, Chard, and Dickson (1997) offered a particularly useful and thorough overview of the model and related research, which we can summarize only briefly in the following introduction.

DI received particular attention as one of the most effective programs involved in Project Follow Through, a federal compensatory education program beginning in

Requests for reprints should be sent to Martha Mac Iver, Center for Social Organization of Schools, 3003 North Charles Street, Suite 200, Baltimore, MD 21218. E-mail: mmaciver@csos.jhu.edu

1967 for low-income students in kindergarten through third grade. Because many educators perceived DI as rigid, it was not eagerly embraced by the educational mainstream (Viadero, 1999). Longitudinal research conducted by developers of a competing preschool curricular model (and subsequently challenged on methodological grounds) also associated DI with higher rates of emotional problems and felony arrests when its students reached late adolescence and early adulthood (Bereiter, 1986; Gersten, 1986; Schweinhart & Weikart, 1997; Schweinhart, Weikart, & Larner, 1986a, 1986b). Plagued by negative publicity like this, DI continued as a sort of underground reform movement until the late 1990s, when it was named in a study by the American Institutes for Research as one of only three school reform programs to have a "strong" record of evidence of positive effects on student achievement (Herman et al., 1999). Other groups, including the American Federation of Teachers (AFT), have also identified it as a promising whole-school reform model (AFT, 1998).

Much of the research documenting positive achievement outcomes for DI was based, however, on special education student populations, as Slavin and Fashola (1998) noted. In fact, of the studies included in a recent meta-analysis of the effects of DI (Adams & Engelmann, 1996), more than one half used a special education student sample. Recognizing the important, documented effects of DI for learning-disabled and other special education students (e.g., Gersten, 1985; White, 1988), as well as the impact of DI on achievement in subjects such as mathematics, language, and spelling (see studies cited in Adams & Engelmann, 1996; Herman et al., 1999), we decided to focus this special issue more specifically on studies of DI in reading among regular education populations. As the following review of relevant literature on DI reading demonstrates, much of the research was published more than 1 decade ago, and was often based on student test scores from the early 1970s. It is essential for educators and policymakers to have access to more recent studies of DI, and this special issue seeks to address that need by gathering several studies from the late 1990s together in one place. After reviewing the previous research base for DI reading, we present a brief summary of each of the research articles, case studies, and commentaries included in this issue.

The best evidence for an effect of DI on reading achievement for regular education students comes from several reanalyses of data from Project Follow Through (Stebbins, St. Pierre, Proper, Anderson, & Cerva, 1977). As a "planned variation approach," Project Follow Through was designed so that the relative effectiveness of the different models could be evaluated. Beginning in the late 1960s, follow-through programs were implemented in roughly 4,000 classrooms distributed over more than 170 school districts and continued for more than 1 decade in some cases. The original Follow-Through evaluation (Stebbins et al., 1977) concluded that basic skills models (including DI) were the most effective of the programs studied. Although there has been considerable debate about the methodology of the Follow-Through study (Anderson, St. Pierre, Proper, & Stebbins, 1978; Bereiter & Kurland, 1981–1982; Gersten, 1984; Guthrie, 1977; House, 1979; House, Glass, McLean, & Walker, 1978; Wisler, Burns, & Iwamoto, 1978), it still provides a useful database for analyzing the impact of DI as a school reform program.

Becker and Carnine (1980) presented evidence that students in DI schools outperformed students in other Follow-Through reform models on the Metropolitan Achievement Tests (MAT; reading, math, spelling, and language) as well as the Wide Range Achievement Test (WRAT). By the end of third grade, after 4 years of DI, students in the follow-through sites were also performing at approximately grade level (50th percentile) in all areas except MAT reading (which Becker & Carnine, 1980, defined as testing primarily reading comprehension skills). On the MAT reading subtest, DI students were, on average, at the 40th percentile. Four of the nine cohorts of third-grade students at a New York City DI site (1973–1981) were achieving at grade level or above (higher than 45th percentile) on the MAT or the Stanford Achievement Test reading test after 4 years of DI (Meyer, Gersten, & Gutkin, 1983). The Meyer et al. report of the Abt evaluation summary of effects on Cohorts 2 and 3 indicated that the reading effect was significant only when a pooled comparison group was used, and only in one of the two cohorts under study (p. 247). Meyer et al. also presented evidence that reading achievement at this New York City DI site was significantly higher than the district as a whole.[1] A subsequent study (Gersten, Darch, & Gleason, 1988) noted that participation in a DI kindergarten appeared to be crucial: Students with 4 years of DI (including kindergarten) significantly outperformed control students on the MAT reading test at the end of third grade, whereas there was no difference between control students and those students who had experienced just 3 years (first through third grade) of DI.

Several other studies built on the early Follow-Through studies by examining later achievement effects on children who participated in the DI reform. Becker and Gersten (1982) analyzed fifth- and sixth-grade achievement effects for students from five different sites who all experienced 4 years of DI. They found strong, significant effects of DI on the WRAT reading test (a measure of decoding) for both fifth and sixth graders (as well as effects in spelling and math problem solving). The effect of DI on MAT reading (comprehension focused) and word knowledge was not as pronounced, in that most comparisons were not significant, but none favored the comparison group. Gersten et al. (1988) reported significantly higher ninth-grade reading scores on the California Achievement

---

[1]In one analysis, they compare average reading scores for the New York City direct instruction cohorts for each year 1973 through 1981 against pooled comparison group data from two cities over the time period 1973 through 1974. Another analysis relies on aggregate average grade equivalent scores, because neither normal curve equivalent scores nor individual level data were available.

Test (CAT)[2] for East St. Louis DI students (compared to control students)[3] 6 years after students had received the 4-year intervention. The effects were significant for students without DI kindergarten (effect size = +0.31, $p < .05$), as well as for those who attended a DI kindergarten (effect size = +0.49, $p < .01$). Similarly, Gersten and Keating (1987) reported significantly higher ninth-grade achievement scores on the CAT in reading and mathematics for DI cohorts from an anonymous city (called Finley), as well as a nearly significant effect of early DI on ninth-grade reading scores in Flint, Michigan. DI students from Flint were also significantly less likely than their comparison group to have an attendance problem (10 or more absences per year) in high school or to be retained in grade (Gersten & Keating, 1987). Meyer (1984) followed the Follow-Through DI students in New York City through high school to ascertain the long-term academic effects of the intervention. Compared to control groups, significantly more of the DI students graduated from high school (59.5% vs. 37.6%), applied to college (34% vs. 18.5%), and were accepted to college (34% vs. 17%). Significantly more of the control students were retained (32.6% vs. 21.4%) or dropped out of school (46% vs. 27.7%). DI students scored significantly higher on ninth-grade reading and math tests as well.

Apart from the studies based on the original Project Follow Through data, the only other longitudinal study (examining students who have experienced a DI intervention for at least 3 years) appears to be the study of the Alliance of Quality Schools in Broward County, Florida (Varela-Russo, Blasik, & Ligas, 1997, 1998).[4] DI is one component of a larger reform strategy in a group of 32 schoolwide Title I elementary schools within that district. More than 80% of students in the schools implementing this reform program were eligible for free or reduced-price lunch. Analysis of nearly 1,000 students who experienced DI for at least 3 years, compared to a demographically similar group of control students, indicated that DI in reading was able to nearly close the reading achievement gap between program and control students in third and fourth grades (though both groups were achieving at just the 37th percentile on the reading

---

[2]We assume (though the authors do not directly specify) that the reported average grade equivalents and percentiles for reading for direct instruction and control groups refer to a "total reading" score on the California Achievement Test (a combination of vocabulary and comprehension).

[3]Except for asserting that comparison students are "demographically similar students who received the district's typical curriculum in the early grades," this article does not report how the comparison groups for this ninth-grade analysis were selected. Because the sample sizes for the ninth-grade control groups are nearly three times larger than those for the control group at the end of third grade, the study does not appear to follow the same control students over time.

[4]A revised and updated version of these reports appears in Maria R. Ligas' contribution to this special issue. Despite numerous popular articles about the effectiveness of direct instruction at Wesley Elementary School in Houston, Texas over the past 2 decades (e.g., Manzo, 1998; Palmaffy, 1998), there do not appear to be any published reports (with the exception of, "On Track: Fifteen Years of Student Improvement," 1992) that systematically analyzed the impact of the reform on achievement measures for students at the school.

comprehension subtest of the Stanford Achievement Test–Eighth Edition). However, DI students' reading scores decreased, on average, in fifth grade, falling below the comparison group and reopening the gap. One of the recommendations in the 1997 report was to "enhance the elements of the Alliance program to strengthen reading and math achievement in Grade 5" (Varela-Russo et al., 1997, p. 19).

Although Camden, NJ was not part of the original Follow-Through study, it began implementing DI in at least one school in 1978, and received a Follow-through grant in 1988 to implement DI in one elementary school. Several published studies of DI in Camden[5] yielded mixed results regarding the impact of 1 or 2 years of DI on reading achievement for second graders. A 1-year experimental study of DI in two second-grade classrooms (with randomly selected children and teachers) yielded a significant positive effect of DI on Comprehensive Test of Basic Skills (CTBS) reading vocabulary scores (DiObilda & Brent, 1985–1986). A small sample size ($n =$ 47, in each group) may have prevented the positive effect of DI on comprehension scores from reaching statistical significance. Brent, DiObilda, and Gavin (1986) also reported a positive effect of 2 years of DI instruction by experienced teachers on second-grade reading scores, whereas students with an inexperienced DI teacher performed no better than control students. In a larger study of Camden second graders who had experienced 2 years of DI, Brent and DiObilda (1993) found no effects of DI on CTBS reading scores, concluding the program was "as effective as traditional programs that are aligned with a specific standardized test" (p. 337).

Other short-term studies of the impact of DI on reading achievement were similarly mixed. In a 1-year study in which 24 second-grade students were randomly assigned either to DISTAR reading or "Johnny Right to Read" programs, Summerell and Brannigan (1977) found significantly greater gains in reading comprehension (measured by the paragraph meaning subtest of the Stanford Achievement Test) for the DISTAR group, but no significant differences on the word meaning subtest. A study of a 15-week remedial reading program (averaging a total of 45 hr of instruction) for second through sixth graders, in which a total of 72 students were randomly assigned either to DISTAR or another structured reading program, found that both groups made equivalent gains (Richardson, DiBenedetto, Christ, Press, & Winsberg, 1978). One-year quasi-experimental studies of the impact of DI in reading on first graders found evidence of an effect on language ability (measured by the Slosson Intelligence Test; Sexton, 1989), spelling and word analysis (measured on the Iowa Test of Basic Skills; Snider, 1990), and reading vocabulary (measured by the Gates McGinitie Reading Test; Bowers, 1972). However, Bowers did not find evidence of a significant effect of DISTAR on reading comprehension,[6] and Snider found no difference between DISTAR and control groups on reading and vocabu-

---

[5]The school where direct instruction was implemented was typical of the district in which 60% of children lived in poverty, and over one half of families received welfare.

[6]Our reading of Bowers (1972) differs from that of Adams and Engelmann (1996, p. 53).

lary subtests of the Iowa Test of Basic Skills. Gersten, Carnine, Zoref, and Cronin (1986) presented evidence of considerable growth in reading achievement among first graders in a DISTAR program (from the 18th percentile on the CTBS Level A reading readiness test in spring of the kindergarten year to the 46th percentile on the CTBS Level B total reading score in spring of the first-grade year), but there was no control group in that particular study. Many short-term experimental studies of DI techniques, generally with small groups of remedial students, have indicated significant effects of DI (e.g., Kaiser, Palumbo, Bialozor, & McLaughlin, 1989).

Although there is considerable evidence that DI has a significant effect on decoding skills in reading as well as on vocabulary skills, there is much less evidence of an impact of the program on reading comprehension. It is possible that the impact of DI on reading comprehension might be more pronounced in sites where implementation is further advanced, given that it often takes several years for a reform effort to take root sufficiently to produce positive results (Fullan, 1999). Several studies of DI have reported a high correlation between achievement results and fidelity of implementation (Gersten & Carnine, 1980; Gersten et al., 1986) or levels of DI experience among teachers (Brent et al., 1986). It may simply take time for teachers to gain sufficient experience and implementation to be solidified before an effect emerges. Given this consideration, the dearth of longitudinal studies other than the Follow-Through study of DI is unfortunate.[7] There may indeed be a reading comprehension effect that simply has not been uncovered yet in the studies to date.

DI advocates have directly addressed the issue of their difficulties in achieving an effect on comprehension scores. Becker (1977) argued that standardized tests of reading comprehension assume a working vocabulary that gives children from middle class homes (where they develop such a vocabulary) an advantage over children whose families do not similarly contribute to such vocabulary development. Because of this, he outlined a specific plan to build vocabulary development into the program. In addition, DI advocates have outlined the importance of teaching reading comprehension skills directly (Carnine, Silbert, & Kameenui, 1997; Gersten & Carnine, 1986). Short-term experimental studies have shown convincingly the effectiveness of DI in strategies for summarizing passages and drawing inferences (Adams, Carnine, & Gersten, 1982; Carnine, Kameenui, & Woolfson, 1982; Carnine & Kinder, 1985; Carnine, Stevens, & Clements, 1982; Patching, Kameenui, Carnine, Gersten, & Colvin, 1983; Ross & Carnine, 1982).

Because most of the published research on DI is more than 10 years old, and questions remain about its effectiveness in improving reading comprehension, we believe the studies included in this special issue represent a particularly important contribution to the literature on DI and whole-school reform efforts. Four longitu-

---

[7]The absence of a peer-reviewed research study on Wesley Elementary is particularly disappointing in this regard.

dinal research studies from the late 1990s examine the impact of DI on reading achievement in Broward County (Florida), Houston, Fort Worth, and Baltimore. Maria R. Ligas analyzed the impact of the 5-year Alliance of Quality Schools project in Broward County, Florida, which utilized DI Reading Mastery as the major component of reading instruction. Growth scores in reading comprehension for alliance school students in Grades 3 through 8 were compared to district averages, adjusted so that program and comparison students had the same demographic characteristics. Coleen D. Carlson and David J. Francis presented results of their external evaluation of the Rodeo Institute for Teacher Excellence program in which the DI Reading Mastery curriculum was implemented over a 4-year period in kindergarten, first-, and second-grade classrooms in a total of 20 schools. Their longitudinal study of experimental and comparison school cohorts analyzes the impact of DI reading instruction on several standardized measures of reading achievement. O'Brien and Ware provided a detailed evaluation of how both DI and Open Court reading programs were implemented in a total of 61 schools in the Fort Worth Independent School District in 1998–1999 and 1999–2000. They analyzed the impact of these programs on reading achievement for kindergarten, first, and second graders. Mac Iver and Kemper examined the effects of DI reading in a 4-year longitudinal study of kindergarten and second-grade cohorts at six experimental and six comparison schools in Baltimore. The study focuses on reading achievement for these cohorts, primarily in third and fifth grades, respectively, after 4 years, as well as on 1-year effects of DI reading for all third- and fifth-grade students at the study schools in 1999–2000.

In this special issue, we also include two case studies focused on particular schools, written by advocates of DI. Muriel Berkeley, who has served as Executive Director of the Baltimore Curriculum Project, presented a case study of City Springs Elementary, one of the schools included in the Mac Iver and Kemper (2002, this issue) research study. Berkeley described the transformation of City Springs (which was also the subject of the PBS documentary, "The Battle of City Springs") from a chaotic school into an oasis of order. Her article documents the dramatic growth in student achievement at the school over the past 5 years since implementation of DI in reading began. She also analyzed the systemic factors that impede full implementation of DI and may limit the achievement effects of the program elsewhere in the district. Bonita Grossen, who is currently leading implementation of a "new generation" of DI programs in secondary schools throughout the country, described components of the BIG Accommodation model and analyzed its effects on reading and mathematics achievement over a 2-year period in a Sacramento middle school. She also discussed developments in the DI teacher-training model and electronic progress monitoring of student achievement.

The commentary by Jerry Silbert (2002/this issue) of the University of Oregon provides an insightful look at these studies from the DI developers' point of view. Barak Rosenshine (2002/this issue), well known for his many publications on school effectiveness, reading instruction, and explicit teaching, followed DI research closely over the past 3 decades, and offers a thoughtful critique of these studies.

We believe this set of articles, published together in this special issue of *JESPAR,* represents a significant contribution to the current national discussion about reading instruction and the utility of whole-school reform models in seeking to raise the achievement of students placed at risk of academic failure. With updates expected for at least a couple of these studies in the next year, we hope to begin a continuing dialogue among researchers regarding DI.

ACKNOWLEDGMENTS

The guest editors wish to thank research assistants Kathleen Romig and Naomi Graeff for their help in bibliographic research and compiling the literature review, and Rafeeq Hasan for help in manuscript and table preparation for this special issue. We are also deeply indebted to *JESPAR* assistant editor Sarah Heneghan, who shepherded the editing process under a very tight production schedule.

REFERENCES

Adams, A., Carnine, D., & Gersten, R. (1982). Instructional strategies for studying content area texts in the intermediate grades. *Reading Research Quarterly, 18,* 27–55.

Adams, G. L., & Engelmann, S. (1996). *Research on Direct Instruction: 25 years beyond DISTAR.* Seattle, WA: Educational Achievement Systems.

American Federation of Teachers (AFT). (1998). *Six promising schoolwide programs for raising student achievement.* Retrieved June 12, 2001, from http://www.aft.org/edissues/whatworks/wwreading.htm

Anderson, R. B., St. Pierre, R. G., Proper, E. C., & Stebbins, L. B. (1978). Pardon us, but what was the question again? A response to the critique of the Follow Through evaluation. *Harvard Educational Review, 48,* 161–170.

Becker, W. C. (1977). Teaching reading and language to the disadvantaged—What we have learned from field research. *Harvard Educational Review, 47,* 518–543.

Becker, W. C., & Carnine, D. W. (1980). Direct Instruction: An effective approach to educational intervention with the disadvantaged and low performers. In B. B. Lahey & A. E. Kazdin (Eds.), *Advances in clinical child psychology* (Vol. 3, pp. 429–473). New York: Plenum.

Becker, W. C., & Gersten, R. (1982). A follow-up of Follow Through: The later effects of the Direct Instruction model on children in fifth and sixth grades. *American Educational Research Journal, 19,* 75–92.

Bereiter, C. (1986). Does Direct Instruction cause delinquency? *Early Childhood Research Quarterly, 1,* 289–292.

Bereiter, C., & Kurland, M. (1981–1982). A constructive look at Follow Through results. *Interchange, 31*(12), 1–22.

Berkeley, M. (2002/this issue). The importance and difficulty of disciplined adherence to the educational reform model. *Journal of Education for Students Placed At Risk, 7,* 221–239.

Bowers, W. M. (1972). *Evaluation of a pilot program in reading for culturally disadvantaged first grade students.* Unpublished doctoral dissertation, University of Tulsa, Oklahoma.

Brent, G., & DiObilda, N. (1993). Effects of curriculum alignment versus Direct Instruction on urban children. *Journal of Educational Research, 86,* 333–338.

Brent, G., DiObilda, N., & Gavin, F. (1986). Camden Direct Instruction Project 1984–1985. *Urban Education, 21,* 138–148.

Carlson, C. D., & Francis, D. J. (2002/this issue). Increasing the reading achievement of at-risk children through Direct Instruction: Evaluation of the Rodeo Institute for Teacher Excellence. *Journal of Education for Students Placed At Risk, 7,* 141–166.

Carnine, D., Kameenui, E., & Woolfson, N. (1982). Training of textual dimension related to text-based reference inference. *Journal of Reading Behavior, 14,* 335–340.

Carnine, D., & Kinder, D. (1985). Teaching low-performing students to apply generative and schema strategies to narrative and expository material. *Remedial and Special Education, 6*(1), 20–30.

Carnine, D., Silbert, J., & Kameenui, E. (1997). *Direct Instruction reading* (3rd ed.). Upper Saddle River, NJ: Prentice Hall.

Carnine, D., Stevens, C., & Clements, J. (1982). Effects of facilitative questions and practice on intermediate students' understanding of character movies. *Journal of Reading Behavior, 14,* 179–190.

DiObilda, N., & Brent, G. (1985–1986). Direct Instruction in an urban school system. *Reading Instruction Journal, 29,* 2–5.

Fullan, M. G. (1999). *Change forces: The sequel.* Philadelphia: Falmer.

Gersten, R. (1984). Follow Through revisited: Reflections on the site variability issue. *Educational Evaluation and Policy Analysis, 6,* 109–121.

Gersten, R. (1985). Direct Instruction with special education students: A review of evaluation research. *The Journal of Special Education, 19,* 41–58.

Gersten, R. (1986). Response to "Consequences of three preschool curriculum models through age 15." *Early Childhood Research Quarterly, 1,* 293–302.

Gersten, R., & Carnine, D. (1980). Measuring implementation of a structured educational model in an urban school district: An observational approach. *Educational Evaluation Policy Analysis, 4,* 67–69.

Gersten, R., & Carnine, D. (1986). Direct instruction in reading comprehension. *Educational Leadership, 43*(7), 70–78.

Gersten, R., Carnine, D., Zoref, L., & Cronin, D. (1986). A multifaceted study of change in seven inner-city schools. *The Elementary School Journal, 86,* 257–276.

Gersten, R., Darch, C., & Gleason, M. (1988). Effectiveness of a Direct Instruction academic kindergarten for low-income students. *The Elementary School Journal, 89,* 227–240.

Gersten, R., & Keating, T. (1987). Long-term benefits from Direct Instruction. *Educational Leadership, 44*(6), 28–31.

Grossen, B. J. (2002/this issue). The BIG Accommodation model: The direct instruction model for secondary schools. *Journal of Education for Students Placed At Risk, 7,* 241–263.

Guthrie, J. T. (1977). Follow Through: A compensatory education experiment. *Reading Teacher, 31,* 240–244.

Herman, R., Aladjem, D., McMahon, P., Masem, E., Mulligan, I., O'Malley, A., et al. (1999). *An educators' guide to schoolwide reform.* Washington, DC: American Institutes for Research.

House, E. R. (1979). The objectivity, fairness, and justice of federal evaluation policy as reflected in the Follow Through Evaluation. *Educational Evaluation and Policy Analysis, 1,* 28–42.

House, E. R., Glass, G. V., McLean, L. D., & Walker, D. F. (1978). No simple answer: Critique of the Follow Through Evaluation. *Harvard Educational Review, 48,* 128–160.

Kaiser, S., Palumbo, K., Bialozor, R. C., & McLaughlin, T. F. (1989). The effects of Direct Instruction with rural remedial students: A brief report. *Reading Improvement, 26,* 88–93.

Kameenui, E. J., Simmons, D. C., Chard, D., & Dickson, S. (1997). Direct Instruction reading. In S. A. Stahl & D. A. Hayes (Eds.), *Instruction models in reading* (pp. 59–84). Mahwah, NJ: Lawrence Erlbaum Associates, Inc.

Ligas, M. R. (2002/this issue). Evaluation of Broward County alliance of quality schools project. *Journal of Education for Students Placed at Risk, 7,* 117–139.

MacIver, M. A., & Kemper, E. (2002/this issue). The impact of Direct Instruction on elementary students' reading achievement in an urban school district. *Journal of Education for Students Placed At Risk, 7,* 197–220.

Manzo, K. K. (1998, June 10). Drilling in Texas. *Education Week, 17,* 32–37.

Meyer, L. A. (1984). Long-term academic effects of the Direct Instruction Project Follow Through. *The Elementary School Journal, 84,* 380–394.

Meyer, L. A., Gersten, R., & Gutkin, J. (1983). Direct Instruction: A Project Follow Through success story in an inner-city school. *The Elementary School Journal, 84,* 241–252.

Nadler, R. (1998). Failing grade. *National Review, 50,* 38–39.

O'Brien, D. M., & Ware, A. M. (2002/this issue). Implementing research-based reading programs in the Fort Worth Independent School District. *Journal of Education for Students Placed At Risk, 7,* 167–195.

On Track: Fifteen Years of Student Improvement. (1992, Winter). *Direct Instruction News.* Houston, TX: Wesley Elementary School.

Palmaffy, T. (1998). No excuses: Houston educator Thaddeus Lott puts failing schools to shame. *Policy Review, 87,* 18–23.

Patching, W., Kameenui, E., Carnine, D., Gersten, R., & Colvin, G. (1983). Direct instruction in critical reading skills. *Reading Research Quarterly, 18,* 406–418.

Richardson, E., DiBenedetto, B., Christ, A., Press, M., & Winsberg, B. (1978). An assessment of two methods for remediating reading deficiencies. *Reading Improvement, 15,* 82–95.

Rosenshine, B. (2002/this issue). Helping students from low-income homes read at grade level. *Journal of Education for Students Placed At Risk, 7,* 273–283.

Ross, D., & Carnine, D. (1982). Analytic assistance: Effects of example selection, students' age, and syntactic complexity. *Journal of Educational Research, 75,* 294–298.

Schweinhart, L. J., & Weikart, D. P. (1997). The high/scope preschool curriculum comparison study through age 23. *Early Childhood Research Quarterly, 12,* 117–143.

Schweinhart, L. J., Weikart, D. P., & Larner, M. B. (1986a). Child-initiated activities in early childhood programs may help prevent delinquency. *Early Childhood Research Quarterly, 1,* 303–312.

Schweinhart, L. J., Weikart, D. P., & Larner, M. B. (1986b). Consequences of three preschool curriculum models through age 15. *Early Childhood Research Quarterly, 1,* 15–45.

Sexton, C. W. (1989). Effectiveness of the DISTAR Reading I Program in developing first graders' language skills. *Journal of Educational Research, 82,* 289–293.

Silbert, J. (2002/this issue). Commentary. *Journal of Education for Students Placed At Risk, 7,* 265–271.

Slavin, R., & Fashola, O. (1998). *Show me the evidence!* Thousand Oaks, CA: Corwin.

Snider, V. E. (1990). Direct instruction reading with average first graders. *Reading Improvement, 27,* 143–148.

Stebbins, L. B., St. Pierre, R. G., Proper, E. C., Anderson, R. B., & Cerva, T. R. (1977). *Education as experimentation: A planned variation model* (Vol. 4-A). Cambridge, MA: Abt Associates.

Summerell, S., & Brannigan, G. (1977). Comparison of reading programs for children with low levels of reading readiness. *Perceptual and Motor Skills, 44,* 743–746.

Varela-Russo, C., Blasik, K., & Ligas, M. R. (1997, July). *Alliance of Quality Schools Evaluation Report.* Broward County, FL: The School Board of Broward County.

Varela-Russo, C., Blasik, K., & Ligas, M. R. (1998, September). *Alliance of Quality Schools Evaluation Report.* Broward County, FL: The School Board of Broward County.

Viadero, D. (1999, March 17). A direct challenge. *Education Week, 18,* 41–43.

White, W. A. T. (1988). A meta-analysis of the effects of Direct Instruction in special education. *Education and Treatment of Children, 11,* 364–374.

Wisler, C. E., Burns, G. P., Jr., & Iwamoto, D. (1978). Follow Through redux: A response to the critique by House, Glass, McLean, and Walker. *Harvard Education Review, 48,* 171–185.

Evaluation of Broward County Alliance of Quality Schools Project

Maria R. Ligas
The School Board of Broward County, Florida

This article examines the evaluation of the Alliance of Quality Schools project, a 5-year project focusing on at-risk students in Broward County, Florida. The purpose of the evaluation was to determine the effect that the project had on selected academic and behavioral student indicators after its 5th year of implementation. This article focuses only on the findings related to the effect that the project has had on reading performance. Findings related to mathematics performance and student behavior can be found by reviewing the 5th-year evaluation report (Ligas, 1999).

The project's mission, based on the philosophy that all children can learn, is to help the greatest number of at-risk students achieve at their highest performance level. In addition to a strong emphasis on Direct Instruction (DI), the Alliance of Quality Schools (AQS) initiative utilizes Accelerated Reader and Computer Assisted Instruction. The project has been evaluated yearly, from the 1994–1995 school year to the 1998–1999 school year. Fifth-year evaluation findings related to student achievement indicated that the effect of the project on academic achievement for elementary and middle school students enrolled at the Alliance schools has varied by grade level and year. The highest increases in student performance occurred at the 4th-grade level for reading and at the 5th-grade level for mathematics. These increases seem to be closely aligned to the grade levels targeted for school accountability by the state of Florida.

EVALUATION OF ALLIANCE OF QUALITY SCHOOLS

The Alliance of Quality Schools is a Broward County Public Schools (BCPS) initiative that arose from the need to provide educational support to students and staff of eligible Title I schools operating schoolwide projects. The project was dedicated to the belief that all children can learn, under a philosophy and process for continuous school improvement, as set forth in Broward County School Board Policy 1403 (The School Board of Broward County [SBBC], Florida, 1995). Under Policy

Requests for reprints should be sent to Maria Ligas, Office of Research and Evaluation, Research Services, 600 SE 3rd Avenue, 3rd Floor, Fort Lauderdale, FL 33301. E-mail: ligasmaria@hotmail.com

1403, the SBBC established an accountability and school improvement system based on the performance of students and educational programs. The system supports the framework for school improvement and accountability and shares the belief that all students can learn at different rates and with different preferential styles.

PROGRAM DESCRIPTION AND COMPONENTS

The Alliance of Quality Schools is a research-based, learner-verified academic and behavioral intervention model involving reading, spelling, writing, and mathematics. Major goals of the Alliance of Quality Schools are, (a) to provide students with high-quality instruction that will enable them to function academically at grade level; and (b) to enhance and support student achievement in all academic areas through quality staff development and research-proven, effective educational strategies and technology.

To enhance commonality of procedure throughout the school, all staff members receive training in research-based academic curriculum and classroom management. In addition, during the summer term, a 5-day preservice training occurs through the Summer Institute. This program is meant to ensure that teachers have the opportunity to apply what they have learned. The training includes specific teaching techniques, program rationale, and expected student outcomes (Colvin, 1994). In each classroom, an average of 20 min per day is allocated to classroom visitation by school support staff, including the principal, assistant principal, and other support staff members.

Teaching is facilitated through on-site curriculum facilitators, school coaches, and consultants. Curriculum facilitators ensure that teachers adhere to schedules, follow program procedures, and use the classroom libraries effectively. They also arrange, coordinate, and monitor in-service training; monitor student progress; and assist in regrouping children who may be performing academically too high or too low for their assigned group. The purpose of on-site coaching is to provide staff with feedback on program implementation, not evaluation of teacher performance.

School Coaches are external coaches assigned to two alliance schools. They go to each site 2 days per week, alternating schools on Fridays to accommodate the needs of their two assigned schools. The coaches are responsible for (a) providing on-site feedback to each staff member in their classroom at least four times each year, (b) providing on-site assistance and coaching to members of the Behavior Team (BT) in the area of effective instruction, (c) assisting the curriculum facilitator in developing ease of entry procedures for incoming students, and (d) assisting in diagnosing the needs of students who are not making adequate progress academically or behaviorally.

Also, the Alliance model calls for each Alliance school to be involved in implementing a schoolwide management plan that teaches students school routines and expectations on an ongoing basis (Colvin, 1994; Cotton, 1990). Staff members receive specific training on the topic of managing students during the Summer Institute, with continuing staff development and on-site coaching offered throughout the school year. Each Alliance school has a BT specialist or in-house expert who provides modeling for staff working with difficult students. Students who are identified as needing additional assistance have individualized behavior plans developed by the staff.

A family component, in conjunction with other programs such as Even Start, Head Start, First Start, and Home Instructional Program for Preschool Youngsters, strives to improve students' and parents' basic skills and attitudes toward education. This component also aims to improve parenting skills, children's preliteracy and school readiness skills, and the overall quality of parent–child relationships.

Accountability

The Alliance program provides ongoing assessment through in-program mastery checks and staff development based on the demonstrated needs of the students. This continuous assessment helps the teachers determine how well they are implementing the new approaches and identify whether students are learning at the desired rate of proficiency (Colvin, 1994). Also, yearly evaluation findings provide relevant information for program improvement.

Curriculum

Alliance staffs assess students to ensure that they are receiving instruction in a curriculum that will enable them to perform academically on or above grade level in all subjects. All Alliance schools utilize a *unified comprehensive curriculum* approach, which includes the implementation of Direct Instruction (DI).

DI.   DI is an intensive intervention designed to increase the amount and quality of learning by systematically developing important background knowledge, applying that knowledge, and linking it to new knowledge. DI includes activities that carefully account for individual differences in required background knowledge. In this way, all students can build hierarchies of understanding, not just those who come to school with the appropriate background knowledge (Carnine, Silbert, & Kameenui, 1997; Colvin, 1994).

DI has been documented to be successful with at-risk first, second, and third graders in increasing basic and cognitive skills, in improving student self-concept and self-esteem, and in gaining parental support (Abt Associates, 1977; Gersten &

Dimino, 1990; Haney, 1977). Research results have suggested that the instructional sequence underlying DI practices reduces the disruptive behavior of students (Nelson, Johnson, & Marchand-Martella, 1996).

Implementation of DI.   The Alliance project uses DI as the foundational core of the program; however, it never intended to use the Reading Mastery (RM) series as the only instructional tool. In addition to using the scope and sequence of RM as the foundation, school staffs are encouraged to adapt and personalize the teaching and learning process according to students' needs. Schools have the ability to move into additional reading basals as the principal sees fit, based on data.

During the implementation of DI in the primary grades, all Grade K–2 classes start with Language for Learning (Direct Instruction System for Teaching Arithmetic and Reading Language) and RM as the reading core. Daily supplements with grade-level books occur from 60% to 80% of the time.

Schools are encouraged to have students complete RM II and transition into the reading approach that the school feels is the best fit for the student population. Some classes in Grades 3 through 5 use RM as the reading basal for all students. Some schools use a combination of RM III through VI and a reading series from Houghton Mifflin's, *Invitation to Literacy* (Cooper et al., 1996), McGraw-Hill's, *A New View* (Aoki et al., 1995), or both.

In the fall, teachers are provided staff development pertaining to the correct use of RM. Alliance coaches, all former district teachers with proven success and personalization of DI, provide the staff development. Six Alliance staff members are national staff developers in DI, as acknowledged by Science Research Associates. Elementary school Alliance Coaches spend the majority of their time with Grades 3 through 5 due to the district-wide focus on the state assessment. They also spend about 20% to 30% of their time in the primary grades.

Every 20 lessons, teachers are asked to follow up on students' fluency level and accuracy measures in RM to ensure that every student is being taught to mastery. Teachers are taught to instruct their students through the use of RM by holding to the integrity of the sequence of instruction. They are also instructed on how to personalize the teaching and learning process to meet the needs of the students. For example, if teachers feel that students need more work on sequencing, they would do a *story retell* after the lesson (in a story retell, students retell the story in sequence, identifying the beginning, middle, and end of the story).

Junior Great Books.   The Junior Great Books reading series was added to the Alliance program in the 1998–1999 school year for Grades 3 through 8. In each Alliance school, at least one teacher at each grade level was provided staff development and materials to infuse Junior Great Books into the curriculum offerings of the school. The goal of the Junior Great Books program is for students to develop the skills, habits, and attitudes of successful readers. The program builds students' analytic and interpretive skills through the use of open-ended, interpretive questions that encourage students to explore literature from their own point of view. The program is shaped around a discussion of literary texts including a culturally diverse mix of classic and modern literary and expository pieces. The selections are age appropriate by grade level. The foundation of the Junior Great Books model is its Shared Inquiry method. Discussions under this method start with a question that challenges students to think critically about the reading assignment, develop their own interpretations, and support these interpretations with evidence from the text. Throughout the discussion, teachers nurture thoughtful dialogue by building on the students' responses. Therefore, students gain experience in communicating complex ideas and in supporting, testing, and expanding their own thoughts.

Corrective Reading (CR).   At the beginning of each school year, middle school students are assessed in reading. Students are administered a group diagnostic test and reading program placement tests. Based on these results, academically deficient students are remediated using DI CR decoding, comprehension program and technology, or both. Some students may work in the program if they experience problems in recognizing words; others may work in the program if their reading difficulties are related to processing and understanding the meaning of ideas expressed in text. Some students may work in both decoding and comprehension programs. Each program has four levels, and placement tests are provided so students may enter at the appropriate instructional level.

Computer-Assisted Reading Instruction.   During the 1998–1999 school year, the Alliance of Quality Schools program adopted the reading software developed by the Computer Curriculum Corporation (CCC). This model of instructional technology components includes multiple measures of assessment, implementation plans, professional development, and ongoing support. The philosophy behind the CCC model is that students will achieve greater results when they (a) spend time on the content deemed important by state and local curriculum standards and testing objectives; (b) focus their efforts on concepts and skills that are organized into homogeneous strands, moving fluidly between strands as appropriate; (c) are placed at an appropriate level to begin the course work, based on their performance in an initial sequence of sessions; (d) can move forward at their own pace when their performance in a particular area satisfies criteria that take into account the fact that the learning process is dynamic; (e) receive tutoring intervention automatically, returning to prerequisite content when the pattern of their responses indicates that the students are having difficulty performing; and (f) are automatically assisted in retaining new concepts that have been learned.

Accelerated Reader.   The Accelerated Reader program was added to each Alliance elementary school during October 1997. The Accelerated Reader is a reading computer software system with the following three-step process that supports increased reading achievement:

1. Students independently select books from more than 11,000 outstanding and popular titles on the Accelerated Reader book lists. The titles range in reading level from first grade through high school.
2. Students read the book that they have selected at their own pace.
3. After reading a book independently, students log on to a computer and take a test on the book that they have completed. Each test consists of 5, 10, or 20 multiple-choice questions that are carefully designed to verify that the student has read the book. With the test completed, the computer gives instant feedback on the number of questions the student has answered correctly, and awards reading points based on the book's length, reading level, and number of correct responses.

Teachers are able to print out a summary of the number of books read, tests passed and with what performance level, and the reading level of the books. In addition, at-risk reports are produced indicating those students that have read books that are either too easy or too difficult, based on comprehension errors. The software also allows teachers to create their own tests.

The Alliance program has added a systematic approach to provide feedback on the number and types of books read by the students along with a reading comprehension measure to gauge the students' knowledge level based on reading certain books. All of these books used to measure reading comprehension have been made available to students at their local school library. The program has also included a daily review of mathematics concepts and applications for the students, combined with additional training and materials provided for each Grade 5 teacher.

Achieving High Standards in Writing.   Starting in the 1997–1998 school year, Alliance staff implemented a developmental, systematic, cooperative approach for learning to write and writing to learn. Following the procedures developed by Rothstein and Gess (1995), the Alliance staff developed a scope and sequence for writing instruction in Grades K–5. In addition, Gess acted as a consultant and provided on-site modeling of this approach at each of the Alliance elementary schools during the 1997–1998 school year. Based on the instructional needs of students, the writing process that the Alliance program implemented moves from high structure support (frames and outlines) to student-initiated writing responses.

Curriculum Supervision.   Alliance of Quality Schools staff worked with Bondi as a consultant to develop and implement a Deliberated Curriculum model

(Wiles & Bondi, 1996). This curriculum defined essential skills that would be taught on a daily basis at each grade level. The skills were aligned to the instructional needs of the students. Students' progress in mastering these skills was reflected in the lesson plans. A reteaching sequence of reading, writing, and mathematics took place based on this highly diagnostic and prescriptive approach.

RELATED EVALUATION FINDINGS

A July 1996 BCPS evaluation of the Alliance program (Younkin, 1996) concluded that analyses of performance measures (such as discipline records and scores on Informal Reading Inventory, Florida Writes, and Stanford Achievement Test) indicated a significant increase in the performance levels of the students in the Alliance schools at the end of its second year of implementation.

The following school year, a second evaluation of the Alliance program (Ligas, 1997a) revealed these findings: (a) increased achievement for alliance students on the Stanford Achievement Test–Eighth Edition (SAT8) Total Reading and Total Mathematics subtests over 1995–1996 levels, (b) increased performance on the Florida Writing Assessment, and (c) decreased number of disciplinary referrals.

Also, a comparison of fifth-grade Alliance and district students suggested that the gap between Alliance and other district schools was closing in every academic area. Recommendations resulting from the 1996–1997 evaluation were to (a) provide increased support to Alliance schools with a high number of, or an increase in, student office referrals during the past 2 years; (b) continue to expand the Alliance of Quality Schools to additional elementary and middle schools; and (c) enhance the elements of the Alliance program to strengthen reading and mathematics achievement in Grade 5.

Students in need of reading remediation at two Title I middle schools had received Sylvan services from 1995–1996 to 1997–1998. Because of this, the Alliance program was not offered at these two middle schools in 1997–1998. Although evaluations of the Sylvan program conducted by the Research and Evaluation Department (Hodges, 1996; Ligas, 1997b; Ligas, 1998b) demonstrated small, relative effects on reading comprehension, they also revealed that student performance expectations did not match those contractually agreed on by Sylvan Learning Systems, Inc., and the SBBC. Therefore, the Sylvan program was discontinued at these two middle schools.

Findings of the 1998 evaluation of the Alliance program (Ligas, 1998a) revealed that the impact of the project on academic achievement for elementary and middle school students varied by grade level and year. The findings also indicated that student behavior had improved, with a decrease in the number of referrals at the elementary school level and in incident data and disciplinary actions at the middle school level. The evaluation also revealed that achievement gains in Reading Comprehension (SAT8) for students participating in the CR program at Alliance middle schools surpassed those registered for both Sylvan students and comparable students district wide. As a result of this evaluation, the Alliance program was expanded to three other middle schools, including the two schools that had implemented the Sylvan program. To strengthen the Alliance program at the middle school level, students in all grades received "daily openers" in reading comprehension and mathematics, in addition to test preparation materials. Daily openers are short-time educational activities of about 5 to 10 min done at the beginning of the school day.

PROJECT IMPLEMENTATION

On April 5, 1994, the SBBC approved the Alliance of Quality Schools as a school improvement program. Shortly thereafter, planning and implementation activities involving teachers, school-based and district administrators, parents, and community members began. These activities included a demonstration for parents, teachers, administrators, and community members regarding DI and technology, as well as a detailed explanation of the Alliance concept.

At all schoolwide Title I schools, staff members were given a detailed implementation concept of the Alliance of Quality Schools model and asked to vote on program acceptance. An 80% faculty agreement was required for the school to be considered as an implementation site. This ensured that teachers and administrators had a commitment to the Alliance program and its goals. To determine which schools displayed the greatest need for the Alliance approach, the following four factors were analyzed: (a) the number of students on free and reduced-price meals, (b) the mobility rate, (c) the number of students above age for grade, and (d) the results on the Stanford Achievement Tests.

Each of the four criteria was given equal weighting, and magnet schools were excluded from consideration. Ten elementary schools were accepted as alliance partners during the first year. In 1995–1996, 13 elementary schools were added to the project. In the third year (1996–1997), 6 schools were added, for a total of 29. In 1997–1998, the district's fourth year of Alliance, 6 more schools were added, 3 at the elementary level, and, for the first time, 3 at the middle school level. In 1998–1999, 5 more schools were added, 2 at the elementary level and 3 at the middle school level. These additions raised the Alliance partner total to 40 (34 elementary and 6 middle) schools.

COST IMPACT

During the first year implementation of the Alliance program, a formative evaluation report (Knight, 1995) estimated that, as of February 1995, the Alliance project served 9,314 students enrolled in 10 elementary schools with a budget of

$3,347,006. Ninety percent of the Alliance coordinator's salary and benefits were funded by Title I. Funding for a curriculum facilitator and a home–school parent partner for each Alliance school also came from Title I. The number of elementary schools, and therefore, the number of students served, had progressively increased during the last 5 years, with 34 elementary schools and 26,226 students served during the 1998–1999 school year. However, the total allocation for each year remained the same. This translated into a reduction of per student cost from $163 in 1995–1996 to $114 in 1998–1999.

Total costs beyond Full-Time Equivalent (FTE) funding for the Alliance project for middle schools during the 1997–1998 school year was $403,434. In the 1998–1999 school year, funding of $511,172 for the Alliance middle schools was provided by Title I. That year, with the addition of three middle schools, the number of Alliance students at this level almost doubled, from 4,569 students in 1997–1998 to 8,746 students in 1998–1999. This translated into a reduction in cost beyond FTE funding of $58 per Alliance middle student for 1998–1999, down from $88 per alliance middle student in 1997–1998.

PURPOSE OF THE EVALUATION

The purpose of the evaluation was to determine the effect that the Alliance of Quality Schools project had on selected academic and behavioral student indicators after its fifth year of implementation.

The evaluation also examined how Alliance middle school students who participated in the CR program compared, in terms of reading comprehension achievement, with other Title I middle school students. Finally, the evaluation addressed the effect of the CCC software program on the reading performance of a selected group of CR students.

EVALUATION QUESTIONS

The evaluation posed several questions:

1. What was the impact of the Alliance of Quality Schools project on student academic performance during the 1998–1999 school year?

2. What was the effect of the Alliance of Quality Schools project on academic performance for students who participated in the Alliance project for the last 5 years, when compared to similar district students who did not participate in the Alliance project during the same period?

3. How did students who participated in the CR program of the Alliance of Quality Schools project compare (in terms of SAT8 Reading Comprehension

Normal Curve Equivalent [NCE] gain scores) with other Title I students who did not participate in this program?

4. How did middle school students who participated in the CR program and used the CCC software for 12 hr or more compare, in terms of SAT8 Reading Comprehension scores, with other CR students at the same middle school who did not use the CCC software or who used it for less than 5 hr?

METHOD

The evaluation utilized a time series design. This design allowed measurement of the project's impact on the achievement of the students enrolled in Alliance schools across 5 years of implementation.

Participants

Elementary school level.   The distribution of race and ethnicity for all elementary students enrolled in the 34 Alliance schools during the 1998–1999 school year shows that the majority of students enrolled were identified as Black (77.8 %), followed by Hispanic (11.3%), and White (9.2%). The Asian, Native American, and multiracial categories each comprised less than 1% of the enrolled Alliance population. A similar race and ethnic distribution was found for the 1994–1995 to 1998–1999 school years in the participating Alliance elementary schools, as shown in Figure 1. There has been a slight decrease in the proportion of Black students as well as a slight increase in the proportion of Hispanic and White students enrolled in Alliance schools since the program's inception in the 1994–1995 school year.

Table 1 illustrates the composition of the Alliance schools in terms of exceptional student education (ESE) status from the 1994–1995 to 1998–1999 school years. For purposes of the evaluation, gifted students, although part of the ESE group, were included in the non-ESE status category. There has been a very slight increase in the proportion of ESE students enrolled in Alliance schools during the last 5 years. Table 1 also shows the composition of the Alliance elementary schools in terms of free or reduced lunch (FRL) status from 1994–1995 to 1998–1999. In 1994–1995, the 10 original Alliance schools had 84% of their students participating in FRL fees. This figure decreased slightly in 1995–1996 to 79.9%, became stable at 82% for the 1996–1997 and 1997–1998 school years, and increased back to 84% during the 1998–1999 school year. The distribution of students in alliance schools classified as limited English proficient (LEP) students is also illustrated in Table 1. The proportion of students classified as LEP remained the same (12.9%) for the 1994–1995 and 1995–1996 school years. However, this proportion increased slightly for the 1996–1997 school year (14.2%) and for the 1997–1998 school year (14.5%), then decreased slightly (13.7%) during the 1998–1999 school year.

Middle school level. The race and ethnicity distribution for the three Alliance schools at the middle school level in the 1997–1998 school year is presented in Figure 2. There was a slight decrease in the proportion of White students and students categorized in the "other" race and ethnic group. Hispanic student enrollment in Alliance middle schools remained stable from 1997–1998 to 1998–1999.

Table 2 illustrates the ESE status for Alliance middle schools, with 16% of enrolled students identified as having an ESE status in each of the 2 years. Sixty-five percent of all students enrolled at Alliance middle schools in 1997–1998 and 64% of

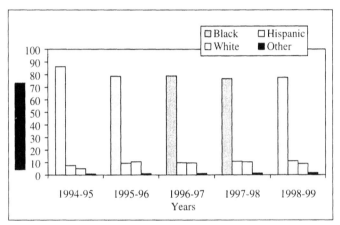

FIGURE 1 Enrollment in Alliance elementary schools by race and ethnicity, 1994–1995 to 1998–1999.

TABLE 1
Enrollment in Alliance Elementary Schools by ESE, FRL, and LEP Status, 1994–1995 to 1998–1999

Status	1994–1995 n	%	1995–1996 n	%	1997–1997 n	%	1997–1998 n	%	1998–1999 n	%
ESE										
ESE	1,248	13.7	3,063	14.9	3,551	15.1	4,487	17.2	4,085	15.6
Non-ESE	7,881	86.3	17,497	85.1	19,897	84.9	21,562	82.8	22,141	84.4
FRL										
FRL	7,640	83.7	16,425	79.9	19,194	81.9	21,320	81.8	22,060	84.1
Non-FRL	1,489	16.3	4,135	20.1	4,254	18.1	4,729	18.2	4,166	15.9
LEP										
LEP	1,182	12.9	2,651	12.9	3,337	14.2	3,773	14.5	3,597	13.7
Non-LEP	7,947	87.1	17,909	87.1	20,111	85.8	22,276	85.5	22,629	86.3

Note. ESE = exceptional student education; FRL = free or reduced lunch; LEP = limited English proficiency.

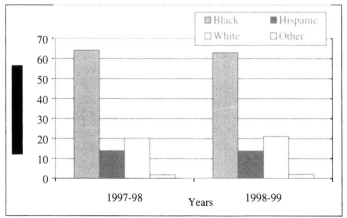

FIGURE 2   Enrollment in Alliance middle schools by race and ethnicity, 1997–1998 to 1998–1999.

TABLE 2
Enrollment in Alliance Middle Schools by ESE, FRL, and LEP Status, 1997–1998, 1998–1999

	1997–1998		1998–1999	
Status	n	%	n	%
ESE				
ESE	710	15.5	1,392	15.9
Non-ESE	3,859	84.5	7,354	84.1
FRL				
FRL	2,981	65.2	5,552	63.5
Non-FRL	1,588	34.8	3,194	36.5
LEP				
LEP	225	4.9	717	8.2
Non-LEP	4,344	95.1	8,029	91.8

Note.   ESE = exceptional student education; FRL = free or reduced lunch; LEP - limited English proficiency.

students enrolled at Alliance middle schools in 1998–1999 received FRL services. The proportion of students identified as LEP in alliance middle schools increased from about 5% in 1997–1998 to 8.2% in 1998–1999.

RESULTS

What was the impact of the Alliance of Quality Schools project on student academic performance for the 1998–1999 school year? Academic performance of students enrolled in Alliance schools was analyzed by comparing 1997–1998 and 1998–1999 Reading Comprehension and Mathematics applications subtest scores on the SAT8 for Grades 3–8. Only results on reading performance are presented here.

1. All students enrolled in the BCPS in Grades 3–8 during 1998–1999, and who took the SAT8 during the 1998 and 1999 spring administrations, were included in this analysis. Students who met the aforementioned criteria and were enrolled in 1 of the 34 Alliance elementary and 6 Alliance middle schools for the 1998–1999 school year were identified. Their scores for both years on the Reading Comprehension subtest of the SAT8 were compared with the scores of district elementary students enrolled in the same grade. Percentile scores for the Reading Comprehension subtest on the SAT8 were transformed into NCE scores and then averaged to allow for statistical analyses of means.

Table 3 presents the mean NCE scores and standard deviations for Alliance and district students on the 1998 and 1999 SAT8 Reading Comprehension subtest by grade level. As Table 3 shows, Alliance students in Grade 4 achieved the highest increase in NCE score gains (7.8) for this subtest of all Alliance grade subgroups. This increase was also higher than the one achieved by Grade 4 district students (6.7) over the same 2-year period. Both of these groups registered medium standardized effect sizes (.45 for the Alliance group and .32 for district group).

Table 3 also shows that Alliance students in Grades 7 and 8 achieved higher gains in average Reading Comprehension NCE scores (2.0 and 2.2, respectively) than did their district counterparts, who registered increases of 1.2 and .6 points, respectively, at the same grade levels. Also, Grades 3, 5, and 6 registered the highest losses (–1.9, –.9, and –.9) compared to the changes registered for other students in the district (–.4, –.5, and .5) at their respective grade levels. All of the standardized effect sizes for these groups were negligible.

Overall, in the 1998–1999 school year, Alliance students in Grades 4, 7, and 8 demonstrated increases in average scores in reading comprehension from their 1997–1998 levels. Third, fifth, and sixth graders showed decreases in the reading comprehension area.

2. What was the effect of the Alliance of Quality Schools project on student academic performance for students who participated in the Alliance project for the last 5 years, when compared to similar district students who did not participate in the Alliance project? Two groups of fifth-grade students and two groups of sixth-grade students were identified to answer this question. One of the fifth-grade groups was comprised of fifth-grade students enrolled in the 10 elementary schools that started Alliance participation in 1994–1995 and the 13 schools that started Alliance participation in 1995–1996. These students were

TABLE 3
Means and Standard Deviations on Stanford Achievement Test–Eighth Edition Reading
Comprehension Normal Curve Equivalents for Alliance and District Groups by Grade Level,
1998–1999

	RC 1998		RC 1999			
Groups	M	SD	M	SD	Differences in Means	d
Alliance						
Grade 3 (n = 3,521)	38.38	19.09	36.53	18.00	−1.85	.10
Grade 4 (n = 3,478)	33.90	17.59	41.74	17.88	7.84	.45
Grade 5 (n = 3,342)	40.18	17.08	39.25	17.44	−0.93	.05
Grade 6 (n = 2,387)	41.04	18.83	40.14	19.80	−0.90	.05
Grade 7 (n = 2,309)	40.45	20.40	42.45	20.35	2.00	.10
Grade 8 (n = 2,342)	40.82	19.93	42.99	22.42	2.17	.11
District						
Grade 3 (n = 12,201)	48.67	20.54	48.28	21.16	−0.39	.02
Grade 4 (n = 12,537)	46.70	20.89	53.36	19.55	6.66	.32
Grade 5 (n = 12, 438)	52.78	20.08	52.27	19.55	−0.51	.03
Grade 6 (n = 12, 691)	49.36	19.83	49.90	21.53	0.54	.03
Grade 7 (n = 12, 305)	50.32	21.55	51.50	20.63	1.18	.05
Grade 8 (n = 11,820)	52.27	20.51	52.82	22.37	0.55	.03

Note.   RC = reading comprehension.

also enrolled at the same Alliance school since the 1994–1995 school year. A weighted sampling process was used to identify a comparison group of fifth-grade students who attended the same Non-Alliance district elementary school for the last 3 years. This sampling process guaranteed that the comparison group was similar to the Alliance participants in terms of their race and ethnicity, ESE status, FRL status, and LEP status. Mobility and retention factors were controlled by identifying students in each group who were enrolled in the same school as second graders in 1995–1996 and who were promoted regularly from year to year. Percentile scores for the Reading Comprehension subtest on the SAT8 were transformed into NCE scores and then averaged to allow for inferential statistical tests.

Figure 3 and Table 4 illustrate the achievement of Alliance and district fifth graders in Reading Comprehension NCE scores for the 1995–1996, 1996–1997, 1997–1998, and 1998–1999 school years. As shown in Figure 3, the gap between the Alliance and the district groups in 1995–1996 was .8 NCE points in favor of the district group. This difference decreased to .7 NCE points in 1996–1997. In 1997–1998, the gap widened to a difference of 1.9 NCE points; and in 1998–1999, the gap became even wider, with a difference of 2.5 NCE points in favor of the district group. A repeated measures multivariate analysis of variance (MANOVA)

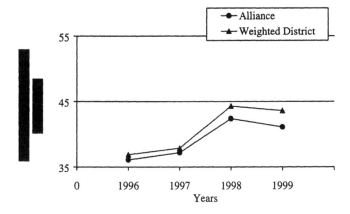

FIGURE 3   Stanford Achievement Test–Eighth Edition Reading Comprehension Normal Curve Equivalent means for 1998–1999 fifth graders by group and year.

TABLE 4
Means and Standard Deviations on Stanford Achievement Test–Eight Edition Reading Comprehension Normal Curve Equivalent Scores for Grade 5, by Group × Year

	1995–1996		1996–1997		1997–1998		1998–1999	
Groups	M	SD	M	SD	M	SD	M	SD
Alliance	36.1	19.0	37.2	17.9	42.4	16.4	41.1	17.1
Weighted district	36.9	19.6	37.9	18.3	44.3	18.0	43.6	17.1

Note. $n = 1,143$ (for each group).

with repeated measures in one factor was performed to identify any statistically significant differences between the results for the Alliance and the district comparison groups on the SAT8 Reading Comprehension subtest. The repeated measures MANOVA test revealed no significant interaction effect of Group × Year, $F(3, 6,852) = 5.22$, $p < .001$, $\eta^2 = .06$. Also, a significant difference was revealed for fifth-grade student performance in reading based on year, $F(3, 6,852) = 301.88$, $p < .001$, $\eta^2 = .26$.

In addition to the previous analyses, two groups of sixth-grade students were identified. One of the sixth-grade groups was comprised of sixth-grade students who were enrolled in the 10 elementary schools that started Alliance participation in 1994–1995 and the 13 schools that started Alliance participation in 1995–1996. These students had attended the same Alliance elementary school for the 1995–1996 to 1996–1997 school years as well as attending one of the six Alliance middle schools in 1998–1999 (AQS, 1996–1999).

The comparison group of sixth graders consisted of those students who attended the same Non-Alliance district elementary school in the third, fourth, and fifth grades, as well as a Non-Alliance district middle school in sixth grade (Non-AQS, 1996–1999). For these analyses, a weighted sampling process was also used to identify a comparison group similar to the Alliance participants in terms of their race and ethnicity, ESE status, FRL status, and LEP status. Mobility and retention factors were controlled by identifying students in each group who were enrolled in the same school as third graders in 1995–1996 and who were promoted regularly from year to year.

Figure 4 and Table 5 present a comparison of reading comprehension NCE scores for the two groups starting in 1995–1996. The gap between the Alliance group and the Non-Alliance district group was then 2.6 NCE points in favor of the Non-Alliance district group. The gap decreased to 1.4 NCE points in 1996–1997 but in-

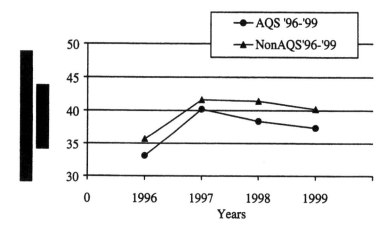

FIGURE 4   Stanford Achievement Test–Eighth Edition Reading Comprehension Normal Curve Equivalent means for 1998–1999 sixth graders by group and year.

TABLE 5
Means and Standard Deviations on Stanford Achievement Test–Eighth Edition Reading Comprehension NCE Scores for Grade 6, by Group × Year

Groups	1995–1996		1996–1997		1997–1998		1998–1999	
	M	SD	M	SD	M	SD	M	SD
AQS 96–99	33.1	17.6	40.2	16.3	38.4	16.9	37.4	18.0
Non-AQS 96–99	35.7	18.8	41.6	17.1	41.4	17.5	40.2	18.6

Note.   n = 549 (for each group); AQS = Alliance group; Non-AQS = Non-Alliance group.

creased again to 3.0 in 1997–1998. In 1998–1999, there was a slight decrease in the gap for a difference of 2.8 NCE points in favor of the Non-Alliance district group.

A repeated measures MANOVA with repeated measures in one factor was performed to identify any statistically significant differences between the results for the Alliance and the district comparison groups on the SAT8 Reading Comprehension subtest. The repeated measures MANOVA test revealed a significant interaction effect of Group × Year, $F(3, 3,288) = 1.84$, *ns*. However, a significant difference was revealed for student performance in reading based on year, $F(3, 3,288) = 113.29$, $p < .001$, $\eta^2 = .20$.

3. How did students who participated in the CR program of the Alliance of Quality Schools project compare (in terms of SAT8 reading comprehension NCE gain scores) with other Title I students who did not participate in this program? To answer this question, four groups of students were identified, as follows:

1. The Alliance CR group for 1998 (CR98) was comprised of 57 Alliance middle school students who received 35 hr or more of instruction in the CR program at Lauderhill, Perry, or Rickards middle schools, only in the 1997–1998 school year.
2. The Alliance CR group for 1999 (CR99) was comprised of 543 Alliance middle school students who received 35 hr or more of instruction in the CR program at Crystal Lake, Lauderdale Lakes, Lauderhill, New River, Perry, or Rickards middle schools, only in the 1998–1999 school year.
3. The Alliance CR98 and CR99 groups were comprised of 40 Alliance middle school students who received 35 hr or more of instruction in the CR program at Lauderhill, Perry, or Rickards in the 1997–1998 school years and at Crystal Lake, Lauderdale Lakes, Lauderhill, New River, Perry, or Rickards middle schools in the 1998–1999 school years.
4. A Title I comparison group of 10,840 Title I middle school students (non-CR) was comprised of Title I students who did not attend Alliance middle schools in the 1998–1999 school years.

All members of each group took the SAT8 Reading Comprehension subtest during the 1997, 1998, and 1999 test administrations. Figure 5 and Table 6 present a comparison of Reading Comprehension NCE scores for the four groups from 1997–1999. As Figure 5 illustrates, Alliance students who participated in the CR program for 2 years (CR98 and CR99), although the lowest performing group in 1997, achieved an average of 1.7 NCE points increase in reading comprehension scores during their first year of participation and a 2.0 NCE increase during their second year. Alliance students who participated in the CR program only in 1998–1999 (CR99) also achieved an average increase of 2.0 NCE points in reading comprehension. Alliance students who had participated in CR only during the 1997–1998 school year (CR98) had achieved a .6 NCE points increase in 1998 over their 1997

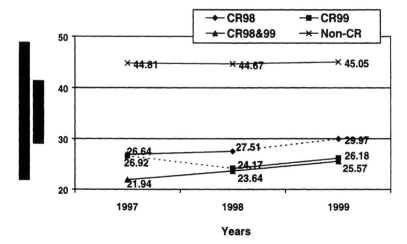

FIGURE 5   Stanford Achievement Test–Eighth Edition Reading Comprehension Normal Curve Equivalent means for corrective reading students by group and year.

TABLE 6
Means and Standard Deviations on Stanford Achievement Test–Eighth Edition Reading Comprehension Normal Curve Equivalent Scores for Corrective Reading Students, by Group × Year

| Groups | n | 1996–1997 | | 1997–1998 | | 1998–1999 | |
		M	SD	M	SD	M	SD
CR (1998)	57	26.9	13.0	27.5	12.1	29.9	15.5
CR (1999)	543	26.6	12.3	24.2	11.8	26.2	14.2
CR (1998 and 1999)	40	21.9	10.0	23.6	12.3	25.6	12.4
Non-CR	10,840	44.8	19.5	44.7	19.9	45.1	20.8

Note.   CR = corrective reading.

scores; however, although they did not participate in the program in 1998–1999, they registered the highest gain in reading comprehension scores this year with a 2.4 NCE points increase.

4. How did middle school students who participated in the CR program and used the CCC software for 12 hr or more compare, in terms of SAT8 reading comprehension scores, with other CR students at the same middle school who did not use the CCC software or who used it for less than 5 hr?

To answer this question, two groups of students were identified, as follows:

1. The Alliance CR CCC group (CCC1) was comprised of 99 Alliance middle school students who used the CCC software for 12 hr or more, in addition to

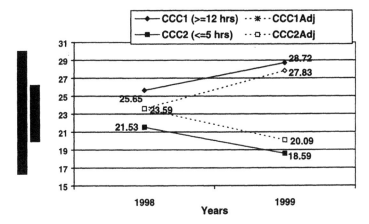

FIGURE 6   Stanford Achievement Test–Eighth Edition Reading Comprehension Normal Curve Equivalent means for two groups of corrective reading students at the same Alliance middle school.

TABLE 7
Adjusted Stanford Achievement Test–Eighth Edition Reading Comprehension Normal Curve Equivalent Means for Two Groups of CCC Corrective Reading Students at the Same Alliance Middle School

| Groups | n | 1997–1998 | | 1998–1999 | | Adjusted Mean |
		M	SD	M	SD	
CCC1[a]	99	25.65	9.8	28.72	11.5	27.83
CCC2[b]	59	21.53	10.7	18.59	10.2	20.09

Note.   CCC = Computer Curriculum Corporation.
[a]$\geq$ = 12 hr. [b]$\leq$ = 5 hr.

receiving 35 hr or more of instruction in the CR program at Lauderhill before the 1999 SAT8 administration.

2. The Alliance CR CCC group (CCC2) was comprised of 59 Alliance middle school students who did not use the CCC software or used it for 5 hr or less, in addition to receiving 35 hr or more of instruction in the CR program at Lauderhill before the 1999 SAT8 administration.

All members of each group took the SAT8 Reading Comprehension subtest during the 1998 and 1999 test administrations. Figure 6 and Table 7 present a comparison of Reading Comprehension NCE scores for the two groups from 1998–1999. As Figure 6 illustrates, there was an initial difference in 1998 Reading Comprehension NCE scores between the two groups (4.12 NCE points) in favor of the CCC1 group. Because of these initial differences, an analysis of covariance (ANCOVA) was performed. The ANCOVA procedure allowed for the comparison of the 1999 mean scores for both groups, after adjusting for the initial differences in 1998 scores. That is, it allowed for the answer to the following question: If both groups had started at the same level in 1998, what would their performance be in 1999? Table 7 shows what the average NCE scores for 1999 would be if both groups had similar NCE scores in 1998. The difference in the average 1999 scores after adjusting for initial differences in average 1998 scores was 7.74 NCE points. This difference was statistically significant at the .001 level, $F(1, 155) = 24.3$, $p < .001$.

SUMMARY

Since 1995, BCPS began implementing the Alliance of Quality Schools project in an effort to assist those elementary students most at risk of failing to achieve to their highest potential. The application of research-based methods (i.e., in the areas of curriculum, behavioral intervention, and leadership), as well as the commitment displayed by school staff, parents, and community from each participating school, has brought about positive results for the students served by this initiative.

The evaluation of the impact of the Alliance of Quality Schools project on student academic performance for the 1998–1999 school revealed that, overall, in the 1998–1999 school year, Alliance students in Grades 4, 7, and 8 demonstrated increases in average scores in SAT8 Reading Comprehension from their 1997–1998 levels. Third, fifth, and sixth graders showed decreases in the reading comprehension area.

This evaluation also investigated the long-term effect of the Alliance of Quality Schools project on student academic performance for students who had participated in the Alliance project for the last 4 or 5 years.

When comparing fifth-grade Alliance students who participated in the Alliance project for the last 4 years to a weighted comparison group of district fifth graders, Alliance students were very close to those of the weighted comparison group in average Reading Comprehension NCE scores during second and third grade. In fourth grade, both groups improved substantially, with an increase of 5.2 NCE points for the Alliance group and of 6.4 NCE points for the district group. The performance of the two groups decreased again in fifth grade, with the Alliance group registering the largest decline. This meant an increase in the gap in reading comprehension between the two groups from 1.9 NCE points in 1998 to 2.5 NCE points in 1999 in favor of the comparison group.

Overall, at the elementary school level, the results show that the greatest increases in reading performance occurred at the fourth-grade level. These increases seemed to be closely aligned to the grade levels targeted for school accountability by the state of Florida during the 1998–1999 school year.

Sixth-grade students attending Alliance schools from 1995–1996 to 1998–1999 had lower Reading Comprehension NCE scores than the weighted comparison district group in third grade in 1996. In fourth grade, both groups improved substantially, and the gap between the two groups decreased to only 1.4 NCE points difference, in favor of the comparison group. The performance of the comparison group remained stable in 1998; however, that of the Alliance group decreased in fifth grade. This meant an increase in the gap between the two groups of 3.0 NCE points. In 1999, the reading comprehension scores for both groups of sixth graders continued to decrease, and the gap in performance was 2.8 NCE points in favor of the comparison group.

As regards the effectiveness of the CR program of the Alliance of Quality Schools project at the middle school level, a comparison, in terms of SAT8 Reading Comprehension NCE gain scores, with other Title I middle school students who did not participate in this program, revealed the following: Alliance students who participated in the CR program in 1997–1998 and 1998–1999, although the lowest performing group in 1997, achieved an average of 1.7 NCE points increase in reading comprehension scores during their first year of participation and a 2.0 NCE increase during their second year. Those Alliance students who participated in the CR program only in 1998–1999 also achieved an average increase of 2.0 NCE points in reading comprehension. Alliance students who had participated in CR only during the 1997–1998 school year achieved a .6 NCE point increase in 1998 over their 1997 scores; however, although they did not participate in the program in 1998–1999, they registered the highest gains in reading comprehension scores in 1998–1999, with a 2.4 NCE points increase.

The evaluation also investigated the effect of the addition of CCC software to CR instruction, by comparing a group of Alliance middle school students who participated in CR and used the CCC software for 12 hr or more, in terms of SAT8 Reading Comprehension average NCE scores, with other Alliance middle school students at the same school who did not use the CCC software or used it for less than 5 hr. After adjusting for initial differences in 1998 reading comprehension NCE scores, the group of Alliance students who participated in the CR program and used the CCC software for 12 hr or more outperformed the group of students who did not use the CCC software or used it for less than 5 hr, by 7.74 NCE points in 1999. This difference was statistically significant at the .001 level.

CONCLUSIONS

The purpose of this article was to report on the findings of a 5th-year evaluation of the Alliance of Quality Schools project, as these findings related to student outcomes in reading achievement. Although the evaluation results provided here represent an effort to understand the reading performance of students receiving instruction under a project that utilized DI as the foundational core of its program, the evaluation was not intended as an evaluation of the effects of DI on reading achievement. A controlled experimental design would be required to identify these effects. The Alliance of Quality Schools project, because of its comprehensive nature, involved the implementation of several coordinated components to address the needs of at-risk students, in both the academic and behavioral areas. In conclusion, effects noted here for the program result from the implementation of these other components, as well as from the implementation of DI, and it is very difficult to parcel out effects attributable only to DI.

Also, after reviewing the findings of the 1998 and 1999 evaluations of the Alliance of Quality Schools project in terms of SAT8 performance in reading comprehension for the Alliance fifth-grade cohorts, it is important to note that their achievement in reading increased every year since 1995; this finding holds true for the fifth-grade cohorts who were part of the district weighted comparison groups during the same years. This confirms an overall trend of improvement for the district and makes it more difficult to ascertain the exclusive impact of DI on the performance of Alliance students.

As a result of this evaluation, the SBBC took the following actions:

1. Identified and implemented strategies to ensure that available student performance and behavior data is used at the school and classroom levels to determine what needs to be provided for continued student growth.

2. Continued the focus of providing electronic databases for individual school and classroom use, which include the utilization of multiple benchmarks tied to the Sunshine State Standards, as well as providing staff development to support its use.

3. Identified and implemented a set of criteria to be used for assigning different levels of support to alliance schools.

4. Implemented the provision of annual updates by the coordinator of the Alliance of Quality Schools project that includes information regarding student participation, attendance, and discipline, as well as student performance. Contingent on resources, the next formal evaluation for the Alliance project will be considered by the Research and Evaluation Department in the year 2002–2003.

REFERENCES

Abt Associates. (1977). *Education as experimentation: A planned variation model* (Vol. 4). Cambridge, MA: Abt Associates.

Aoki, E. M., Flood, J., Hoffman, J. V., Lapp, D., Martinez, M., Sullivan Palincsar, A., et al. (1995). *A New View*. New York: Macmillan/McGraw-Hill.

Carnine, D., Silbert, J., & Kameenui, E. (1997). *Direct Instruction reading* (3rd ed.). Upper Saddle River, NJ: Prentice Hall.

Colvin, G. (1994). *Procedures for establishing a proactive schoolwide discipline plan.* Eugene: University of Oregon, U.S. Department of Education.

Cooper, J. D., Pikulski, J. J., Au, K. H., Calderon, M., Comas, J., Lipson, M. Y., et al. (1996). *Invitations to literacy.* Boston: Houghton Mifflin.

Cotton, K. (1990). *School improvement series, close up #9: School-wide and classroom discipline.* Portland, OR: Northwest Regional Educational Laboratory.

Gersten, R., & Dimino, J. (1990). Reading instruction for at-risk students: Implications of current research. *OSSC Bulletin, 33*(5), 1–33.

Haney, W. (1977). *Reanalysis of follow-through parent and teacher data.* Boston: Huron Institute.

Hodges, E. V. E. (1996). *Sylvan Learning Systems, Inc.: Program evaluation.* Fort Lauderdale, FL: The School Board of Broward County.

Knight, K. (1995). *Alliance of Quality Schools: Formative evaluation report.* Fort Lauderdale, FL: The School Board of Broward County.

Ligas, M. R. (1997a). *Alliance of Quality Schools: Evaluation report.* Fort Lauderdale, FL: The School Board of Broward County.

Ligas, M. R. (1997b). *Sylvan Learning Systems, Inc.: Program evaluation.* Fort Lauderdale, FL: The School Board of Broward County.

Ligas, M. R. (1998a). *Alliance of Quality Schools: Evaluation report.* Fort Lauderdale, FL: The School Board of Broward County.

Ligas, M. R. (1998b). *Sylvan Learning Systems, Inc.: Program evaluation.* Fort Lauderdale, FL: The School Board of Broward County.

Ligas, M. R. (1999). *Alliance of Quality Schools: Evaluation report.* Fort Lauderdale, FL: The School Board of Broward County.

Nelson, J. R., Johnson, A., & Marchand-Martella, N. (1996). Effects of Direct Instruction, cooperative learning, and independent learning practices on the classroom behavior of students with behavioral disorders: A comparative analysis. *Journal of Emotional and Behavioral Disorders, 4,* 53–62.

Rothstein, E., & Gess, D. (1995). *Teaching writing: A developmental, systematic, cooperative approach for learning to write and writing to learn* (5th ed.). Suffern, NY: The Write Track.

The School Board of Broward County. (1995). *Policy handbook.* Fort Lauderdale, FL: Author.

Wiles, J., & Bondi, J. (1996). *Supervision: A guide to practice* (4th ed.). Englewood Cliffs, NJ: Prentice Hall.

Younkin, W. F. (1996). *Alliance of Quality Schools: Evaluation report.* Fort Lauderdale, FL: The School Board of Broward County.

JOURNAL OF EDUCATION FOR STUDENTS PLACED AT RISK, 7(2), 141–166

Increasing the Reading Achievement of At-Risk Children Through Direct Instruction: Evaluation of the Rodeo Institute for Teacher Excellence (RITE)

Coleen D. Carlson and David J. Francis
Texas Institute for Measurement, Evaluation, and Statistics
University of Houston

This article describes an evaluation of a program, the Rodeo Institute for Teacher Excellence (RITE), which addresses at-risk students' failure to develop reading skills. The evaluation included all Grade K–2 students participating in the program and in comparison schools selected to serve as a control group. Results indicated that the RITE program was successful at increasing the reading abilities of students in at-risk schools. Children who began the RITE program early and who spent more years in the program outperformed all other students. Intervention with teachers was related to improvement in observed teaching skills (behavior management and teacher corrections), and successful implementation of programmatic teaching techniques was related to student performance. These findings close the trainer–teacher–student feedback loop by showing that teacher behavior relates to student performance.

Failure to develop basic reading abilities during the first few years of school has been shown to be related to a number of academic, economic, and socioemotional difficulties (Lipson & Wixson, 1997; Pressley & Hampston, 1998; Snider & Tarver, 1987; Wharton-McDonald, Pressley, & Hampston, 1998). Juel (1988) reported that approximately 88% of first-grade students whose performance scores were in the lower quartile in reading comprehension remained at performance levels below the 50th percentile through fourth grade. Others have reported similar findings in that students who have been poor readers in the early elementary years remain poor readers throughout school; the problem intensifies with each new year. Concern over early reading and the prevention of early reading problems has resulted in two national research reviews in the last 3 years, one commissioned by the National Research Council (Snow, Burns, & Griffin, 1998), and the other by the

Requests for reprints should be sent to Coleen D. Carlson, Texas Institute for Measurement, Evaluation, and Statistics, 126 Heyne Building, Department of Psychology, University of Houston, Houston, TX 77204–5022. E-mail: coleen.carlson@times.uh.edu

U.S. Congress, coordinated by the National Institute for Child Health and Human Development (National Reading Panel Report, 2000).

Central to the acquisition of early reading ability is the speed and comprehensiveness with which children learn the process of decoding. For many students, learning the alphabetic principle is easy. Many students enter school having already experienced a variety of literacy-related activities, and many already have at least some knowledge of letters and sound–symbol (letter–sound) correspondence. However, other students have had significantly fewer literacy-related opportunities prior to those first provided within the school setting and enter school with little to no knowledge of the alphabetic principle. At least in part due to these more limited experiences, these same children have been shown to be those who are less likely to develop automatic decoding skills (Adams, 1990). Although being at risk for reading difficulties is not a circumstance limited to students from lower economic strata or to those living in urban settings, the prevalence of lower reading performance levels and less developed reading abilities for students from this background in urban settings tends to be significantly higher.

For at-risk students, the effectiveness of the reading instruction they receive in the early school years is of utmost importance. There has been considerable debate over the past decade about what constitutes the most effective beginning reading instruction. In the empirical literature of reading instruction, explicit decoding instruction has increasingly been cited as a more effective instructional approach (Stahl, McKenna, & Pagnucco, 1994) than more implicit methods. Studies have shown that the standardized tests scores of students participating in programs that explicitly teach phonemic awareness, phonics, and letter–sound associations increase or are at higher levels than those of students in other types of programs (Adams, 1990; Pflaum, Walberg, Karegaines, & Rahsher, 1980). Other studies of tutoring intervention have shown that the more successful interventions with at-risk students include higher occurrences of modeling, word study practices, and more time spent practicing skills (Juel, 1996; Leslie & Allen, 1999).

Program effectiveness is only partially attributable to the content of the instructional program itself. The teacher's implementation of the program is equally important to the successful development of reading skills in at-risk children. Because many teachers are not adequately prepared for the task of teaching reading to at-risk children, teacher training and professional development are also important factors in decreasing the number of students who fail to develop basic reading skills (Brady & Moats, 1997).

The Rodeo Institute for Teacher Excellence (RITE) was designed to provide severely at-risk Grade K–2 students with explicit instruction in phonemic awareness and decoding through a consistent curricula, adequate materials, and skilled teachers. The RITE program was modeled after a successful program implemented in one elementary school within the district that saw dramatic skill gains in its students. At the core of the RITE program is phonics-based instruction and an emphasis on professional development. The foundation of this program rests in the reading mastery (RM) curriculum (Englemann & Bruner, 1995). Using these instructional materials, the RITE program strives to strengthen teachers' skills in reading instruction through intensive teacher training and year-long support provided by trainers who work within the schools and consult with teachers, providing feedback on program planning and implementation. During the summer, each teacher attends in-depth, hands-on phonics instruction training using the RM materials. During the school year, each school is assigned a master trainer, who provides daily on-site support and holds monthly meetings with all teachers to discuss issues and concerns in an open forum.

In addition to the teaching skills directly related to the RM curricula, the RITE program also strives to provide teachers with strong classroom management techniques. Many of the teacher skills focused on in the RITE program are similar to those that have been presented in literature on the best teaching practices. Specifically, the RITE program emphasizes the consistent and complete use of the "model–test–retest" correction technique from the RM curriculum. This technique directs students' attention to mistakes, provides them with a model of the correct response, tests their knowledge after the modeling has occurred, and continues this practice until students are firm in their knowledge. Furthermore, the program also emphasizes the use of positive reinforcement in the form of teacher praise and verification for correct student responses. Finally, the program emphasizes strong classroom management skills. The ability of the teacher to provide an environment that is safe, consistent, and that allows the student time to focus on the tasks at hand is both an important goal of this program and necessary to its success. Because students receive reading instruction in this program in small, skill-leveled groups, it is imperative that those students not in a reading group remain on task and engaged in active learning activities (e.g., independent reading, listening center activities).

The RITE program completed its fourth year of implementation during the 2000–2001 academic year. Each year, the program has increased in size, beginning in 6 schools during the 1997–1998 school year and ending the 2000–2001 school year in 20 schools. The external evaluation of the RITE program initially focused only on student performance levels and gains. Over time, the evaluation expanded to include observations of teacher performance within the classroom; trainer reports of intervention provided to teachers; and examination of the links between student, teacher, and trainer performance.

PARTICIPANTS

Program Group

The external evaluation included students from all kindergarten, first-, and second-grade classrooms from all years of the RITE program. Third-grade performance levels were also examined for those students who had participated in the program at some point during their kindergarten, first-, or second-grade year; and for whom data were available from the district on the state-mandated assessment, the Texas Assessment of Academic Skills (TAAS). Table 1 describes the number of students beginning each year in each grade, as well as the number of students from each grade level who participated in the program across years. Roughly equal numbers of boys (51%) and girls (49%) participated in the RITE program, and the majority of the RITE students were of African American (65%) or Hispanic (28%) descent. The remainder of the participants were White (3%), Asian American (3%), and American Indian (1%).

In the 2000–2001 academic year, 277 teachers from 20 schools participated in the RITE program. Of these teachers, 137 were new to the RITE program, 74 were returning for their second year, 47 for their third year, and 19 for their fourth year. Of the 20 RITE schools, 4 were entering their fourth year in the program, 3 were entering their third year in the program, 6 were entering their second year, and 7 were beginning their first year with the program.

Comparison Group

Twenty comparison schools were selected to serve as a control group for each of the RITE program schools. Each year, as schools were added to the RITE program, comparison schools were selected from the non-RITE schools in the district. These schools were selected based on the degree to which school characteristics matched those of one of the RITE schools. The characteristics examined included the percentage of students who

1. Received free or reduced-price lunch.
2. Belonged to an ethnic minority group.
3. Were limited English proficient.
4. Met the minimum state-mandated reading performance requirement.

All non-RITE schools in the district were compared to the participating RITE schools during the RITE schools' first year of participation in the program. If the percentages in all four categories for a comparison school were within a 10% range of the percentage at a particular RITE school, then that comparison school was placed in a pool of possible matches for that RITE school. Because each RITE school had more than one possible comparison school, the next step was to identify the comparison school that was geographically closest to the RITE school. The comparison school within the pool of possible matches for a RITE school that was geographically closest to that RITE school was selected as that RITE school's match.

The comparison group provided a means for judging the performance of students in the program relative to expectations for similar students who were participating in

TABLE 1

RITE Students by Grade Within and Across Program Years

RITE Program Students Over Time

Grade	Year Entered Program	Kindergarten	First Grade	Second Grade	Third Grade
Kindergarten	1997–1998	413 (1997–1998)	259 (1998-1999)	181 (1999–2000)	137 (2000–2001)
	1998–1999	607 (1998–1999)	420 (1999–2000)	271 (2000–2001)	—
	1999–2000	969 (1999–2000)	611 (2000–2001)	—	—
	2000–2001	1460 (2000–2001)	—	—	—
First grade	1997–1998	—	440 (1997–1998)	268 (1998–1999)	192 (1999–2000)
	1998–1999	—	494 (1998–1999)	252 (1999–2000)	163 (2000–2001)
	1999–2000	—	1045 (1999–2000)	624 (2000–2001)	—
	2000–2001	—	1036 (2000–2001)	—	—
Second grade	1997–1998	—	—	457 (1997–1998)	301 (1998–1999)
	1998–1999	—	—	462 (1998–1999)	314 (1999–2000)
	1999–2000	—	—	986 (1999–2000)	546 (2000–2001)
	2000–2001	—	—	993 (2000–2001)	—

Note. RITE = Rodeo Institute for Teacher Excellence.

other district programs. Although not equivalent to randomizing, it was an attempt to provide a baseline performance standard for children with similar demographic characteristics that were attending schools of similar composition in similar geographic regions of the same district. Insofar as the district has had an active program targeting improved reading performance, it is critical that any outcomes associated with participation in the RITE program be judged relative to outcomes that could have reasonably been expected for these students had their school not participated in the RITE program. Due to the emphasis on improved reading performance at the district level, each of the comparisons schools was required to provide a reading curriculum for kindergarten, first, and second grades. However, within the comparison schools, the curricula across grades was not as standardized as it was in the RITE program, nor was not the same level of support provided to teachers regarding program implementation and implementation skill development.

MEASURES

The skill assessments administered at each grade were chosen to capture the multicomponent nature of academic reading skills in kindergarten and Grades 1 and 2, as well as the central importance of the TAAS examinations for Texas public school children in Grades 3 and beyond. In the first year of the program (1997–1998), all kindergarten students were administered the Word Identification subtest of the Woodcock–Johnson Mastery Test–Revised (Woodcock & Johnson, 1979) in the fall and spring of the school year. In 1998–1999, the assessment plan was modified, and individual assessments of students by trained pyschometricians were eliminated in favor of collecting district-mandated assessments, in an effort to reduce the overall cost of the evaluation program and to reduce the testing burden to students. Unfortunately, because this was the first year of a new assessment program within the district, some problems were experienced with the data collection mechanisms at the district level, specifically in the transfer of data from teacher-administered assessments in the fall and spring to district reporting forms. As a result, no data were available that year for the kindergarten students. In the 1999–2000 and 2000–2001 academic years, all kindergarten RITE and comparison school students' scores from both the winter and spring district-administered screening section of the Texas Primary Reading Inventory (TPRI) were collected. In each of the four program years, all first- and second-grade RITE and comparison school students' Word Reading and Reading Comprehension scores from the district-administered Stanford Achievement Test–Ninth Edition (SAT9) were collected. In the 2000–2001 academic year, Word Reading scale scores from the SAT9 were also available for kindergarten students. For those students who participated in the RITE program at some point during kindergarten, first, or second grade, and who have since reached third grade, the Texas Learning Index from the district-administered TAAS were also collected.

Woodcock Reading Mastery Test–Revised (Woodcock & Johnson, 1979)

In 1997–1998, all RITE and comparison kindergarten students were administered the Word Identification subtest in the fall and spring of the school year. The Word Identification task asks students to read words presented one at a time and consists of a total of 20 items. Internal consistency reliability coefficients for this subtest were .91 and .92, respectively, for the fall and spring administrations.

TPRI

The TPRI is a teacher-administered instrument developed to assist the teacher in identifying students' skills and skill levels and to guide instruction (Texas Education Agency [TEA], 1998). By district mandate, the TPRI was administered to kindergarten students by their classroom teacher in the winter and spring of each school year (beginning in 1998–1999). In kindergarten, the TPRI screen consists of measures of Phonological Awareness—specifically, Letter–Sound Identification and Blending Onset and Rime.

Letter–sound identification. The Letter–Sound Identification section of the TPRI screen consists of 10 letters of which the child must correctly provide the associated sound for 8 to "pass" the screen. The letters on this screen are considered to be 10 of the more difficult letters for children to learn the associated sounds, including: L, O, N, I, R, E, H, W, U, and Y. This portion of the TPRI screen has reliability (coefficient alpha) of .90 and a bivariate correlation with end of Grade 1 reading of .54.

Phonological awareness. In the Phonological Awareness (Blending Onset and Rime) section of the TPRI, the child is presented with isolated pairs of onset and rimes and asked to put the two parts together to make a word. There are eight items on the screen; a score of six out of eight correct is considered passing. This portion of the TPRI screen has reliability (coefficient alpha) of .91 and a bivariate correlation with end of Grade 1 reading of .50.

SAT9

The SAT9 is a norm-referenced standardized test that is designed to measure performance in the areas of reading, spelling, study skills, language, mathematics, science, and social science. The SAT9 is a district-mandated achievement test, and, for this evaluation, students' scores on the Word Reading and Reading Comprehension subtests were collected from the district research and accountability department.

TAAS

The TAAS is a state-mandated, criterion-referenced assessment given to all third-grade students in the spring of each academic year (TEA, 1990). In this evaluation, the Texas Learning Index (TLI) scores from the reading portion of the TAAS were collected for all RITE and comparison school children once the child reached third grade. The TLI score is a modified t score of the student's raw score. Specifically, the TLI is a t score that is anchored at the exit level passing standard rather than the mean of the distribution. A TLI score of 70 or above is considered passing, or indicates that the student has met the minimum standards for that grade level.

Teacher Observations

During the 2000–2001 school year, all kindergarten, first-, and second-grade classrooms were observed in each of the RITE program schools. Each classroom was observed at two time points (the fall of 2000 and the spring of 2001) and on two different days at each time point. During each observation session, a trained research assistant observed the teaching of a lesson for a period of approximately 20 to 25 min. Therefore, each teacher was observed for an average of approximately 80 to 100 min over the course of the year. A different observer conducted each of the two observations at a given time point in a particular classroom, and at each time point, one observation was conducted during instruction with the highest reading group, and the other with the lowest reading group in each classroom. Therefore, the possibility that teacher behaviors and techniques are simply a result of the ability level of the group being taught is minimized.

During the observation, two areas were alternately the focus of observations: teacher corrections (i.e., whether the teacher, in response to student errors, provided the group or individual with corrections that followed the RITE program model–test–retest paradigm), and teacher responses to student responses (i.e., whether praise, verification of the student response, or both, was provided; or whether no teacher response was provided). During an observation, the unit of focus in the classroom observations was considered to be a response. Therefore, information was recorded for each and every response requested by a teacher or provided by a child. The time that the observer spent in the classroom was divided into six segments. The observer rated each of the two aforementioned categories during three different segments. Therefore, during one observation period, each category was focused on three times. Hence, across the two observation sessions in a given time period within the year, each category was observed six times. The decision to focus on these two techniques was based on the importance that the RITE program placed on these key programmatic instruction techniques.

In addition to the two programmatic instructional techniques described earlier, classroom management is also an important aspect of the RM program. Consequently, observers also recorded the number of behavioral interruptions that occurred that caused a break in the flow of the reading group and the number of children outside of the reading group who, during the session being observed, were not engaged in independent activities.

Trainer Support Survey

Each RITE trainer was asked to complete a feedback survey on teachers in their schools. Trainers were asked to rate the level of preintervention problems, postintervention problems, and the general amount of intervention they provided each teacher in four different areas. Of the four areas rated, two focused on general classroom teaching, and two on skills specific to aspects of the RITE program. Specifically, the two general classroom teaching skill items were "classroom management–organization" and "disciplinary techniques–behavior management." The three programmatic teaching skills reported on included "understanding key concepts of the program" and "appropriate use of teacher corrections."

The scale for rating teachers' problems pre- and postintervention was a 4-point Likert-type scale, ranging from 1 (*no problem*) to 4 (*seriously problematic*). Ratings of the level of intervention provided were also reported on a 4-point Likert-type scale, ranging from 1 (*no help was ever provided*) to 4 (*the area was addressed specifically on numerous occasions*). Trainers' ratings of the four areas were averaged into the two teaching skills categories according to the list mentioned earlier (general classroom management and programmatic teaching).

PERFORMANCE ANALYSES

Preliminary Analyses

Prior to performing all analyses, all performance scores were examined for outlying values (e.g., specific children whose scores were much higher or lower than the majority), and the data was then checked to ensure the accuracy of the scores. Next, the number of teachers and children in the RITE and comparison schools were compared to ensure relative equivalence. Each year, attrition analyses were conducted to examine the performance levels of students who left the program school versus those who remained in the program school into the next grade (Little & Rubin, 1987;

Shafer, 1997). No significant differences in performance were found between the attrition and non-attrition groups in any analyses. Furthermore, attrition was not related to student characteristics such as gender and ethnicity. Based on these results, it is reasonable to consider that factors other than student performance and student demographic characteristics are responsible for attrition and that, for the sake of analyses, the data meet the assumptions for missing at random (Little & Rubin).

Within-Grade Analyses

The first set of analyses examined student performance in each grade separately. Because children learn and perform in similar settings (e.g., classrooms) and receive instruction from similar sources (e.g., teachers), scores for all students in the same classroom are not independent of one another. This lack of independence among observations must be taken into account in the analyses and makes the use of conventional analyses problematic. Instead, to account for the non-independence of students' performance, multilevel modeling techniques were employed in all analyses. The two levels in these analyses included the individual and the classroom (or teacher). Inclusion of the second level (teacher) addresses the possible non-independence among scores for children in the same classroom.

All within-grade analyses examined performance differences between comparison and RITE students as a function of the number of years of program experience. Therefore, we can compare the relative performance levels of all first graders and all second graders as a function of the number of years the children have participated in program schools. For kindergarten students, performance was examined as a function of RITE versus comparison only, as all kindergarten students had only 1 year in the program. Table 2 presents the total number of students included in the within-grade analyses for each grade level by number of years in the RITE program.

Kindergarten analyses.   The analysis of kindergarten students' performance was conducted for students in the 1997–1998, 1999–2000, and 2000–2001 academic years. During the 1998–1999 school year, no kindergarten assessment data was available. In 1997–1998, kindergarten students were administered the Word Identification subtest of the Woodcock–Johnson Mastery Test–Revised (Woodcock & Johnson, 1979). In the 1999–2000 school year, TPRI data were available for each student; and in 2000–2001, TPRI as well as SAT9 Word Reading data were available for kindergarten students.

Analyses of the 1997–1998 kindergarten data examined group differences in spring performance using fall performance as a covariate, in addition to examining group differences in fall performance, and evidence for differential effectiveness of the fall covariate (i.e., heterogeneity of regression). Results indicated that groups did not differ in the fall, $F(1, 412) = .08, p \leq .78$; and there was no evidence for heterogeneity of regression. However, after controlling for fall performance levels in Word Identification skills, the RITE kindergarten students' performance levels were significantly higher than those of the comparison students, as shown in the top section of Table 3, $F(2, 412) = 17.42, p \le .0001$. Therefore, RITE kindergarten students showed statistically greater gains in Word Reading skills over the course of the academic year than did comparison students. Although there was a small difference between groups at the pretest, it is important to bear in mind two facts when considering this difference. First and foremost, the difference is not statistically significant, indicating that we cannot reject the possibility that the groups are equivalent at the pretest. Second, the difference is small, such that even if we reject the notion that the groups are equivalent at the pretest, they are not largely different.

Analysis of the pass rates on the TPRI across the kindergarten year included two cohorts of kindergarten students (those from the 1998–1999 school year, as well as those from the 1999–2000 school year). Analyses examined differences in RITE and comparison students pass rates on both the winter and spring TPRI, as well as the relative gain in the number of students attaining passing status over the kindergarten year. From these analyses, we can ascertain not only whether more RITE children are passing the skills sections of the TPRI than comparison children at the end of the kindergarten year, but whether children are more likely to drop their at-risk status as identified by the TPRI screening when they receive kindergarten instruction through the RITE program.

Table 4 presents the pass versus no pass and RITE versus comparison group status for middle and end-of-year TPRI scores. Results of these analyses indicate that there were significant group differences (RITE vs. comparison) in students' TPRI pass rates in both the winter and spring. Specifically, in the middle of the kindergarten year, more RITE kindergarten students were passing the Letter–Sound Identification sections of the TPRI: RITE = 65%, comparison = 42%, $\chi^2 = 32.95, p \le .001$;

TABLE 2
Total Number of Students by Number of Years in the RITE Program Through the
2000–2001 Academic Year

Treatment Group	Grade Level	Number of Years in the RITE Program			
		0	1	2	3
COMP	Kindergarten	2,105	—	—	—
	First grade	3,924	—	—	—
	Second grade	2,838	—	—	—
RITE	Kindergarten	—	2,842[a]	—	—
	First grade	—	3,015	1,290	—
	Second grade	—	2,898	1,144	452

Note.   COMP = comparison; RITE = Rodeo Institute for Teacher Excellence.
[a]Unavailable data in the 1998–1999 school year.

TABLE 3
Kindergarten Woodcock–Johnson and SAT9 Performance Means and
Percentiles

	Treatment Group	
Subtest	RITE	Comparison
Woodcock–Johnson Word Identification Fall (1997–1998)		
M	0.84	0.75
SD	0.22	0.18
Woodcock–Johnson Word Identification Spring (1997–1998)		
M	16.76*	6.90*
SD	1.29	1.21
SAT9 Word Reading (2000–2001)		
M	457.71**	435.66**
SD	54.92	44.52
Below 25th Percentile	13%	22%
Above 50th Percentile	69%	49%

Note.   RITE = Rodeo Institute for Teacher Excellence; SAT9 = Stanford Achievement Test–Ninth Edition.
$*p \leq .0001$, after controlling for beginning of the year performance. $**p \leq .0001$.

and there was no significant differences in pass rates on the Phonological Awareness section of the TPRI (i.e., Blending Onset Rimes) between RITE and comparison school students: RITE = 19%, comparison = 15%, $\chi^2 = .44, p \leq .51$. At the end of the year, results indicated that more RITE children were passing both the Letter–Sound Identification: RITE = 91%, comparison = 78%, $\chi^2 = 26.32, p \leq .001$; and the Phonological Awareness sections of the TPRI screen: RITE = 68%, comparison = 50%, $\chi^2 = 28.32, p \leq .001$. Although there were no program group differences in the percentage of students moving from failing to passing from the middle to the end of the year on the Letter–Sound Identification section of the TPRI (RITE = 27%; comparison = 39%), more RITE children were moved from failing to passing status on the Phonological Awareness section of the TPRI over the course of the year than comparison children (RITE = 50%; comparison = 39%).

The final set of kindergarten analyses examined group differences in the SAT9 Word Reading skills for the 2000–2001 kindergarten students. These analyses compared average performance levels across the RITE and comparison groups, as well as the percentage of children performing at or below the 25th percentile, as well as those performing at or above the 50th percentile. Although the comparison of mean scores across groups provides useful information about general levels of performance, examining the distribution of percentile scores within and between groups provides important information about whether the RITE program is reduc-

TABLE 4
Kindergarten TPRI Pass Rates From Middle to End of Year

| | | | End of Year | |
| | | Middle of | | |
TPRI Subtest	Group	the Year	No Pass	Pass
		No pass	8%	27%
Letter–Sound Identification	RITE	Pass	1%	64%
		No pass	19%	39%
	COMP	Pass	3%	39%
		No pass	31%	50%
	RITE	Pass	1%	18%
Phonological Awareness		No pass	46%	39%
	COMP	Pass	4%	11%

Note. COMP = comparison; RITE = Rodeo Institute for Teacher Excellence; TPRI = Texas Primary Reading Inventory.

ing students' risk for low achievement or producing achievement levels that exceed normative expectations. Results indicated significant differences in RITE versus comparison students SAT9 Word Reading levels, such that the RITE kindergarten students were performing at significantly higher average skill levels than comparison students by the end of the kindergarten year (see lower section of Table 3), $F(1, 1,459) = 99.47$, $p \leq .0001$. Furthermore, RITE kindergartners were less likely to score below the 25th percentile, and significantly more likely to score above the 50th percentile than comparison students.

Taken together, results of the kindergarten analyses indicate that students in the RITE program show significantly higher levels of phonemic awareness and word reading skills than peers not in the program. Furthermore, in regard to word reading, the RITE kindergarten students are not only performing at higher levels than their nonprogram peers, but are also performing above national norms as indexed by percentile scores on the SAT9 Word Reading subtest.

First- and second-grade analyses. Two types of analyses were conducted in the examination of all first- and second-graders performance; and for each of these types of analyses, SAT9 Word Reading and Reading Comprehension performance were examined separately. The first set of analyses compared average performance levels on the SAT9 skills tests as a function of the number of years of experience the students had in the RITE program. The second set of analyses examined the average percentage of children across these same experience groups who were performing at or below the 25th percentile as well as those performing at or above the 50th percentile. Average performance levels are presented in Table 5 for first and second grades, respectively.

TABLE 5
First and Second Grade End of Year Stanford Achievement Test–Ninth Edition Means and
Percentile Performance

Subtest	RITE Years			Comparison Years		
	3	2	1	3	2	1
First grade						
Word Reading						
M	—	541.51	516.98	—	509.83	506.79
SD	—	55.48	52.87	—	51.79	51.79
Below 25th percentile	—	8%	20%	—	26%	23%
Above 50th percentile	—	73%	52%	—	48%	47%
Reading Comprehension						
M	—	549.86	533.12	—	518.31	516.31
SD	—	49.37	47.97	—	47.71	45.18
Below 25th percentile	—	11%	19%	—	26%	24%
Above 50th percentile	—	78%	60%	—	55%	52%
Second grade						
Word Reading						
M	580.30	562.27	553.98	555.21	553.98	551.01
SD	43.65	46.05	41.44	42.76	44.53	41.67
Below 25th percentile	16%	27%	33%	33%	31%	32%
Above 50th Percentile	61%	44%	36%	38%	36%	37%
Reading Comprehension						
M	589.75	578.32	574.64	571.01	569.32	569.57
SD	30.86	34.99	32.91	31.56	35.23	33.59
Below 25th percentile	12%	24%	29%	34%	34%	32%
Above 50th percentile	66%	51%	43%	39%	38%	36%

Note.   There were no significant differences between the comparison groups as a function of the number of years the students has been in the school. First Grade: Word Reading ($F = 1.21, p \leq .19$); Reading Comprehension ($F = 1.98, p \leq .16$); Second Grade: Word Reading ($F = 3.02, p \leq .09$); Reading Comprehension ($F = .86, p \leq .43$). RITE = Rodeo Institute for Teacher Excellence.

Results (shown in Table 6) indicate that the number of years in the RITE program was significantly related to both Word Reading and Reading Comprehension. Follow-up contrasts for each grade-level analysis indicate that performance scores increased significantly as the number of years of experience in the RITE program increased. Therefore, all RITE students are performing at levels significantly higher than comparison students; and within the RITE program, students who finish first or second grade with more years of program experience outperform their program peers (see Tables 5 and 6).

Additional analyses were conducted to examine the effect of number of years in the same school on performance levels for comparison students. Because the number of years in the RITE program is confounded with the number of years the student remains in the same school, it was important to examine the effect of number of years

TABLE 6
First and Second Grade SAT9 Performance Predicted by Number of Program
Years

Grade and SAT9 Subtest	F	p
First-grade Word Reading[a]	71.72	.0001
Follow-up contrasts		
Comparison versus 1 year	17.00	.0001
Comparison versus 2 years	143.42	.0001
1 year versus 2 years	69.90	
First-grade Reading	92.11	.0001
Comprehension[a]		
Follow-up contrasts		
Comparison versus 1 year	65.19	.0001
Comparison versus 2 years	168.67	.0001
1 year versus 2 years	40.58	.0001
Second-grade Word Reading[b]	27.65	.0001
Follow-up Contrasts		
Comparison versus 1 year	2.99	.080
Comparison versus 2 years	7.81	.0070
Comparison versus 3 years	63.10	.0001
1 year versus 2 years	14.78	.0001
1 year versus 3 years	75.00	.0001
2 years versus 3 years	27.25	.0001
Second-grade Reading	27.45	.0001
Comprehension[b]		
Follow-up contrasts		
Comparison versus 1 year	9.17	.0030
Comparison versus 2 years	21.97	.0001
Comparison versus 3 years	74.07	.0001
1 year versus 2 years	3.79	.0050
1 year versus 3 years	39.77	.0001
2 years versus 3 years	19.75	.0001

Note. Number of program years were used a predictor for this analyses. Comparison students were considered irrespective of the number of years in the same school based on analyses indicating no significant differences between these groups. SAT9 = Stanford Achievement Test–Ninth Edition.

[a]First-grade analyses, $df = 2, 6981$. [b]Second-grade analyses, $df = 3, 6,139$.

in the same school on performance within the comparison schools. Results indicated that there were no significant effects of number of years in the same school and first- and second-grade performance levels within the comparison schools (see Table 5). Based on this, all analyses were conducted collapsing the comparison students into one category (zero program years). These results strengthen the findings for the effects of number of years in the RITE program as they suggest that the effects are not simply an artifact of student stability within the same school environment.

As with the kindergarten analyses, first- and second-grade performance score distributions were also examined in terms of the percentages of students scoring below the 25th percentile and above the 50th percentile as a function of the number of years in the RITE program (see Table 5). As can be seen in this table, the greater the number of years in the program, the less likely students are to perform below the 25th percentile and the more likely they are to perform above the 50th percentile. The greatest performance differences are seen with students who at the end of second grade have had 3 years of program experience, or who at the end of first grade have had 2 years of program experience. Put another way, the program effects were greatest for students who began the program in kindergarten, and next largest for students who began the program in Grade 1.

Third-grade analyses.   The final set of analyses of student outcomes compared third-grade TAAS performance of students in the RITE and comparison schools. (Third graders also took the SAT9, but evaluators did not have these scores available for analysis.) There are three groups of children who have participated in the RITE program who have completed the third grade. One group participated in the program for the entire 3 years (Grades K–2), the second participated in first and second grade (2 years), whereas the other participated for 1 year (second grade only). Hence, in the third-grade analyses, there are four groups of third-grade children being compared: those with 3 years in the program; those with 2 years, 1 year, and 0 years in the program; or comparison children.

The first set of analyses compared average performance levels on the reading portion of the TAAS across the four groups, and the second examined the percentage of children passing the reading portion of the TAAS, as shown in Table 7. Analyses indicated that average TAAS TLI scores for children in third grade who participated in the RITE program for 3 years (Grades K–2) were significantly higher than those for students who participated for 2 years, 1 year, or in a comparison school, as shown in Table 8. Furthermore, students participating for 2 years (first and second grade) have significantly higher average scores than those who participated in second grade only (1 year), who in turn have higher average scores than students from the comparison schools. As with the first- and second-grade analyses, an additional analysis was conducted to examine the effect of number of years in the same school on performance levels for comparison students. Results indicated that there was no significant effect of number of years in the same school on third grade TAAS reading TLI scores within the comparison schools (see Table 7). Based on this, all analyses were conducted collapsing the comparison students into one category (zero program years).

TAAS pass rates are calculated based on the students TLI score (70 or greater is equivalent to passing). Passing the TAAS at Grade 3 means a student has met the minimum expectations for the end of third grade. Analyses indicated a similar pattern to that found with the average TLI score analysis mentioned earlier, χ^2 = 26.44, $p < .001$. Specifically, as students spend more time in the RITE program, they are significantly more likely to meet or exceed the state-mandated reading skills requirement (see Table 7).

Longitudinal Analyses

The two groups of students who showed the highest performance levels in the Grade 1, Grade 2, and Grade 3 analyses mentioned earlier were those students who began the program in kindergarten. Although grade-level analyses inform us about the performance levels of students with varying years of experience in the RITE program, these analyses tell us little about the gains being made within a specific group of students over time. The longitudinal analyses examined the degree to which performance in a higher grade could be attributed to gains made the previous year, or whether there were additional gains being made above and beyond performance gains in previous program years.

Longitudinal analyses were conducted for the cohort of children who had participated in the entire span of the RITE program (Grades K–2) and for whom data were available in each year of the program (first kindergarten cohort beginning kindergarten in 1997–1998 and completing second grade in the 1999–2000 school year).

Analyses of performance from kindergarten through first grade were conducted by a series of models predicting SAT9 scores at the end of the first-grade year after controlling for performance levels on the Woodcock–Johnson Word Identification subtest in the kindergarten year. This analysis allowed us to examine differences in first-grade performance levels above and beyond the gains seen in the kindergarten year. Therefore, we can ascertain not only whether RITE children are performing at higher levels than comparison children at the end of first grade, but also whether ad-

TABLE 7
Third Grade Texas Assessment of Academic Skills Means and Percentage Passing by Number of Program Years

	RITE Years			Comparison Years		
Statistic	3	2	1	3	2	1
M	79.86	78.05	75.04	72.47	71.89	71.08
SD	16.44	18.26	21.22	22.66	24.02	23.46
Percentage passing	82%	79%	73%	68%	66%	65%

Note.   There were no significant differences between the comparison groups as a function of the number of years the students have been in the school ($F = .24$, $p \leq .62$). RITE = Rodeo Institute for Teacher Excellence.

TABLE 8
Third-Grade Performance Predicted by Number of Program Years

TAAS	F	p
Reading TLI[a]	15.58	.0001
Follow-up contrasts		
Comparison versus 1 year	14.94	.0001
Comparison versus 2 years	27.11	.0001
Comparison versus 3 years	15.49	.0001
1 year versus 2 years	5.17	.0200
1 year versus 3 years	5.04	.0200
2 years versus 3 years	0.52	.4700

Note. Comparison students were considered irrespective of the number of years in the same school based on analyses indicating no significant differences between these groups. TAAS = Texas Assessment of Academic Skills; TLI = Texas Learning Index.
[a]Third-grade analyses, $df = 3, 5,040$.

ditional differential performance gains occurred in the first-grade year that were not attributable solely to the differential performance gains observed in kindergarten.

Analyses indicated that there were significant group differences (RITE vs. comparison) in students' SAT9 Word Reading and Reading Comprehension skill levels at the end of first grade after controlling for end of kindergarten Word Identification skills, as shown in Table 9. Therefore, not only do RITE first-grade students with 2 years of program experience end first grade at higher performance levels, these students show differential performance gains across the first-grade year that cannot be attributed solely to gains seen in the kindergarten year.

Analyses of performance from first through second grade were also conducted for this cohort by a series of models predicting SAT9 scores at the end of the second-grade year after controlling for performance levels on the same SAT9 subtests at the end of the first-grade year. These analyses examined differences in performance at the end of second grade that were above and beyond any gains seen in the first-grade year. Therefore, these analyses examined whether RITE children performed at higher levels than comparison children at the end of second grade, and whether additional development occurred in the second-grade year that was not attributable solely to performance gains in the first grade.

Results indicated that there were no significant differences in RITE and comparison students' average Word Reading or Reading Comprehension scores at the end of the second-grade year after controlling for end of first-grade performance (see Table 9). Although all students' Word Reading and Reading Comprehension performance levels increased over the second-grade year, results suggest that performance at the end of second grade for the cohort with 3 years in the RITE program has more to do with gains made in previous years rather than gains made in the second-grade year.

Teacher Implementation Analyses

Teacher correction techniques. In observing teachers' corrections of errors in students' responses, the first piece of information recorded was whether an error was made. If so, the observer then recorded whether the teacher provided a full, partial, or no-correction for the erroneous response. The percentage of errors was calculated by dividing the number of errors observed by the number of responses observed. On average, errors were observed in 15% of the student's responses in the fall and in 10% of the responses in the spring. At each time point, the percentage of errors observed across all classrooms ranged from 1% to 30%.

The number of years a teacher is in the RITE program will likely influence their skill in implementing the key aspects of the program. To examine this, teacher corrections were examined as a function of the number of years of experience that the teacher had with the RITE program, as shown in Table 10. In the beginning of the year, fourth-year teachers showed lower use of full corrections than all other teachers. However, by the end of the year, there were no differences in full correction usage based on teaching experience.

Examination of the teachers' responses to students' responses showed little to no variation in the percentage of time the teacher provided praise or verification over the course of the year. Overall, RITE teachers praised student responses an average of 20% of the time, and provided verification of responses an average of 30% of the

TABLE 9
End of Grade-1 Performance Controlling for End of Kindergarten Performance in K–2 Cohort

SAT9 Subtest	Predictor	F	p
End of Grade 1[a]			
Word Reading	WJ Word Identification end of Kindergarten	11.83	.0007
	Group (RITE vs. COMP)	17.42	.0001
Reading Comprehension	WJ Word Identification end of Kindergarten	7.01	.0090
	Group (RITE vs. COMP)	22.09	.0001
End of Grade 2[b]			
Word Reading	Word Reading end of Grade 1	187.40	.0001
	Group (RITE vs. COMP)	.80	.4400
Reading Comprehension	Reading Comprehension end of Grade 1	299.60	.0001
	Group (RITE vs. COMP)	1.32	.3300

Note. COMP = comparison; SAT9 = Stanford Achievement Test–Ninth Edition; WJ = Woodcock–Johnson.

TABLE 10
Percentage of Teacher Corrections Over Time and by Number of
Program Teaching Years

	Time Point	
Program Years	Fall	Spring
1 year	60%	76%
2 years	57%	77%
3 years	67%	76%
4 years	46%	77%

time. Furthermore, there were no differences in the average use of praise or verification as a function of the number of years teaching in the RITE program.

These results are not surprising given that the increased use of programmatic correction techniques was a primary focus of the RITE training program in the current year. Based on the evaluation of teacher behaviors in prior years, RITE trainers this year increased efforts to improve teachers' use of full corrections in response to student errors. The average gains seen across the year for all teachers were consistent with this general emphasis. At the same time, emphasis on praise and verification were reduced as previous years' evaluations have not found these two teacher behaviors to be as strongly linked to student outcomes. Not surprisingly, these teacher behaviors are relatively stable over the current year.

Trainer Intervention Analyses

General classroom teaching skills. Table 11 shows the average pre and postintervention ratings for general classroom teaching skills, as well as the average level of reported intervention by number of years teaching in the RITE program. First- and second-year RITE program teachers' general teaching skills were rated as more problematic than third- and fourth-year teachers. On average, trainers reported providing more intervention to these teachers than to either third- or fourth-year teachers. Furthermore, first- and second-year teachers were rated by trainers as showing the most improvement in these teaching skills over the course of the year. Although trainers reported providing more intervention with teachers where ratings were more problematic, it was encouraging to note that the correlation of reported intervention levels with the observed decrease in these behaviors was negative—meaning that for all teachers, the more intervention provided, the more problematic behaviors decreased in the areas of classroom management, organization, and disciplinary technique or behavior management ($-.59, p \le .0001$). Although en-

TABLE 11
Trainer Reported Problems and Intervention Levels by Number of Program Teaching Years

Type of Rating	Number of Years of RITE Teaching			
	1	2	3	4
Classroom management				
Pre-intervention problems	2.0	1.8	1.2	1.3
Post-intervention problems	1.4	1.3	1.2	1.3
Level of intervention	2.4	2.2	1.6	1.8
Programmatic teaching				
Pre-intervention problems	1.9	1.8	1.4	1.3
Post-intervention problems	1.2	1.2	1.2	1.1
Level of Intervention	2.8	2.6	1.8	1.8

Note.   RITE = Rodeo Institute for Teacher Excellence.

couraging, because the same person made both ratings (intervention and observed improvement), it is also possible that the correlation simply reflects rater bias. To examine this possibility, the relation between reported level of general classroom teaching skills and examiner observation of behavioral interruptions in the classroom was examined. The correlation between the two was significant, indicating that the more reported intervention on the part of the trainer, the greater the decrease in the behavioral interruptions observed by examiners in the classroom over the course of the year ($-.29, p \leq .01$). Here, the ratings of teacher behaviors and level of intervention required were made by trainers, whereas the observations of teacher behaviors used to assess teacher behavior change were made by classroom observers who work for the evaluation team. These individuals are not involved in the rating or training of teachers and do not have contact with the trainers. In that sense, the observations used to measure teacher behavior and teacher behavior change are made independently of the trainers' ratings of teachers. Therefore, it seems that trainer intervention with general classroom management skills is related to the teacher's ability to better manage the behavior of the children in the classroom.

Program-specific teaching skills.   Table 11 also shows the average pre and postintervention ratings for program-specific teaching skills, as well as the average level of reported intervention. On average, first- and second-year RITE program teachers' program-specific skills were rated as more problematic than the skills of third- and fourth-year teachers, and trainers reported significant improvement in these skills after intervention for first- and second-year teachers. In addition, by the end of the year, trainers were reporting, on average, relatively few problems with these skills for all teachers. Although trainers reported providing more intervention with teachers where ratings were more problematic, it was encouraging to note that the correlation of reported intervention levels with the reported decreases in problematic program implementation skills was significant—meaning that for all teachers, the more intervention provided, the greater the rated decrease in problematic behaviors in the areas of program implementation skills ($-.54, p \le .0001$). Again, although this relation was encouraging, the fact that both of these ratings (intervention and observed improvement) were made by the trainer leaves open the possibility that the correlation is an artifact of the rater. To examine this possibility, the level of intervention required to improve program implementation skills as rated by the trainer was correlated with teacher correction techniques in the classroom as rated by the classroom observer. The correlation between the two was significant and positive, indicating that the more reported intervention on the part of the trainer, the greater the increase in the teachers' use of full corrections over the course of the year ($.21, p \le .01$). Therefore, it seems that trainer intervention with program implementation skills is related to teachers' increased use of full correction techniques in the classroom.

It is interesting to note that this pattern did not hold true for teachers' implementation of verification responses. There was no relation between reported levels of intervention for program-specific skills and the degree to which teachers used verification in their responses to children. It may be the case that when reporting levels of intervention for program implementation techniques, trainers focused more heavily on teacher correction behaviors than teacher responses to students' correct responses (or praise and verification responses).

LINKING TEACHER IMPLEMENTATION TO STUDENT PERFORMANCE

An important element of any program's success lies in the degree to which implementation of the key components of the program relates to desired outcomes for students. To gain support for the specific program being used, it is important to first establish that key components of the program are indeed related to desired outcomes, and that the degree to which implementation of the key components is followed is correlated with higher desired outcomes. This type of evidence provides strong support for the specific program as a route for obtaining desired outcomes.

In this evaluation, the degree to which full implementation of program-specific components were related to increased student achievement was examined. This portion of the evaluation focused on teachers usage of full correction techniques at the beginning and end of the school year. Simultaneous examination of the relation of usage at these two time points to student outcomes allows for the determination of the relative influence of implementation levels at the beginning and end of the year.

The relations between fall and spring levels of teacher corrections were examined simultaneously for each student outcome in each grade. In all models, the interaction between fall and spring levels of teacher corrections was included to allow for the possibility of different outcomes based on the difference in the level of corrections across the year. Results indicated that teacher corrections related significantly to children's performance levels, and that the pattern of the relation was similar across all grades.

Results indicated that teachers' use of correction techniques in both the fall and spring was related to students' performance on the majority of skills, as shown in Table 12. Specifically, the higher the level of usage, the higher the students' performance levels. The interaction between fall and spring corrections was also significant in all models. Follow-up analyses indicated that students of teachers who used low levels of correction over the course of the year performed at significantly lower levels than all other students. Therefore, teachers' high use of correction techniques for all or at least part of the school year was more effective than no use of full correction techniques.

DISCUSSION

Student Outcomes

This evaluation indicated that the RITE program was very successful at increasing the reading abilities of students in at-risk schools and who would likely themselves be at risk for reading difficulties. Children who began the RITE program early and

TABLE 12
Student Performance Predicted From Fall and Spring Teacher Corrections

Performance Measure	Predictor	F	p
Kindergarten[a]			
Word Reading	Fall corrections	6.13	.01
	Spring corrections	5.68	.02
	Interaction	6.01	.01
Grade 1[b]			
Word Reading	Fall corrections	15.70	.0001
	Spring corrections	20.60	.0001
	Interaction	28.04	.0001
Reading Comprehension	Fall corrections	28.44	.0001
	Spring corrections	20.03	
	Interaction	35.28	
Grade 2[c]			
Word Reading	Fall corrections	14.20	.0001
	Spring corrections	19.80	.0001
	Interaction	16.76	.0001
Reading Comprehension	Fall corrections	25.89	.0001
	Spring corrections	19.68	.0001
	Interaction	27.54	.0001

[a]Kindergarten analyses, $df = 3, 1,459$. [b]First-grade analyses, $df = 3, 1,646$. [c]Second-grade analyses, $df = 3, 1,877$.

who spent more years in the program outperformed their schoolmates with less program experience, those who began the program later, and those who never participated in the program (comparison school students). The most profound effects of the RITE program were seen in the first 2 years of schooling, especially when students began the program in kindergarten. By the end of kindergarten, students showed prereading skill development levels greater then their nonprogram peers; they also demonstrated greater gains in these skills over the course of the kindergarten year. At the end of first grade, children with 2 years in the program again outperformed their peers, both those with less program experience and those who had not participated in the program. Furthermore, these first graders also showed differential gains during the first-grade year that could not be accounted for by the gains experienced in kindergarten alone.

In second grade, RITE students with previous experience in the program continued to perform at higher levels than their peers with less program experience and comparison students. However, these children did not show differential gains across the second-grade school year. Therefore, in second grade, growth rates in reading skills were comparable for RITE and comparison school children, whereas overall performance level differences between the groups were maintained.

Based on these findings, we conclude that the program has accelerated students' development of prereading and reading skills. By second grade, the acceleration of this development has slowed, such that skill development in second grade continues at rates that are comparable to those of nonprogram students. Therefore, we also conclude that the second-grade program as currently implemented does not fully capitalize on the performance gains experienced by children who participate in the program in kindergarten and first grade. However, it is important to recognize that students in the comparison schools have not caught up to the RITE program children by the end of second grade. In fact, third-grade students who have participated in the RITE program were significantly more likely to pass the minimum skills requirement on the reading section of the TAAS than were students in the comparison schools. Nevertheless, RITE must consider steps that can be taken to further improve outcomes for students in second grade and beyond, including finding ways to strengthen the impact for students whose first year in the program is in second grade, and ways to better capitalize on the gains made in kindergarten and Grade 1. Currently, the leadership of the RITE program is considering enhancements to the language and literacy components of the program, and in particular, working with teachers to increase the amount of book reading and language development activities employed in Grades K–2.

Teacher Implementation and Trainer Support

At the beginning of the year, first-year teachers were rated as having more problematic general classroom and program-specific teaching skills. Not surprisingly, trainers on average also reported providing first-year teachers with more support (intervention) with general classroom teaching as well as with program-specific teaching skills. Analyses within this year's evaluation indicated that the more intervention the trainer reported providing to a teacher, the more improvement there was in the observed teaching skills discussed earlier (behavior management and teacher corrections). Most notable was the success of the RITE trainers focus on full correction techniques and the gains seen in the majority of the teachers' implementation of these techniques over the course of the school year. Because the level of intervention was related to observed positive development of these skills, and, as we saw earlier, there was still room for the development of these skills, it would be important to continue high levels of intervention with all teachers, regardless of the number of years in the program.

Student Performance and Teacher Implementation

Implementation of the more advanced teaching techniques required by the RITE program was significantly related to student performance. Teachers who showed higher levels of implementation all year or part of the year had students who were performing at significantly higher skill levels than teachers who showed low levels of implementation all year.

These findings are important in that they indicate that teaching techniques that are specific to delivery of the RITE program are related to better student performance. Furthermore, taken with the previous discussion of the effects of trainer intervention, these results also support the importance of the training component of the program. Specifically, we saw that trainer intervention was related to teachers' improved adherence to program teaching techniques, and that teacher adherence to program teaching techniques resulted in better student outcomes. These results close the trainer–teacher–student feedback loop by showing that teacher behavior relates to student performance. Insofar as room remains for improvement in teacher adherence to program teaching techniques, trainers' support of teachers must be continued and strengthened. As trainers increase their support of teachers, the RITE program can expect more improvement in teachers' adherence to program teaching techniques, and as a result, greater gains in student performance can be expected.

ACKNOWLEDGMENTS

The RITE program and the research associated with it are supported by The Houston Livestock Show and Rodeo.

We wish to thank the RITE teachers, administrators, and trainers; as well as the individual students who take part in the RITE program.

REFERENCES

Adams, M. J. (1990). *Beginning to read: Thinking and learning about print.* Cambridge, MA: MIT Press.

Brady, S., & Moats, L. C. (1997). *Informed instruction for reading success: Foundations for teacher preparation.* Baltimore: International Dyslexia Association.

Englemann, S., & Bruner, E. C. (1995). *The SRA reading mastery rainbow.* New York: McGraw-Hill.

Juel, C. (1988). Learning to read and write: A longitudinal study of 54 children from first through fourth grades. *Journal of Educational Psychology, 85,* 112–126.

Juel, C. (1996). What makes literacy tutoring effective? *Reading Research Quarterly, 31,* 268–288.

Leslie, L., & Allen, L. (1999). Factors that predict success in an early literacy intervention project. *Reading Research Quarterly, 34,* 404–424.

Lipson, M. Y., & Wixson, K. K. (1997). *Assessment and instruction of reading and writing disability: An interactive approach* (2nd ed.). New York: Plenum.

Little, R. J., & Rubin, D. B. (1987). *Statistical analysis with missing data.* New York: Wiley.

National Reading Panel Report. (2000, April 13). Testimony of Duane Alexander, Director, National Institute of Child Health and Human Development before the Labor, Health and Human Services, and Education Subcommittee, Senate Appropriations Committee, Washington, DC.

Pflaum, S. W., Walberg, H. J., Karegaines, M. L., & Rahsher, S. P. (1980). Reading instruction: A quantitative analysis. *Educational Researcher, 9*(7), 12–18.

Shafer, J. L. (1997). *Analysis of incomplete multivariate data.* London: Chapman & Hall.

Snider, V. E., & Tarver, S. G. (1987). The effect of early reading failure on acquisition of knowledge among students with learning disabilities. *Journal of Learning Disabilities, 20,* 351–356.

Snow, C. E., Burns, M. S., & Griffin, P. (Eds.). (1998). *Preventing reading difficulties in young children.* Washington, DC: National Academy Press.

Stahl, S. A., McKenna, M. C., & Pagnucco, J. R. (1994). The effects of whole language instruction: An update and reappraisal. *Educational Psychologist, 29,* 175–186.

Texas Education Agency (TEA). (1990). *Texas assessment of academic skills: Technical report.* Austin: Author.

Texas Education Agency (TEA). (1998). *Texas primary reading inventory: Technical manual.* Austin: Author.

Wharton-McDonald, R., Pressley, M., & Hampston, J. (1998). Literacy instruction in nine first-grade classrooms: Teacher characteristics and student achievement. *The Elementary School Journal, 99*(2), 101–128.

Woodcock, R. W., & Johnson, M. B. (1979). *Woodcock–Johnson Psychoeducational Battery–Revised.* Allen, TX: DLM.

JOURNAL OF EDUCATION FOR STUDENTS PLACED AT RISK, 7(2), 167–195

Implementing Research-Based Reading Programs in the Fort Worth Independent School District

Daniel M. O'Brien

The Cecil and Ida Green Center for the Study of Science and Society
University of Texas at Dallas

Anne M. Ware

Fort Worth Independent School District
Research and Evaluation

Within only 2 school years, the Fort Worth Independent School District implemented direct instruction of prereading and early reading skills in kindergarten, first, and second grade for more than 14,000 students in 61 elementary schools. This article describes the reading programs adopted by the district, the implementation activities, and the evaluation.

The article first examines the programs selected, the selection process, and the roles of district personnel and external advisors in motivating, legitimizing, and attracting funding for the implementation. The article then reviews the evaluation of the implementation process, including feedback mechanisms, coaching, classroom observations, and district-wide monitoring of lesson progress and mastery. The article evaluates student gains by comparing performance on standardized reading tests with prior year performance and national norms. Finally, the article analyzes variation in reading program effectiveness using a value-added regression framework.

The study finds that the reading programs have a positive impact on student reading achievement, especially for disadvantaged students in kindergarten.

The nationwide focus to "leave no child behind" (Paige, 2001) has gained substantial momentum during the past decade, with the publication of new studies demonstrating the importance of prereading and early reading skills, and the role of direct

---

Requests for reprints should be sent to Daniel M. O'Brien, Green Center, University of Texas at Dallas, P.O. Box 830688, MS GC 21, Richardson, TX 75083–0688. E-mail: obri@utdallas.edu

instruction in improving these skills in young students.[1] With a new superintendent, and armed with this research, the Fort Worth Independent School District (FWISD) engaged reading experts from around the country, developed objectives for a new reading initiative, hired an experienced director of reading, applied for and won several large grants, convinced the school board to invest an additional $1 million of local funds, and launched what was one of the largest implementations of direct instruction reading programs ever attempted. During the 1998–1999 school year, 32 FWISD elementary schools, or more than 6,000 K–2 students and 430 teachers, began using one of two programs, reading mastery (RM) or open court (OC).[2] The following school year, the reading programs were implemented on 29 additional campuses, serving more than 14,000 K–2 students. This left only 9 of the 70 FWISD elementary schools still using whole language programs.

To assess the effectiveness of the new reading programs, the district planning and evaluation staff worked with an external evaluation advisory committee, comprised of district and university reading and evaluation experts. This committee helped to design and guide a broad evaluation of the implementation. The district plan included limited resources for both an outcome and process evaluation. The process evaluation focused on improving instruction by (a) disseminating student skill development information to teachers, support staff, and principals; (b) providing coaching and mentoring resources to individual teachers; and (c) identifying instructional practices that work. The outcome evaluation used statistical analysis to (a) study the effectiveness of the overall reading initiative on district-wide student reading performance; (b) compare student performance between programs, schools, and classrooms; and (c) identify sources of variation in reading gains, including strength of implementation, teacher training, and lesson pacing. Results of these evaluations have been shared with district and other interested reading professionals at two FWISD conferences: the Texas Association of School Administrators conferences and the Council of Great City Schools meetings, as well as other meetings with district teachers, principals, and administrators.

This article describes the FWISD reading program implementation and its evaluation. We begin by describing the research basis for the FWISD reading approach,

---

[1] A summary of the research that was especially influential is found in Marilyn Adams's (1996), *Beginning to Read: Thinking and Learning About Print.* This text includes an extensive list of references. Numerous studies, including Project Follow Through, support the use of direct instruction in early reading instruction (G. L. Adams & Engelmann, 1996; Meyer, 1984). Even the influential American Federation of Teachers supports a balanced program including "direct teaching of decoding ... " (AFT, 1999, p. 7). Additional references are also available from the Texas Education Agency (1997).

[2] In addition, by January 1999, direct instruction was being used for corrective reading programs in 43 elementary schools, 20 middle schools, and 8 high schools. We limited the discussion in this article to reading programs in Grades K–2; there was also evidence that corrective reading made a difference for students in older grades. During 1999–2000, corrective reading was used for remedial reading instruction in all of the district's elementary, middle, and high schools.

the planning phase of the implementation, reading program descriptions, and demographic characteristics of program students. We focus on what factors motivated the choice of programs as well as how district and external advisors interacted to motivate and legitimize reading program selection and implementation.

The second section reviews methods and findings of the formative evaluation, emphasizing classroom observation strategies and feedback mechanisms. We then discuss the outcome evaluation, comparing district performance on standardized reading tests with prior year performance and national norms. We examine differences in school-year gains by program and race or ethnicity. Sources of variation in student progress, such as gender, special education, income, and English proficiency are assessed using a value-added regression framework. Finally, we present an overview of our findings and conclusions, as well as a description of evaluation improvements that are being considered.

BACKGROUND

The FWISD is the 38th largest school district in the United States (National Center for Education Statistics, 2000) with more than 78,000 students; 9,117 total staff; 4,596 teachers; and an annual operating budget approaching $.5 billion. Like most large city school districts, the student population is diverse: 87% are non-White, 53% are economically disadvantaged, and 23% are enrolled in bilingual or English as a Second Language programs (FWISD, 2001). Many of these students began kindergarten or the first grade lacking basic prereading skills. During the 1995–1996 school year, led by a new superintendent, FWISD established 11 education imperatives aimed at meeting the district's education mission. Imperative 1 was that all students would be able to read by the end of Grade 2.

> The heart of the district's reform efforts is a comprehensive practical approach to improved reading instruction. The reading initiative stresses direct instruction, staff development, a choice of models, expanded materials, dynamic and entrepreneurial leadership and rigorous formative and evaluative assessment. (McKenzie Group, Inc., 2000, p. 19)

The following section describes how the district arrived at this juncture.

IDENTIFYING THE NEED

Prior to the 1998–1999 school year, most of the reading instruction in FWISD was based on the whole language approach made popular during the prior decade. Advances in reading research, however, led educators and researchers to question this approach and advocate a balanced reading program with an emphasis on insuring that all students learn basic prereading and reading skills. A balanced reading program, they decided, would focus on three specific areas, as defined by Marilyn Adams (1996): phonological awareness, or recognizing the sounds that make up oral language; graphophonemic knowledge, or relating the sounds to pictures and letters; and time set aside for the practice of reading and writing.

Based on various test scores, FWISD recognized that many students were not reading at grade level. In 1997 and 1998, the 2 years prior to the implementation of direct instruction, first- and second-grade students scored below grade level and well below the 50th percentile on the Gates–MacGinitie reading test. In addition, results from the high-stakes accountability test mandated by the Texas Education Agency (TEA), called the Texas Assessment of Academic Skills (TAAS), indicated that district students in Grades 3 through 8 were performing poorly in comparison to students throughout the state.

Table 1 summarizes TAAS reading passing rates by grade for the 1996–1997 school year. The first panel gives passing rates by grade for all Texas students by race or ethnicity, and for students who are eligible for the federal free and reduced-price lunch program. The second panel gives the same statistics for students attending FWISD. The third panel represents the difference in passing rates.

In each grade and for each subgroup, the passing rate for FWISD students was lower than that of students throughout the state. The differences were especially large for Hispanic, African American, and economically disadvantaged students, whose FWISD passing rates ranged from 2.9% to 13.7% lower than the statewide average. Note that the percentages for all students were larger than for the individual categories. This was due to the larger proportion of students in Fort Worth who were African American or Hispanic (71.6%) or economically disadvantaged (58.7%) than the statewide averages (51.7% and 48.1%, respectively).[3]

Based on these unacceptable reading scores, the district began a full-scale investigation of alternatives by enlisting the aid of a group of reading experts, led by Douglas Carnine of the University of Oregon.[4] The group made an assessment of current district practices, ascertained that FWISD reading instruction did not ade-

---

[3]As shown through the comparison of characteristics and performance of students who received each reading program, there was also substantial variation between schools. Students in several of the Fort Worth Independent School District campuses were primarily nonminority and not economically disadvantaged; these students' test scores exceeded statewide averages. For the schools targeted for the new programs, there were higher proportions of minority and economically disadvantaged students and lower test scores.

[4]Carnine was joined by Jean Osborn, University of Illinois; David Chard, University of Texas; Ramon Alvarez, Rio Hondo Intermediate School; and Marsha Sonnenberg, Planning Council for the Governor's Texas Reading Initiative. Ms. Sonnenberg was later hired to lead the reading initiative for the district. It was due in large measure to her efforts and those of her Chief of Staff, Lucinda Randall, that the reading initiative was fully and successfully implemented

TABLE 1
Percentage of Students Passing 1996–1997 TAAS Reading for Students in All Texas
Districts and in the Fort Worth Independent School District

	Grade 3	Grade 4	Grade 5	Grade 6	Grade 7	Grade 8
State of Texas						
All students	81.5	82.5	84.8	84.6	84.5	83.9
African American	69.3	69.5	70.8	74.1	74.8	74.0
Hispanic	73.8	75.5	77.4	75.4	75.0	74.2
White	89.3	90.2	92.4	93.7	93.6	93.0
Economic disadvantage	72.0	73.0	75.7	74.3	74.0	72.7
Fort Worth ISD						
All students	70.0	70.4	74.7	70.1	70.4	71.5
African American	61.5	59.2	67.9	62.3	61.8	64.4
Hispanic	62.8	66.7	67.0	62.3	64.0	63.1
White	87.3	87.9	91.3	91.3	91.3	91.2
Economic disadvantage	62.1	62.4	65.7	60.6	62.2	61.2
Difference						
All students	−11.5	−12.1	−10.1	−14.5	−14.1	−12.4
African American	−7.8	−10.3	−2.9	−11.8	−13.0	−9.6
Hispanic	−11.0	−8.8	−10.4	−13.1	−11.0	−11.1
White	−2.0	−2.3	−1.1	−2.4	−2.3	−1.8
Economic disadvantage	−9.9	−10.6	−10.0	−13.7	−11.8	−11.5

Note. From Texas Education Agency, Academic Excellence Indicator System, http://www.tea.state.tx.us. TAAS = Texas Assessment of Academic Skills.

quately address phonemic awareness and graphophonemic knowledge, and recommended the addition of phonics-based instruction (Carnine, 1997). Following the recommendations of the team, FWISD administrators reviewed direct instruction curricula, participated in school visits around the country to see these programs in action, and hired a reading director to lead the implementation of direct instruction. At about the same time that FWISD was formulating its reading initiative, the Texas governor began a reading initiative calling for "all students to read on grade level by the end of Grade 3" (TEA, 1997). To help school districts implement research-based programs, grant funding was made available through the Academics 2000 program and through the Texas Reading Academy (TEA, 2000; TRA 2000). The district applied for these funds in each program implementation year (1998–1999 and 1999–2000), receiving Academics 2000 grants of $750,000 for each year and TRA grants of $450,000 and $575,000. Based on the experts' recommendations and support from the superintendent and administration, the FWISD school board committed an additional $1 million to the initiative. The experts and district personnel agreed to implement two phonics intensive direct instruction reading programs, OC and RM, in Grades K–2.

SELECTING THE SCHOOLS

The approach taken by the district was to implement the new reading programs in the lowest performing schools first, expanding the programs to other campuses as funding became available. During the initial program year, 32 campuses were identified as most needing direct instruction of reading and prereading skills. In the second year, an additional 29 campuses were included. The assignment of programs to the campuses and to students was far from random.[5] Principals from each of the 32 initially identified schools chose the program. Eighteen principals selected RM; the remaining 14 chose Open Court Collection for Young Scholars. During the second program year, each first-year campus retained its existing program; 2 additional campuses implemented RM; and 25 of the remaining 34 campuses implemented an updated version of the OC program.

DESCRIPTION OF THE READING PROGRAMS

Both versions of OC offer a reading and writing program designed to serve K–6 students. OC can be used in regular classrooms, or with special education, limited English proficient, or other students who read below grade level (TCER, 1997). The program focuses on prereading and reading skills, including the alphabet, phonological awareness and phonics, and blending. The program's reading books reinforce the skills taught in the daily lessons. Students learn 43 common English sounds and frequent spelling patterns, then use blending as a strategy to decode common words. Dictation, spelling, and word-building games help students progress from spelling words by sound to writing whole words and complete sentences. Learning units are organized around specific themes and include systematic instruction in phonemic awareness, phonics, comprehension, and writing. As students progress through the program, they are introduced to fiction and nonfiction literature. Instruction involves whole-class lessons and independent activities designed to address individual needs. The program also encourages independent and group reading and the use of supplemental literature.

RM is also targeted at students in Grades K–6 and can be used for regular, special education, and limited English proficient students. Somewhat more structured than OC, the program uses fast-paced, scripted teacher–student interaction. Teachers read from scripts created by the program. The program materials include 120 to 160 oral and written activities for each of six levels. Beginning with phonological and letter–sound relations, RM teaches decoding using sounding out, rhyming, and blending. Daily reading selections allow decoding skills to be com-

---

[5]We discuss the implications of this nonrandom assignment for statistical inference later in the article. The reading programs were implemented either for all students or no students in Grades K–2 at each campus during each school year.

bined with comprehension strategies. Literature collections introduce and reinforce various literary forms. Teachers direct small groups of students determined
through placement tests to be at similar reading levels. Teachers assess the students' progress periodically with informal mastery tests; students can speed up or
slow down their pace depending on the results of these tests.

STUDENT CHARACTERISTICS

To compare student characteristics across programs, we grouped district elementary schools into four categories: RM schools, or the 18 schools that implemented
RM during 1998–1999 and 1999–2000, as well as the 2 schools that implemented
RM during the 1999–2000 year; OC schools, or those 14 campuses that implemented OC in 1998–1999 and 1999–2000; OC 2000 schools, or those 25 campuses
that implemented OC only in 1999–2000; and finally traditional program (TP)
schools, or those campuses that implemented a curriculum based on the whole language approach to reading instruction.[6]

As noted earlier, there were wide differences in student characteristics between the
programs. Table 2 shows the number of students and selected characteristics of students in the elementary schools that implemented each reading program. The differences were stark. For example, 74.6% of the students in the OC schools were Hispanic,
as contrasted with 13.2% in the TP schools and 18.1% in the RM schools. Fully 66.9%
of the students in the TP schools were Anglo, whereas 69.9% of the students in the RM
schools were African American. Whereas only 26.9% of the TP schools' students
were eligible for the federal free and reduced-price lunch program, more than 80% of
the students in OC and RM schools were eligible. Finally, more than 50% of the OC
students were limited English proficient, compared to less than 5% in the TP schools.

Student characteristics across programs also differed in terms of reading ability, as measured by TAAS performance. To compare TAAS test scores across
grades, we generated a z score, with a mean of zero and variance of one, for district
students with valid TAAS test scores for each grade. The mean score for each
grade and program in Table 2 is the average number of standard deviations by
which students in that grade and program exceeded or fell short of the average of
all district students taking the test. In each grade, TP students exceeded the mean
by almost .5 *SD*. Students in the RM and OC schools scored between .25 and .43
SD below the mean. It was clear that the schools selected for reading programs

---

[6]The extent to which direct instruction may be used in the traditional schools is unknown. Teachers
there generally continued to use the program in place before the reading initiative began. This could
have included some phonics training. No doubt there has also been some leakage of materials and information about direct instruction that may have influenced the pedagogy in some of the traditional school
classrooms. No classroom observations were done in the traditional schools.

TABLE 2
Selected 1996–1997 Characteristics of Fort Worth Elementary Schools by Reading Program Type

Program	No. students	% African American	% Hispanic	% White	% Federal Lunch Program
Traditional program	4,130	17.8	13.2	66.9	26.9
Open court	9,553	12.9	74.6	10.8	87.0
Open court 2000	17,063	23.0	42.0	32.4	62.9
Reading mastery	10,485	69.9	18.1	10.2	81.7
Total	41,231	40.6	40.6	25.2	69.7

Program	% LEP	% Special Education	Mean z Score		
			Grade 3	Grade 4	Grade 5
Traditional program	4.1	11.9	0.47	0.45	0.49
Open court	51.2	9.4	−0.32	−0.32	−0.43
Open court 2000	25.8	11.7	0.13	0.23	0.23
Reading mastery	13.5	10.6	−0.25	−0.37	−0.31
Total	26.4	10.9	0.00	0.00	0.00

Note.   From Texas School Microdata Panel Enrollment and Texas Assessment of Academic Skills files.

were those with the lowest family incomes, highest proportion minority of students, and lowest reading achievement in Grades 3 through 5.

PROGRAM IMPLEMENTATION ACTIVITIES

The implementation of the new reading programs for 14,000 K–2 students in 61 elementary schools was a monumental task. For example, during the first implementation year, there were 41 separate training sessions for teachers and 23 sessions for principals. In April 1998, there was a 2-day session for OC school principals and a 1 and a half-day session for RM school principals; these sessions focused on program implementation and monitoring. The major teacher training sessions for OC and RM spanned 2 full days at the beginning of August. Follow-up sessions for both programs were held throughout September and October. Many of the sessions were open to any teachers who felt that they needed additional training. Other sessions, requested by principals, were for the entire reading staff in a school or for those who would benefit from additional training. Initial sessions were taught by professional experts from the companies that developed the programs. Mentor teachers who had become expert in the correct method of teaching OC or RM taught some of the follow-up sessions. In the second year of implementation, training sessions were offered on an even more frequent basis, but for smaller groups. The smaller groups allowed for training that could address the specific needs of teachers with varying levels of expertise.

Teacher training also included classroom coaching by consultants and mentor teachers at regular intervals and on an as-needed basis. The consultants observed reading instruction and provided constructive feedback to teachers and reading staff. The coaches also provided small group training at individual campuses. In 1998–1999, OC coaches visited each school at least four times, for a total of about 650 classroom visits. In the same year, RM coaches visited each school at least six times, for a total of about 1,240 classroom visits. Mentor teachers also provided support for classroom teachers at the school level. The duties of mentor teachers included observing, coaching, training, and facilitating data collection. In the third year of implementation, the mentor teachers served as trainers in place of outside consultants.

ORGANIZING FOR READING EVALUATION

The Academics 2000 and TRA grants that helped to fund reading program implementation in the district each required that FWISD report implementation progress and measure reading improvement. The district therefore budgeted funds to add a full-time reading evaluation manager. Guidance for the evaluation was provided by an external evaluation advisory committee consisting of three district personnel, including the director of reading, the director of research and evaluation, and the reading evaluation manager, as well as reading and evaluation experts recruited from various universities.[7] The committee met prior to the implementation and twice during each of the first 2 years of implementation. These 2-day meetings focused on continuously improving the evaluation design, examining the progress of the implementation, interacting with FWISD reading staff, and preparing findings for the district administration. The committee added value in each of these areas and was especially important in establishing and maintaining the effectiveness and legitimacy of the program evaluation.[8]

THE FORMATIVE EVALUATION

The FWISD staff and external evaluation committee recognized early in the process that there was no practical way to randomly assign students to program treat-

---

[7]The FWISD External Evaluation Advisory Committee consisted of Anne Ware, Director of Reading Evaluation; Paul Brinson, Director of Research and Evaluation; Marsha Sonnenberg, Director of Reading; Craig Darch, Auburn University; David Francis, University of Houston; Allen Henderson, Texas Wesleyan University; John Kain, University of Texas at Dallas; Dan O'Brien, University of Texas at Dallas; and Jerry Silbert, University of Oregon.

[8]The director of reading was also instrumental in enhancing the reputation and legitimacy of the programs through constant interaction with the superintendent; communication with district administrators, principals, teachers, and parents; and through organizing public events, including two reading conferences and many public presentations. From the early stages, reading progress reports included statistical information such as mean test scores, number of personnel trained, and other reading program data available, in part, due to the evaluation design and participation of internal and external personnel.

ments. The committee also observed that reading achievement would not only depend on what program was being used, but also on the preparation of and fidelity to the materials and pedagogical techniques inherent to the programs' strengths. Finally, the committee recognized that participants at all levels of the organization would learn by doing; it would be essential to quickly disseminate guidance and performance feedback to the support staff, classroom teachers, and parents.

District staff developed three major components of the process evaluation based on experiences at the schools they visited, as well as recommendations of the external evaluation team: (a) Observe each classroom teacher at least twice during each school year; (b) gather and analyze as many additional classroom- and school-level measures as are feasible, including those generated as part of each reading program; and (c) provide feedback from tests, observations, and other data to administrators, principals, teachers, and parents in a timely fashion.

CLASSROOM OBSERVATIONS

A major difficulty in large-scale education program evaluation is that abstract data may not represent what is actually happening in the classroom. For example, to establish what math or reading method is being used in a particular classroom, it is not sufficient to know what books are ordered for that classroom or school. Stories abound of teachers relegating new texts to the closet to continue to employ pedagogies learned in college that they have used for years.

FWISD attempted to capture the fidelity of program implementation through individual classroom observations conducted by trained research assistants. The purpose of these observations was to objectively assess the degree to which teachers implemented key aspects of the reading programs. The classroom observation procedures were designed with input from the external evaluation advisory committee, reading coaches, and a teacher advisory committee. The observations were not related to individual teacher evaluations, and no one except for the individual teachers and selected research staff had access to the data collected from each observation. Teachers were given advance notice of the observation visits and received a written report of the data gathered from each observation. To assess reliability, 20% of the observations were conducted by two observers. Observation procedures were piloted during December 1998. Five part-time college students were recruited, trained in the programs, and began visiting classrooms during reading periods in the spring of 1999. The observers were scheduled to visit each program classroom at each campus once each semester during each evaluation year. During the first program year, a total of approximately 600 RM and 300 OC classroom observations were conducted. In the second year of implementation, observations were continued with the original 32 schools, whereas additional observations were conducted in a subsample of the schools new to the program, for a total of approximately 400 OC and 600 RM observations.

Open Court

OC observations lasted approximately 20 min. Observers recorded details of classroom instruction and student participation of OC instruction and assigned a qualitative rating to each of the following six areas: (a) teacher involvement of students, which assessed the extent to which the teacher actively involved the students in the lesson by using rotation, encouragement, praise, and other teaching strategies; (b) monitoring of student responses, which assessed the degree to which the teacher watched and listened as students responded so that errors or lack of attention could be noticed and corrected; (c) presentation of lesson, which assessed the degree to which the teacher presented the instructional indicators and used the formats correctly; (d) pacing, which assessed the quickness and smoothness of the lesson presentation and the degree to which the lesson kept the students' attention; (e) group participation, which assessed the degree to which group responses involved full and simultaneous class participation; and (f) student focus on lesson content, which assessed the degree to which students were actively engaged in the relevant lesson activity.

Reading Mastery

The highly structured nature of RM allowed more specific numerical measures in each classroom. During six 2-min time intervals, observers recorded frequency counts of specifically defined teacher and student behaviors as follows: (a) number of student responses per minute; (b) number of responses receiving teacher verification or praise; (c) number of errors receiving full, partial, or no correction; and (d) number of group responses with full or partial student participation. Frequency counts were then converted to percentages based on the total number of minutes observed, the total number of each behavior (e.g., errors, group responses) observed, or both.

Teachers received confidential feedback reports following each observation. The reports described the observation procedures and listed the specific rating assigned for each measure. Teachers were encouraged to discuss the report with reading coaches as an additional way to improve their reading instruction. In addition to individual teacher reports, summary reports of the classroom observations were prepared for reading department staff and coaches. These reports were designed to help identify training and coaching needs and listed campus average ratings for each of the observation measures. Comparisons of beginning- and end-year summary reports indicated increased proficiency for most of the observation measures across each year.[9]

---

[9]At the end of the second year, the observation ratings were high and revealed little variability across teachers, suggesting that teachers had acquired the relevant implementation skills. Consequently, in the third year, the observation procedures were changed to include ratings of classroom independent reading activity. Readers are welcome to contact Anne Ware for more information about the observation procedures.

STUDENT LESSON PROGRESS AND MASTERY

It is also possible to assess and assist reading instruction by monitoring the rate at which students progress through the lesson sequence (lesson progress) and performance on in-program mastery tests. Lesson progress, as measured by the number of lessons completed in a RM curriculum, is positively related to grade-level reading performance on standardized tests. In addition, students who are progressing through RM lessons and mastering the content of the lessons are more likely to be successful readers than students who are progressing through the lessons but not mastering the lesson content (Engelmann, 1999). In the first year of implementation, the reading staff, consultants, and external evaluation team members identified end-of-the-year target lessons for each grade level based on students' beginning reading levels, arrival date of materials, and the projected presentation of one lesson per day throughout the school year. Individual student progress toward that target was tracked on a monthly basis for each RM classroom beginning in January 1999. Lesson progress reports summarized these data for teachers, principals, and reading staff in terms of progress toward the first-year target. Based on these summaries, potential regrouping and acceleration of students, as well as teacher training needs, could be addressed by administrators and teachers.

In the second year of direct instruction implementation, research and reading department staff assessed lesson progress by documenting the beginning, middle, and end-of-year lesson number for RM and OC students. For RM students, the staff also assessed mastery of lesson content at the three time periods. This assessment was based on the number of mastery tests each student had taken and passed in each semester of the school year. From these data, reports were prepared to help teachers identify individual student needs and to help administrators identify coaching and training needs. The reports included (a) beginning-of-year lesson placement reports, which helped teachers place students at appropriate reading lesson levels based on recent test scores; (b) mid-year lesson progress reports, which summarized student, class, or grade-level progress toward an end-of-year target lesson, identifying individual students or classes that were not making adequate progress; (c) mid-year lesson mastery reports, which identified students who were progressing through the program but not mastering the lesson content; and (d) end-of-year student lesson reports, which provided campus coordinators with student lesson information, helping them prepare for the coming school year.

USING THE TEXAS PRIMARY READING INVENTORY (TPRI) TO INFORM INSTRUCTION

In support of the governor's reading initiative, Texas law requires each school district and charter school to annually administer a reading skills assessment to K–2 students and to report the results to the state board of education, the local board of education, and each student's parent or guardian. The TEA developed one instrument, the TPRI, and provides a list of other acceptable instruments. Districts using one of the approved tests are allowed to use state funds to purchase test materials; other instruments are used at the district's expense. FWISD chose the TPRI.

This test is administered one-on-one between the reading teacher and each student. Although the number of questions and test sections vary somewhat between grades, there are basically four sections: a screening inventory, a phonemic awareness inventory, a graphophonemic knowledge inventory, and a reading inventory. The screening inventory is designed to identify students who have and have not developed grade-level reading concepts. If students meet the screening criteria, they proceed directly to the reading inventory, required for all students. Students who do not meet the screening criteria are tested for phonological and graphophonemic proficiency to enable teachers to identify individual instructional needs. The reading inventory assesses reading accuracy, fluency, and comprehension.

To reinforce the importance of targeting reading instruction to meet each child's needs, reports prepared by the FWISD reading evaluation staff that summarize each student's performance on each portion of the TPRI are returned to each teacher within approximately 2 weeks of test administration. Summary reports are also produced for each principal and at the district level. Parents are informed of their child's performance through a letter for each TPRI administration, indicating whether the student has met the grade-level screening criteria, and has mastered phonological, graphophonemic skills, or both. The letter also includes accuracy and comprehension scores from the reading portion of the TPRI. Therefore, teachers, parents, and administrators receive regular information on the reading progress and skill needs of each K–2 student.

At the district level, TPRI scores are summarized and compared across reading programs to help the reading staff determine progress and identify needs for each of the programs. Table 3 shows the percentage of students meeting TPRI screening criteria for each grade in the fall of the 1998–1999 school year and in the spring of the 1999–2000 school year by program. These rates, shown in the first three columns of Table 3, range from 56% (RM first grade) to 86% (TP kindergarten). The percentage of students meeting the screening improved in every program during the 2 years of implementation. The increased proportion of students meeting the screening criteria ranged from 3% (TP kindergarten) to 32% (RM first grade).

The three columns farthest to the right illustrate that the gap in the percentage of students meeting the criteria in the direct instruction reading programs and those in the more affluent TPs narrowed dramatically. The only remaining substantial gaps in these rates were in the second grade, with 13% (RM), 8% (OC), and 5% (OC 2000) fewer students meeting the screening criteria. For all kindergarten and first-grade students, the percentage meeting the criteria was either the same or within 2% of the rates for TP students.

TABLE 3
Percentage of FWISD Students Meeting Texas Primary Reading Inventory Screening Criteria by
Test Administration, Grade, and Reading Program

	Percent Passing			Gap With Traditional Program		
Test Date and Program	Kindergarten	Grade 1	Grade 2	Kindergarten	Grade 1	Grade 2
Fall, 1998						
Traditional program	86	72	78	0	0	0
Open court 2000	74	61	70	12	11	8
Open court	77	61	70	9	11	8
Reading mastery	67	56	59	19	16	19
Spring, 2000						
Traditional program	89	89	89	0	0	0
Open court 2000	89	89	84	0	0	5
Open court	91	91	81	–2	–2	8
Reading mastery	88	88	76	1	1	13
Fall to Spring change						
Traditional program	3	17	11	0	0	0
Open court 2000	15	28	14	12	11	3
Open court	14	30	11	11	13	0
Reading mastery	21	32	17	18	15	6

Note. FWISD = Fort Worth Independent School District.

These results should be interpreted with caution for at least four reasons: TPRI was administered by individual teachers who may have felt that more of their students should pass the screening; the statistics shown in the table are for different years, and results may vary from one cohort to another; the TP students may have been approaching a ceiling; and passing the TPRI screening is a crude measure of student performance. However, when we consider that the programs were implemented in the lowest reading performance schools, the TPRI results are very encouraging.

OUTCOME EVALUATION

Each of the grants funding the FWISD reading initiative included a requirement that the district assess the impact of direct instruction programs on students' academic progress. The outcome evaluation fulfilled this requirement by comparing district student performance in each grade for the 2 program implementation years. Over the course of the Fort Worth reading implementation, we attempted to analyze student performance in a variety of ways and to identify factors affecting student performance. In this article, we present three primary analyses. First, we examine whether the reading initiative had an effect on average Fort Worth student performance compared with national norms and compared with district student performance in prior years. We then examine the relative contribution of each reading program. We present and discuss differential program effects by grade and for students of each race and ethnicity. Finally, recognizing that there are large differences in the demographic characteristics of students being instructed using each reading program, we use regression analysis to control for measured systematic differences such as income and race or ethnicity. We present regression results of program performance by grade, school year, and separately by race and ethnicity.

To measure student academic progress in kindergarten, first, and second grades, the district administered the Stanford Achievement Test–Ninth Edition battery of reading tests in the fall and spring of 1998–1999 and 1999–2000. The test form varied across grades and from fall to spring. The district used the manufacturer-recommended test for each grade level and testing date (Harcourt Brace, 1999). In the analyses presented later, we used the normal curve equivalent (NCE) total reading score as the measure of student reading skill. This score was a composite of several grade-appropriate subtests that assessed specific reading skills such as word reading, spelling, and comprehension. The NCE has a mean of 50 and standard deviation of 21.06 and therefore can have values ranging from 1 to 99. This equal interval scale can be used to compare results between test instruments and can be averaged for comparison of mean results between groups of students. Deviations above or below 50 place a student or group of students above or below the average for students in the norm sample. This gives us an easily interpreted benchmark for such comparisons as those involving the number of students with reading skills at or above grade level.

To compare FWISD student performance with national norms, we show mean NCE total reading scores for each test administration by grade and school year in Table 4. Scores are given for all students (total) and by race or ethnicity.[10] The first panel has mean scores for the fall test administration, the second panel has mean spring scores, the third panel has mean gains or losses, and the final panel gives the number of students taking the test. Statistical significance of the gains or losses was measured using a paired differences test. An asterisk is used to indicate that the probability of the mean difference being different than zero is at least 95%.

The first two panels indicate that district students in kindergarten and first grade, with the exception of Hispanic kindergarten students in 1999–2000, started the year scoring above the national norm. Second-grade students were close to the mean with average scores of 47.3 and 49.1 in the two program years. This seemed quite unusual for a central city district with the student demographics discussed earlier. Having discussed this with the representatives of Harcourt Brace, we con-

---

[10]The Texas Education Agency uses five racial or ethnic indicators: Native American, Asian, African American, Hispanic, and Anglo. Only .2% of district students were Native American. Due to their small number, and concerns about confidentiality, mean scores and some other statistics were not presented for Native American students.

TABLE 4
Forth Worth Independent School District Mean SAT9 Normal Curve Equivalent Reading
Scores and Fall to Spring Gains (Losses) by School Year and Grade

	Kindergarten		Grade 1		Grade 2	
	1998–1999	1999–2000	1998–1999	1999–2000	1998–1999	1999–2000
Fall						
Asian	61.0	52.0	64.6	59.6	52.4	55.0
African American	56.5	53.6	53.2	54.2	44.1	44.5
Hispanic	52.9	49.1	52.3	52.8	42.5	46.2
Anglo	66.0	61.7	67.1	66.4	57.8	60.3
Total	58.7	54.2	57.2	57.0	47.3	49.2
Spring						
Asian	65.7	63.9	63.8	62.7	56.5	56.3
African American	59.6	64.1	50.9	53.3	45.0	45.8
Hispanic	58.1	61.3	53.4	54.3	45.8	49.2
Anglo	70.3	71.3	66.1	66.0	61.0	62.1
Total	63.0	65.1	56.6	57.2	49.9	51.3
Gains (losses)						
Asian	4.8*	12.0*	−0.8	3.1*	4.1*	1.3
African American	3.1*	10.5*	−2.3*	−0.9*	0.9*	1.4*
Hispanic	5.1*	12.2*	1.1*	1.4*	3.3*	3.0*
Anglo	4.3*	9.6*	−1.0*	−0.4	3.2*	1.8*
Total	4.2*	10.9*	−0.6*	0.2	2.5*	2.1*
Students						
Asian	75	90	108	92	100	113
African American	783	970	1,144	1,384	1,369	1,456
Hispanic	840	1,142	1,431	1,520	1,683	1,690
Anglo	891	854	1,106	1,062	1,154	1,021
Total	2,589	3,056	3,789	4,058	4,306	4,280

Note. SAT9 = Stanford Achievement Test–Ninth Edition.
*$p < .05$.

cluded that the norms seemed too low, probably based on the students participating in the norm sample. We are more confident, then, in discussing the gains from fall to spring, as these are more independent of test score levels.

As shown in the "total" lines in the table, district students had percentile score gains from fall to spring in four of the six grades and years. Only in the first grade was there a mean loss of 0.6 NCE points in 1998–1999. The 0.2 NCE point mean gain in 1999–2000 is not statistically significant. Kindergarten students had the largest gains of 10.9 NCE points in 1999–2000 and 4.2 points in 1998–1999. The large gains for 1999–2000 are particularly impressive because the test was administered to almost 500 more kindergarten students than in 1998–1999. Second-grade gains were smaller, about 2 NCE points.

By race or ethnicity, 22 of the 24 grade–school, year–race–ethnicity categories were statistically significant. Of these, 19 were positive and only 3, all in the first grade, were negative. Hispanic students made larger gains than the norm sample in each year and grade, ranging from 12.2 NCE points for kindergarten students in 1999–2000 to 1.1 points for first-grade students in 1998–1999. Although African American students in general had the lowest gains, the 1999–2000 African American kindergarten students had larger gains than Anglo students, and the 1999–2000 African American second-grade students had larger gains than Asian students.

Was this performance different than in prior years for the district? During the 2 years prior to the reading program implementation, the district tested first- and second-grade reading skills each spring using the Gates–MacGinitie test. We used these results to compare the performance of each cohort, that is, students in each grade at each of the consecutive years. Because one of the district's goals was for all students to read at or above grade level, we present the percentage of students reading at or above the 50th percentile in first and second grade in Table 5. Within each grade we provided means for those students who were economically disadvantaged, that is, eligible for free or reduced-price lunch under the federal program; for those who were not eligible by race or ethnicity; and for all students.

As shown in the total line for first grade, 55% of the ineligible students tested in 1996–1997 were reading at grade level, as compared to 64% in 1997–1998, 60% in 1998–1999, and 67% in 1999–2000. In the second grade, 44% of ineligible students were at grade level in 1996–1997, as compared to 52% in 1997–1998, 52% in 1998–1999, and 69% in 1999–2000. Generally, the trend was positive. For both grades, a larger proportion of higher income students were at or above grade level in 1999–2000 than in any other year.

The results were more striking for low-income students. In the first grade, only 28% were at grade level in 1996–1997. This increased to 38% for 1997–1998, 57% for 1998–1999, and 52% for 1999–2000. For the second grade, only 21% of students were at grade level in 1996–1997, increasing to 29% in 1997–1998, 46% in 1998–1999, and 48% in 1999–2000. Twice as many low-income students in each grade were reading at grade level in 1999–2000 than in 1996–1997, an increase of more than 800 students in each grade.

If we consider low-income student gains from 1996–1997 to 1999–2000 for first grade by race or ethnicity, we see that 55% more Asian students (25%–70%), 20% more African American students, 28% more Hispanic students, and 24% more Anglo students were reading at or above grade level by the end of Year 2. For second grade, 21% more Asian students, 28% more African American students, 34% more Hispanic students, and 30% more Anglo students were reading at or above grade level. The number of students tested in each grade also increased.

Although we realize that two different test instruments were used in the spring of each year, and that performance did vary between cohorts of students, we believe that the gains shown earlier demonstrated that the focus on reading and im-

TABLE 5

Percentage of Fort Worth Independent School District Students in Grades 1 and 2 Reading at Grade Level and Number of Students by Eligibility for Free or Reduced Price Lunch, Test Instrument, Year, and Race or Ethnicity

Grade and Race/Ethnicity	Ineligible for Free or Reduced-Price Lunch				Eligible for Free or Reduced-Price Lunch			
	Gates–MacGinitie		SAT9		Gates–MacGinitie		SAT9	
	1996–1997	1997–1998	1998–1999	1999–2000	1996–1997	1997–1998	1998–1999	1999–2000
Grade 1								
Asian	70	60	75	77	25	45	52	70
African American	42	52	44	59	28	38	56	48
Hispanic	41	43	45	56	24	36	57	52
Anglo	63	77	76	78	35	46	60	59
Total	55	64	60	67	28	38	57	52
Grade 2								
Asian	52	56	62	76	30	19	50	51
African American	22	32	44	51	10	20	33	38
Hispanic	25	36	48	52	12	18	36	46
Anglo	57	65	53	80	22	39	51	52
Total	44	52	52	69	21	29	46	48
Number of students								
Grade 1								
Asian	40	47	56	43	55	53	52	64
African American	350	391	546	459	1,338	1,265	886	1,306
Hispanic	303	316	526	626	1,123	1,096	966	1,438
Anglo	1,053	892	1,030	1,002	432	402	254	429
Total	1,746	1,646	2,158	2,130	2,948	2,816	2,158	3,237
Grade 2								
Asian	42	41	65	63	56	52	64	73
African American	338	376	1,107	438	1,374	1,238	1,164	1,290
Hispanic	284	299	1,422	527	1,188	1,099	1,482	1,534
Anglo	919	991	365	902	412	387	383	396
Total	1,583	1,707	2,959	1,930	3,030	2,776	3,093	3,293

Note. At grade level is defined as scoring at or above the 50th percentile. SAT9 = Stanford Achievement Test–Ninth Edition.

plementation of phonics-intensive reading instruction in the district had a marked positive effect on reading performance of students throughout the district and that the effect was strongest for economically disadvantaged students, especially for students in the earliest grades.

PROGRAM COMPARISON

We now turn our attention to an analysis of differential gains for students who received instruction within each reading program. Table 6 gives mean NCE scores for students in kindergarten, first grade, and second grade by program for the fall and spring of each school year; and gains (losses) from fall to spring, as well as the number of students in each grade and program for each year. The first and fourth data columns are for all students. Note that there were three reading programs in 1998–1999 (TP, OC, and RM). In 1999–2000, two schools changed from the TP techniques to RM; students in these schools were included with other RM students. There were 25 additional OC schools in 1999–2000. We show these students as a separate category, OC 2000.

For the reasons outlined earlier, we again focus attention on student gains from fall to spring in each year. As seen on the total line, all students had statistically significant and positive gains except for students in the traditional program in 1999–2000, whose gains were not statistically different from those of students in the norming sample. Average gains ranged from 1.8 NCE points for all students in 1998–1999 to 4.8 points for students in OC 2000 in 1999–2000.

Comparing student performance by program, all students in kindergarten and second grade had positive and statistically significant gains. For first-grade students, the results were mixed. In 1998–1999, TP and RM students gained at a lower rate than the norming sample, whereas OC students gained at a faster rate. In 1999–2000, TP and RM students gained at a slower rate. OC 2000 students had statistically significant gains and RM first-grade students gained at about the same rate as the norming sample.

When compared with TP, OC and RM appeared to be particularly effective for kindergarten and first-grade students. In the 1999–2000 school year, OC kindergarten students narrowed the total reading score gap with TP students by 4.6 NCE points; OC 2000 students narrowed the gap by 8.0 points; and RM students narrowed the gap by 9.5 points.

Were the programs particularly effective for minority children? Table 7 shows the kindergarten mean NCE scores and gains by year, program, and race or ethnicity.

The rows labeled total are the same as the means and gains shown for kindergarten students in Table 6. The comparison by race or ethnicity is also informative. In the 1998–1999 school year, gains for African American students in RM exceeded those of African American students in the TP by a small margin (3.5 compared to 2.9

TABLE 6
Fort Worth Independent School District SAT9 Mean Normal Curve Equivalent Reading Scores and Gains From Fall to Spring by School Year, Reading Program, and Grade

Test Date and Grade	1998–1999				1999–2000				
	All Students	Traditional	Open Court	Reading Mastery	All Students	Traditional	Open Court	Open Court 2000	Reading Mastery
Fall									
K	58.7	61.0	54.1	52.4	54.2	67.9	52.9	52.0	51.3
Grade 1	57.2	60.8	52.1	50.3	57.0	70.4	53.6	56.8	52.9
Grade 2	47.3	51.1	42.5	41.1	49.2	60.6	47.6	50.8	42.8
Total	53.6	57.2	48.0	46.7	53.3	66.3	51.1	53.3	48.5
Spring									
K	63.0	64.9	61.3	55.9	65.1	72.1	61.6	64.2	64.9
Grade 1	56.6	59.5	55.5	48.9	57.2	66.2	55.1	58.3	52.0
Grade 2	49.9	53.6	46.6	42.6	51.3	63.1	48.5	53.3	45.0
Total	55.4	58.7	52.3	47.6	57.1	66.9	54.0	58.1	52.6
Gains (losses)									
K	4.2*	3.9*	7.2*	3.5*	10.9*	4.1*	8.7*	12.1*	13.6*
Grade 1	0.6*	-1.3*	3.4*	-1.3*	0.2	-4.1*	1.5*	1.5*	-0.9*
Grade 2	2.5*	2.5*	4.0*	1.5*	2.1*	2.5*	0.9*	2.5*	2.2*
Total	1.8*	1.5*	4.3*	0.9*	3.8*	0.6	3.0*	4.8*	4.2*
Students									
K	2,589	1,865	278	446	3,056	426	450	1,391	789
Grade 1	3,789	2,395	601	793	4,058	520	689	1,828	1,021
Grade 2	4,306	2,569	775	962	4,280	499	746	1,847	1,188
Total	10,684	6,829	1,654	2,201	11,394	1,445	1,885	5,066	2,998

Note. K = kindergarten; SAT9 = Stanford Achievement Test–Ninth Edition.

*$p < .05$.

NCE points). In the second program year, African American students achieved gains of 12.5 NCE points in RM and 10.8 points in OC 2000, as compared with gains of only 1.1 points in the TP schools. Hispanic students in RM also did very well in 1999–2000, gaining more than 17 NCE points, as compared with gains of 4.0 points in the first program year. The use of the same highly scripted program for 2 consecutive years may have been responsible for the increased achievement of RM students.

Hispanic students in the OC program gained 8.3 NCE points in the first program year, as compared with 4.3 points in the TP schools. Gains increased to 10.1 points for OC students, nearly 13 NCE points for OC 2000 students, and 17.5 points for RM students, as compared to less than 1.6 points for Hispanic students in TP schools. Schools using OC and OC 2000 had a high proportion of Hispanic students; these students responded well to the program. Whereas 2 year's experience helped OC students, kindergarten students in OC 2000, in its first year, also did very well.

We have noted earlier that there were substantial differences in the demographic characteristics of students between programs. The differences in race or ethnicity by program are shown in the bottom panel of Table 7. For example, in 1999–2000, only 68 of the 426 TP students (16%) were African American, compared with 529 of the 789 students in RM (67%). Similarly, Hispanic students made up 67% of the OC students and only 14% of the TP students.

Simple comparisons of means such as those shown in Tables 5 through 7 are inadequate for the task of comparing performance across programs because of the large systematic differences in the demographic characteristics of students in each reading program. We controlled for these differences using value-added regression analyses (Hanushek, 1979). The dependent variable in each regression was the spring NCE score, whereas the independent variables included the fall score and student demographic characteristics.

In addition to indicating each student's prior skills, the fall score reflected much of the influence of family, peers, and school on the student. The controls for race or ethnicity, eligibility for free and reduced-price lunch, gender, special education classification, and limited English proficiency reflected the impact of differential student characteristics on reading skill gains during the school year. Table 8 shows estimated coefficients and t statistics for spring total reading NCE score regressions for kindergarten students in 1999–2000. Similar tables for kindergarten students in 1998–1999 and for first and second grade for each implementation year are available from the author (O'Brien).

Each coefficient is an estimate of the number of NCE points that the spring score increases or decreases in relation to a unit change in the explanatory variable. A t statistic greater than 2.0 indicates statistical significance at the 5% level. The standard errors (and t statistics) are adjusted for heteroskedasticity using the Huber–White method (StataCorp, 2001).

There are four regressions shown in Table 8. The two data columns farthest to the left are for all kindergarten students with valid fall and spring scores. Each additional

TABLE 7
For Worth Independent School District Kindergarten SAT9 Mean Total Reading Normal Curve Equivalent Scores and Gains From Fall to Spring by School Year, Reading Program, and Race or Ethnicity

Test Date and Race/Ethnicity	1998–1999				1999–2000				
	All Students	Traditional	Open Court	Reading Mastery	All Students	Traditional	Open Court	Open Court 2000	Reading Mastery
Fall									
Asian	61.0	62.0	57.4	58.6	52.0	72.4	48.1	49.8	51.5
African American	56.5	58.1	58.8	53.9	53.6	58.7	58.7	53.3	52.6
Hispanic	52.9	54.2	52.1	47.6	49.1	59.5	51.8	47.7	45.8
Anglo	66.0	67.0	56.4	52.0	61.7	71.8	53.2	57.7	53.9
Total	58.7	61.0	54.1	52.4	54.2	67.9	52.9	52.0	51.3
Spring									
Asian	65.7	66.4	68.5	61.4	63.9	78.5	57.9	63.8	62.4
African American	59.6	61.0	60.6	57.4	64.1	59.8	60.8	64.1	65.1
Hispanic	58.1	58.5	60.4	51.6	61.3	61.1	61.9	60.5	63.2
Anglo	70.3	71.1	65.2	54.4	71.3	77.1	61.8	69.6	67.3
Total	63.0	64.9	61.3	55.9	65.1	72.1	61.6	64.2	64.9

Gains (losses)									
Asian	4.8*	4.5*	11.1	2.8	12.0*	6.2	9.8*	13.9*	10.9*
African American	3.1*	2.9*	1.8	3.5*	10.5*	1.1	2.2	10.8*	12.5*
Hispanic	5.1*	4.3*	8.3*	4.0*	12.2*	1.6	10.1*	12.8*	17.5*
Anglo	4.3*	4.1*	8.8*	2.3*	9.6*	5.3*	8.6*	11.9*	13.4*
Total	4.2*	3.9*	7.2*	3.5*	10.9*	4.1*	8.7*	12.1*	13.6*
Number of students									
Asian	75	55	7	13	90	9	17	52	12
African American	783	437	51	295	970	68	65	308	529
Hispanic	840	554	179	107	1,142	61	301	612	168
Anglo	891	819	41	31	854	288	67	419	80
Total	2,589	1,865	278	446	3,056	426	450	1,391	789

Note. SAT9 = Stanford Achievement Test–Ninth Edition.

*p < .05 level.

TABLE 8
Fort Worth Independent School District 1999–2000 Kindergarten Spring Normal Curve Equivalent Reading Score Value Added Regressions for All Students and by Race or Ethnicity

Explanatory Values	All Students Coefficient	t	African American Coefficient	t	Hispanic Coefficient	t	White Coefficient	t
Fall score	0.60	46.40	0.61	28.40	0.55	23.00	0.61	26.70
Open court	1.78	1.50	4.32	1.70	7.02	2.80	-1.71	-0.70
Open court 2000	3.77	4.10	10.15	5.20	7.44	3.10	1.94	1.70
Reading mastery	6.69	6.30	12.63	6.50	11.23	4.30	2.59	1.30
Native American	-6.86	-1.60	0.00		0.00		0.00	
Asian American	-1.05	-0.60	0.00		0.00		0.00	
African American	-3.11	-3.70	0.00		0.00		0.00	
Hispanic	-1.51	-1.60	0.00		0.00		0.00	
Free or reduced lunch	-2.96	-4.40	-3.51	-3.20	-2.52	-2.30	-3.66	-2.5
Special education	-8.97	-6.30	-6.24	-2.70	-8.63	-4.10	-11.07	-3.90
Men	-2.58	-4.50	-3.17	-3.10	-2.86	-3.00	-1.81	-1.80
LEP	-0.61	-0.7	2.45	0.7	-0.88	-0.80	-0.40	-0.1
Constant	34.33	26.30	25.51	11.1	31.20	11.20	34.99	16.4
R^2	0.455		0.474		0.352		0.495	
No. of students	2,944		907		1,104		834	

Note. Standard errors adjusted for heteroskedasticity using the Huber–White method. LEP = limited English proficient.

pair of columns is for a regression including only the African American, Hispanic, or Anglo students. The total number of students was 2,944, with 907 African American students; 1,104 Hispanic students; and 834 Anglo students in the regressions. The R^2 statistic indicates that the regressions explain between 35.2% and 49.5% of the variation in the dependent variable, the spring total reading NCE score.

As we might expect, the best predictor of future performance is past performance; the fall score was a significant predictor of spring score. The impacts of each other explanatory variable were as we would expect based on prior research (Kain & O'Brien, 1998, 2000). The Native American, Asian, African American, and Hispanic variables take on a value of one if the student is that race or ethnicity. The coefficients estimate the differential gains for each race or ethnicity compared to the omitted category, Anglo students. All of the race or ethnic coefficients are negative, but only the coefficient for African American students is statistically significant at the 5% level. Therefore, African American kindergarten students scored 3.1 NCE points below Anglo students, controlling for the other explanatory variables. The effect of low income and special education was negative and statistically significant for the regression, including all students as well as each of the regressions by race or ethnicity. All but White men also had lower gains than women, holding the other explanatory variables constant. Although the sign of the estimated coefficients were negative in each regression for limited English proficiency, none of the estimates were statistically significant.

To analyze program-to-program differences, we included program variables that took on a value of one for each student in the RM, OC, or OC 2000 reading programs. The regressions were restricted to students who were in the same program in both the fall and spring; less than 1% of the district's students who had test scores in the spring and fall changed programs. The omitted reading program category was the TP, so the coefficients were mean differences between this program and the TP, holding the control variables constant. The coefficients indicated that for all kindergarten students in 1999–2000, OC 2000 and RM students had larger gains than TP students, whereas OC student gains were not significantly different from TP students, holding the control variables constant.

Program effects differed by race or ethnicity. For African American students, the signs and significance of each program coefficient was the same as for all students, but the estimated gains associated with the programs were larger. For Hispanic students, each of the direct instruction programs was associated with larger gains than the TP. For Anglo students, gains were not statistically different from gains for the TP, holding the other control variables constant.

Table 9 contains the coefficients and t statistics for only the program variables for regression estimates by grade and year. The left two data columns have the estimated coefficients and t statistics for all students, whereas the remaining pairs of columns are for estimates including only African American, Hispanic, or Anglo students. Overall, there were 22 positive and statistically significant coefficients.

TABLE 9
Fort Worth Independent School District Normal Curve Equivalent Reading Score Value Added Regressions by Reading Program and School Year for All Students and by Race or Ethnicity

Program–School Year–Grade	All Students		African American		Hispanic		White	
	Coefficient	t	Coefficient	t	Coefficient	t	Coefficient	t
Open court								
1998–1999 K	2.62	2.80	-0.38	-0.20	3.42	2.90	3.45	1.60
1999–2000	1.78	1.50	4.32	1.70	7.02	2.80	-1.71	-0.70
1998–1999	3.07	5.10	1.07	0.70	3.36	4.40	4.90	3.20
Grade 1								
1999–2000	1.93	2.30	-0.29	-0.20	1.90	1.10	5.08	2.80
1998–1999	0.97	2.30	-1.60	-1.70	2.13	4.30	-0.84	-0.70
Grade 2								
1999–2000	-4.10	-6.30	-5.39	-3.20	1.07	3.30	-3.65	-3.20
Reading mastery								
1998–1999 K	-1.19	-1.50	-0.64	-0.60	-2.33	-1.70	-4.65	-1.60
1999–2000	3.77	4.10	10.15	5.20	7.44	3.10	1.94	1.70
1998–1999	-0.70	-1.30	0.31	0.40	-2.94	-3.00	3.19	1.80
Grade 1								
1999–2000	2.67	4.10	4.39	3.30	2.06	1.20	2.82	3.30
1998–1999	-0.83	-1.90	-1.58	-2.80	0.47	0.60	-1.40	-0.90
Grade 2								
1999–2000	-1.67	-3.00	-4.04	-3.00	1.12	3.60	-0.67	-0.60
Open court 2000								
1999–2000 K	6.69	6.30	12.63	6.50	11.23	4.30	2.59	1.30
1999–2000	0.16	0.20	0.57	0.40	1.62	0.90	-1.04	-0.70
Grade 1								
1999–2000	-2.55	-4.00	-4.10	-3.10	1.60	4.60	-2.61	-2.10
Grade 2								

Note. Standard errors adjusted for heteroskedasticity using the Huber–White method. K = kindergarten.

Each indicates that total reading NCE score gains for the direct instruction program in a year and grade were larger than for the TP, holding the control variables constant. For 28 program grades and years, the coefficients were not statistically significant, indicating that these students had gains that were not statistically different from TP students. The remaining 10 coefficients were negative and statistically significant. For these program years and grades, students had lower gains than similar TP students. In all, for 50 of the 60 years–grades–race–ethnic estimates, students in direct instruction programs had gains as large or larger than students in the more affluent TP schools.

The most positive results were for kindergarten, where 9 of the 20 coefficients were positive and statistically significant, and all of the remaining estimated coefficients were not statistically significant. We can therefore reiterate our prior findings. Intensive phonics-based instruction appears to benefit students in the earliest grade. In FWISD, these programs have generally allowed the poorest minority students to keep pace with students who have similar characteristics but attend more affluent schools.

POTENTIAL CONFOUNDING EFFECTS

As noted earlier, the study design to evaluate these reading implementations was extensive, but far from the random assignment experiment near and dear to every researcher's heart. Some critical factors were very difficult to measure. An important example is time on task. Logically, the more time students spend learning a reading or prereading skill, the more progress they will make in that area. Over 2 years of implementation, classroom observers were unable to identify time on task. Since then, the district has initiated a more intense classroom observation study to be conducted during the spring of 2001 in a sample of classrooms. We hope to identify the time spent in reading instruction and other classroom management factors that influence reading progress.

No data was readily available for three major factors that may have influenced overall student gains. Possibly, the most important was the influence of each student's family background. To help fill this gap, the district has considered asking parents about their educational background at registration. There was also scant data for the classroom reduction initiative. Several of the program schools received funding to hire additional personnel with the goal of reducing class size, but the specific way that this was accomplished at each school, and which students participated, was not readily available. Finally, there were several reading interventions available to some schools in the district. As noted earlier, these included reading recovery teachers who spent time with students outside the normal classroom, and several computer-based reading programs utilized by students during or after normal classroom hours. Again, there was little readily available data on these programs. The district has recognized the potential systematic effect that each of these may have had on reading performance, and hopes to document each in the coming years.

SUMMARY AND CONCLUSIONS

During the 1998–1999 and 1999–2000 school years, the FWISD successfully implemented direct reading instruction for more than 14,000 students in 61 schools. The district director of reading, aided by a group of reading experts, achieved buy-in from district teachers and principals through visits to schools that had effectively employed the new programs. Evaluation of the implementation was the purview of the research and evaluation department, whose director and reading evaluation manager collaborated with university reading and evaluation specialists. Together, this outside influence helped to legitimize the reading programs with internal and external constituents, including the school board and the TEA.

Results of the implementation have been impressive on two fronts. The formative evaluation process resulted in continuous program improvement through regular and timely feedback of program results to teachers, principals, parents, and management. Statistical analyses confirmed what district reading teachers and those most involved in the programs had sensed—that implementation of direct instruction reading programs combined with an emphasis on all students reading by the end of second grade resulted in improved reading skills for students throughout the district. These improvements were especially significant for minority and economically disadvantaged students, and for students in the earliest grade.

The district's future direction includes an ongoing emphasis on reading, the continued use of direct instruction in the earliest grades, the expansion of programs for middle and high school corrective reading, and the continued improvement of reading instruction through the identification of skill areas that need additional emphasis. The evaluation will expand to identify more classroom-specific measures such as time on task, differences in classroom organization, and differences in individualized reading instruction. The evaluation will also include more data, such as student participation in remedial reading programs, use of computer-aided instruction, and availability of other resources by students in each campus or program.

ACKNOWLEDGMENTS

We thank Marsha Sonnenberg, FWISD Director of Reading; Paul Brinson, FWISD Director of Research and Evaluation; Lucinda Randall, John Kain, and the entire reading and evaluation staffs of the FWISD for their efforts, suggestions, and support. We also thank participants in the Fort Worth Reading Symposium, RESET meetings, Council of Great City Schools meetings, and the members of the FWISD External Evaluation Committee for their comments and guidance.

REFERENCES

Adams, G. L., & Engelmann, S. (1996). *Research on direct instruction: 25 years beyond DISTAR.* Seattle, WA: Educational Achievement Systems.

Adams, M. (1996). *Beginning to read: Thinking and learning about print.* Cambridge, MA: MIT Press.

American Federation of Teachers (AFT). (1999). *Teaching reading is rocket science: What expert teachers of reading should know and be able to do.* Washington, DC: Author.

Carnine, D. (1997). Bridging the research-to-practice gap. *Exceptional Children, 63,* 513–521.

Engelmann, S. (1999, July). *Student-program alignment and teaching to mastery.* Paper presented at the 25th National Direct Instruction Conference, Eugene, OR.

Fort Worth Independent School District (FWISD). (2000). *School and community relations quick facts: 2000–2001 FWISD Profile.* Retrieved March 1, 2001, from http://www.fortworthisd.org/fwisd_profile.html

Hanushek, E. A. (1979). Conceptual and empirical issues in the estimation of educational production functions. *Journal of Human Resources, 14,* 351–388.

Harcourt Brace Educational Measurement. (1999). *Stanford 9 technical manual.* San Antonio, TX: Harcourt Brace.

Kain, J. F., & O'Brien, D. M. (1998, April 2–4). *A longitudinal assessment of reading achievement: Evidence from the UTD Texas Schools Project.* Retrieved March 1, 2001, from http://www.utdallas.edu/research/greenctr

Kain, J. F., & O'Brien, D. M. (2000, March 9). *Black suburbanization in Texas metropolitan areas and its impact on student achievement.* Retrieved March 1, 2001, from http://www.utdallas.edu/research/greenctr

McKenzie Group, Inc. (2000). *Fort Worth Independent School District review of education initiatives.* Fort Worth, TX: Fort Worth Independent School District.

Meyer, L. A. (1984). Long-term academic effects of the direct instruction Project Follow Through. *The Elementary School Journal, 84,* 380–394.

National Center for Education Statistics (NCES) (2000). *Characteristics of the 1000 largest public elementary secondary school districts in the United States.* Washington, DC: National Center for Education Statistics.

Paige, R. (2001, February 15). *No child left behind: A blueprint for education reform.* Testimony before the Senate Committee on Health, Education, Labor, and Pensions, Washington, DC (Report No. SD430). Available from http://labor.senate.gov/107 hearings/feb2001/feb2001.html

StataCorp. (2001). *Stata statistical software: Release 7.0.* College Station, TX: Author.

Texas Center for Educational Research (TCER). (1997, August). *Reading programs for students in the lower elementary grades: What does the research say?* Retrieved March 1, 2001, from http://www.tasb.org/tcer

Texas Education Agency (TEA). (1997). *Beginning reading instruction: Components and features of a research-based reading program.* Austin, TX: Author.

Texas Education Agency (TEA). (2000). *Academics 2000: 1999 summary report of local subgrant awards.* Austin, TX: Author.

Texas Reading Academy. (2000). *Fact sheet: 1998 awarded applications.* Austin, TX: Texas Education Agency, Office of Statewide Initiatives.

JOURNAL OF EDUCATION FOR STUDENTS PLACED AT RISK, 7(2), 197–220

The Impact of Direct Instruction on Elementary Students' Reading Achievement in an Urban School District

Martha Abele Mac Iver

Johns Hopkins University

Elizabeth Kemper

Department of Education
North Carolina State University

This article reports the preliminary achievement outcomes of the first 4 years of direct instruction (DI) reading, implemented in 6 Baltimore elementary schools. On the primary measure of reading comprehension, members of the original kindergarten cohort were, on average, reading at grade level (49th percentile) by the end of 3rd grade. Members of the original 2nd-grade cohort were nearing grade level (40th percentile) by the end of 5th grade. However, students at control schools (where other curricula to improve reading achievement were being implemented) were achieving at the same level, so there were no significant differences between the outcomes for the 2 groups (controlling for demographics and pretest factors). Future research, based on a well-established implementation (rather than the problem-filled early years of implementation experienced by these 6 schools) might uncover significant effects that were not evident at the time this article was written. DI appears to be a viable option for raising student reading achievement, even if this study has not yet yielded evidence that DI performs significantly better than other reading curricula.

The call for educators and policymakers to consider the results of research when selecting reform models for high poverty schools (e.g., Slavin & Fashola, 1998) is heeded, at least occasionally. As Muriel Berkeley described elsewhere in this special issue, the search for a curriculum with a research-proven track record led members of the Baltimore Curriculum Project to select DI, even before it was identified as 1 of only 3 school reform models with strong evidence for improved student achievement by the American Institutes for Research report on schoolwide reform models (Herman et al., 1999). This article extends the circle by analyzing the first outcomes of an experiment that was motivated by previous research results.

Requests for reprints should be sent to Martha Abele Mac Iver, Center for Social Organization of Schools, 3003 North Charles Street, Suite 200, Baltimore, MD 21218. E-mail: mmaciver@csos.jhu.edu

The Direct Instruction (DI) reading curriculum, based on the reform model developed by Sigfried Engelmann (1969; Engelmann & Carnine, 1982; Engelmann & Engelmann, 1966) and disseminated by the National Institute for Direct Instruction (NIFDI), was first implemented in six Baltimore city public elementary schools in the fall of 1996. The school system agreed to support this externally initiated and externally funded reform effort, which expanded over the next several years and was institutionalized in the fall of 1998 as an alternative curriculum for 18 schools grouped into one administrative area (the DI area). Under the plan developed by the initiating external partner, the Baltimore Curriculum Project (BCP), schools associated with the project phased in implementation of the entire DI whole-school reform program (reading, language, spelling, and mathematics) over a period of 2 to 3 years. In addition, schools gradually began implementing a social studies and science curriculum developed by the BCP, based on the Core Knowledge sequence (Core Knowledge Foundation, 1995; Hirsch, 1996). Although part of a larger evaluation study, this article focuses only on the impact of the DI reading program in the six original schools.

DESIGN OF THE STUDY

Sample of Schools

Each of the six schools was demographically matched with a similar, within-district school so that it would have a reasonable control against which it could be compared.[1] When the study began, five of the six schools had free or reduced-price lunch rates of 80% or higher, and were among the lowest performing schools in the district. Two of the schools left the BCP in Year 3 (although they continued to implement DI, at least in reading, and remained administratively part of the district's DI area).

Sample of Students

Two cohorts of students in the DI and control schools were followed through the course of the multiyear evaluation. These cohorts were composed of students who were either in kindergarten or second grade during the 1996–1997 school year (primarily in third and fifth grades, respectively, during 1999–2000). Although it would be possible to analyze outcomes for other cohorts receiving DI, and for all

---

[1]Because of differential demographic change in paired schools over the course of the evaluation study, as well as differences in demographic composition of particular paired cohorts, it is still necessary to control for differences between Direct Instruction and control school cohorts in analyses.

children at a particular school, these were the only cohorts for whom pretest or early covariate achievement measures were available from the first year of the study.[2]

Process-Implementation Measures

In the first 3 years of the study, detailed classroom-level observations were made in the DI schools.[3] Data collected provided evidence about the implementation of the DI reform model. Interviews with principals and DI coordinators, as well as focus groups with teachers, were also conducted over 4 years to gauge DI school staff perceptions of the ongoing innovation. In addition, the research team engaged in such activities as professional development sessions, discussions with implementation managers (while shadowing them at a school), discussions with the district's DI area staff, and ongoing discussions with the external partner (BCP staff).

Outcome Measures

The primary student achievement outcome measures used in this study were scores on the reading comprehension subtest of the Comprehensive Test of Basic Skills–Fifth Edition (CTBS–5 B Terra Nova; CTB, 1997). We used a curriculum-based measure (CBM), an individually administered test of oral reading fluency, as a secondary outcome measure. Covariate measures included the Peabody Picture Vocabulary Test (PPVT; Dunn & Dunn, 1981), administered in the fall of 1996 to the kindergarten cohort, and the CTBS–Fourth Edition (CTBS–4; CTB, 1991), administered in the spring of 1997, 1998, and 1999.

The CBM reading inventories are individually administered assessments of student oral reading fluency. These assessments were conducted in the spring of 1999 among second and fourth graders (as well as twice during the 1997–1998 school year in all first- and third-grade classrooms) in the DI and control schools. Students read passages from the DI Reading Mastery (RM) series and a popular elementary school anthology of literature.

The PPVT is a norm-referenced, picture identification test that is used nationally to obtain a measure of students' language ability. It is considered to be a good predictor of future success in reading, and permitted us to control for any prior

---

[2]Unfortunately, the school system did not administer standardized tests in elementary schools in the spring of 1996. The evaluation team administered Comprehensive Test of Basic Skills tests only to the particular cohorts under study.

[3]The observation system was adapted from those in Schaffer and Nesselrodt (1993) and Stringfield et al. (1997). It included measures of time on task and elements of good instruction, as identified in Stallings (1980) and Slavin (1987).

reading readiness "advantage" on the part of some of the children. The PPVT was administered in the 1996–1997 school year to the cohort of kindergarten students at both DI and control schools.

The CTBS–4 is a norm-referenced, multiple-choice test that has been found in a variety of studies to possess reasonable psychometric properties. The two subtests of reading comprehension and mathematical concepts (the more nearly "higher order' subtests in the basic skills area) were administered to all second-grade students in each pilot school in the fall of 1996. The second-grade students in each pilot and each control school were tested with the CTBS–4 in the spring of 1997. In subsequent years, the evaluation team used the results of the Baltimore City Public School System's annual testing of the students using the CTBS–4 (in 1998 and 1999) and the CTBS–5 (in 2000).

IMPLEMENTATION ISSUES

Four of the six original BCP schools have continued their association with the NIFDI, the organization led by the original developer of the DI model.[4] In the judgment of a NIFDI representative, there was a high degree of implementation in Year 4 at three of these schools, but this was not the case in previous years at all of these schools (Davis, 1999). NIFDI considers DI implementation to be "endangered" at the fourth school, primarily because the current principal (the third since implementation began) does not appear committed to following all recommendations made by the NIFDI, and staff turnover has been very high.

Although the developer did not judge levels of implementation to be high prior to Year 4, researchers observed relatively high levels of fidelity to the DI reform model in BCP classrooms during the first 3 years (as well as the fourth year) of the reform.[5] Although observers were not able to judge all dimensions of the technical quality of implementation as defined by the developer, they found teachers were

---

[4]The two schools that were not willing to implement all dimensions of the whole-school reform program as defined by the National Institute for Direct Instruction (NIFDI) did continue implementation of the RM curriculum, even if not according to the exact specifications of the original developer. The one school to which we continued to have access for observation was given high marks in implementation, according to its consultant (JP Associates), and our observations concurred. Given this issue of how fully DI was implemented, analyses of student achievement were conducted for the group of four NIFDI schools, as well as the full group of six.

[5]See evaluation reports from Years 1 through 3. Teacher proficiency in the technical delivery of instruction necessarily has a growth curve, and high rates of teacher turnover at Baltimore Curriculum Project (BCP) schools did have a detrimental effect on institutionalizing the implementation. According to interviews with principals, some (though by no means all) of the teacher turnover had to do with teachers who disagreed with the program and preferred to go elsewhere. By Year 4, however, the mobility of teachers at BCP schools had definitely decreased, compared to previous years (Thrift, 2000).

consistently using DI curricular materials and DI techniques (e.g., correction procedures, management procedures, etc.). Schools were consulting regularly with the developer on implementation issues and generally seeking to implement the recommendations. Compared to other reform programs implemented in urban schools we have studied, we judged the implementation of DI at the BCP schools to be on the high end of the scale.

The key implementation problem in Baltimore, according to the NIFDI, has been the kindergarten program. Although the DI program was designed for a full-day kindergarten, it was not until Year 3 that all the original BCP schools had a full-day kindergarten.[6] (Most of the six original BCP schools had a half-day kindergarten during Year 1 of the program implementation.) There has also been a very high rate of turnover among kindergarten teachers, at least partially due to opposition to the program. By Year 4 of the program, however, a NIFDI representative voiced optimism about all four of the BCP kindergarten programs (although they did not view the fourth as "highly implementing").

The NIFDI representative's discussion of the pivotal role of the kindergarten program revealed some fundamental differences between the developer's view of program implementation and a researcher's approach to program fidelity. NIFDI defines successful implementation as requiring a particular rate of curriculum (lesson) coverage, especially in kindergarten. For example, the current goal is to complete RM 1 by the end of kindergarten. However, because the program also requires that students learn to mastery before teachers are able to progress further with lessons, it appears that the developer's definition of successful implementation incorporates a student outcome component. This blurring of distinctions between implementation and student outcomes (even if not the same outcome measure as used in the evaluation) complicates the evaluation process, especially if the developer claims that implementation is low because a certain number of lessons were not mastered in kindergarten. And, because the developer's rating of implementation is indirectly, if not directly, related to a particular pacing schedule, the developer also judges implementation according to whether schools agree to devote an extra period in the day to DI reading instruction (and therefore lose time otherwise allocated to the Core Knowledge component of the BCP reform). Schools that balk at a "double reading period"[7] are then judged to have low levels of implementation. Although such a demanding standard for implementation is well within the developer's prerogative, a process evaluation cannot disregard the

---

[6]Three of the six matched control schools continued to have half-day kindergarten, even during Year 4 of the implementation.

[7]Regular implementation of the DI program generally includes 1 half hr of reading, 1 hr of language arts, 1 hr of mathematics, and about half an hour of spelling and handwriting. A "double dose" of reading would add at least 45 min more reading instruction to the day (instead of social studies and science instruction).

cases that fail to meet this standard or the reasons they fail to meet it. We argue that there is sufficient evidence of implementation to evaluate the effects of DI after 4 years, although we plan to continue evaluation analyses in subsequent years of implementation.

RESULTS

This section reports on the effects of DI on reading achievement using several analytical lenses:

1. The impact of 4 years of DI on spring 2000 CTBS–5 reading scores for the original kindergarten cohort, controlling for reading readiness (measured by the PPVT).
2. The impact of 3 years of DI on spring 2000 CTBS–5 reading scores for the original second-grade cohort, controlling for spring 1997 CTBS–4 reading comprehension scores.[8]
3. Normal curve equivalent (NCE) gains over time for original cohorts.
4. One-year effects for cohorts of interest (third and fifth grades), controlling for spring 1999 reading score (includes all students, not just those who have remained in the same school over the period of the study).
5. One-year effects for mobile students (students new to school in 1999–2000), controlling for spring 1999 reading score.
6. Effects of DI on a measure of oral reading fluency, spring 1999 (controlling for spring 1998 reading scores).

Table 1 summarizes the regression analysis of spring 2000 reading comprehension and reading vocabulary scale scores[9] for the original 1996–1997 kindergarten and second-grade cohorts (primarily in third and fifth grade at the time of testing).

---

[8]Because the Comprehensive Test of Basic Skills–Fourth Edition scores for control students prior to the spring of 1997 are not available, we have no way of controlling for achievement prior to commencement of Direct Instruction (DI) implementation. We can, however, control for achievement 1 year into implementation, to ascertain if DI had any impact on achievement during the subsequent 3 years of implementation.

[9]The original design of the study included only measures of reading comprehension, and in the spring of 1997, when the Baltimore City Public School System did not administer the Comprehensive Test of Basic Skills to most elementary students, the Johns Hopkins University research team administered only the reading comprehension subtest to the second-grade cohort. Because later reading vocabulary scores were available, we included them in analyses as another measure of reading. We maintain, however, that the reading comprehension measure is the most important (Daneman, 1991; Stanovich, 1991).

TABLE 1
Effect Sizes of Multiple Years of Direct Instruction on Spring 2000 Comprehensive Test of Basic Skills–Fifth Edition Scores, Controlling for Pretest and Demographic Variables

Cohorts	B	SD (Control Group)	Effect Size
Kindergarten			
Reading comprehension	5.86	46.48	.13 ($p = .140$) 6 pairs
	7.70	48.20	.16 ($p = .130$) 4 pairs
Reading vocabulary	−2.40	54.11	−.04 ($p = .130$) 6 pairs
	3.24	52.96	.06 ($p = .600$) 4 pairs
Grade 2			
Reading comprehension	−2.13	40.25	−.05 ($p = .577$) 6 pairs
	.12	43.30	.00 ($p = .982$) 4 pairs
Reading vocabulary	4.86	35.69	.14 ($p = .166$) 6 pairs
	7.46	34.87	.21 ($p = .100$) 4 pairs

Note. Dependent variable is spring 2000 scale score. Effect sizes are for four years of direct instruction for original Kindergarten cohort, 3 years of direct instruction for original Grade-2 cohort. The original kindergarten cohort is primarily in Grade 3 in spring 2000. The original Grade-2 cohort is primarily in Grade 5 in spring 2000. Retained students are included in analyses.

The analyses included retained students in second and fourth grade, respectively, a notably larger group in control schools than BCP schools.[10] Only students who remained at the same school (DI or control school) for the 4-year period were included in this first analysis.[11] We conducted analyses with all six original pairs of schools, as well as with the four pairs of schools that continued with the original consulting group (NIFDI). (Although all schools continued to implement DI reading, implementation at two of the original schools differed somewhat after they changed consultants.)

For the original kindergarten cohort, we examined the effect of 4 years of DI on both reading comprehension and reading vocabulary scores, controlling for pretest scores on the PPVT and demographic variables. Over the 4-year period, the effect of DI on reading comprehension scores was marginal, $F(1, 319) = 2.2, p = .14$, effect size = +0.13 for six pairs; $F(1, 209) = 2.3, p = .13$, effect size = +0.16 for four pairs. There were no significant differences on reading vocabulary scores, $F(1, 305) < 1$, *ns* for six pairs; $F(1, 196) < 1$, *ns* for four pairs.

Because pretest scores (from before program implementation began) for the original second-grade control cohort were not available, our analysis of effects on that

---

[10]We discuss lower retention in grade rates at direct instruction schools compared to control schools in a later section of this article.

[11]The study began in fall 1996 with 712 in the kindergarten cohort (379 at Baltimore Curriculum Project schools, 333 at control schools). Due to student mobility (transfers within or outside the system), only about one half or fewer remained at the same schools after 4 years (including retained students, who were included in analyses).

cohort controlled for spring 1997 reading comprehension test scores (after the first year of DI implementation), as well as demographic variables. This analysis included retained students, but only those students who had remained at the same school over the 4-year period. Over the 3-year period (after the first year of DI), there was a directly positive but nonsignificant effect on reading vocabulary scores, $F(1, 333) = 1.9, p = .166$, effect size = +0.14 for six pairs; $F(1, 210) = 2.7, p = .10$, effect size = +0.21 for four pairs. There was no significant effect of DI on reading comprehension scores for the 3-year period, $F(1,340) < 1$, ns for six pairs; $F(1, 217) < 1$, ns for four pairs. There could, however, have been a significant effect during the first year of DI that we were not able to detect with the data available.

By the fourth year of the study, both original cohorts had been significantly reduced in size due to student mobility (the analysis included only those students who had remained at the same school over the 4-year period), but sample mortality did not appear biased except for retention rates (which we adjusted for by including retained students in the scale score analysis). There were no significant differences between DI and control schools in the readiness or achievement levels of students who were lost due to mobility.

Tables 2 and 3 summarize NCE gains in reading for the original cohorts.[12]

Because NCE scores correspond to particular grade-level versions of the test, these tables include only those students who were promoted on schedule. Although the tests are not strictly comparable, these gains give a reasonable estimate of how much reading growth occurred for each group over the 4-year period. For the original kindergarten cohort, we report the average NCE scores on the PPVT, the first-grade CTBS–4 reading tests, and the third-grade CTBS–5 reading tests.[13] For the original second-grade cohort, we report the average NCE scores on the second-grade CTBS–4 reading comprehension test (spring 1997), third-grade CTBS–4 reading tests (spring 1998), and the fifth-grade CTBS–5 reading tests.

Overall, the students in this study cohort began school below average in reading readiness, as measured by the PPVT. By the end of third grade they were, on average, reading at about grade level (49th percentile).[14] Students who received 4 years of DI beginning in second grade were nearing grade level (approximately the 40th percentile) by the end of fifth grade.

Tables 4 through 7 present average spring 2000 scale scores by school and cohort, including all students who remained at the same school (retained as well as

---

[12]Spring 1999 scores were not reported because they were not available for all schools in the study.

[13]Retained students, who were in second rather than third grade in spring 2000, were analyzed separately because normal curve equivalent scores correspond to particular grade-level versions of the test.

[14]When just the four National Institute for Direct Instruction schools and their controls are included, however, the average reading comprehension achievement is at the 38th percentile, and the average reading vocabulary achievement is at the 33rd percentile.

TABLE 2
Mean Normal Curve Equivalent Scores for Original Kindergarten Cohort at Baltimore Curriculum Project and Control Schools Fall 1996–Spring 2000

| | Kindergarten (1996–1997) | | Spring 1998 CTBS–4 Reading | | | | Spring 2000 CTBS–5 Reading | | | |
| | PPVT | | Vocabulary | | Comprehension | | Vocabulary | | Comprehension | |
	M	%	M	%	M	%	M	%	M	%
All BCP students[a]	29.7	17	41.3	34	40.7	33	46.5	43	49.3	49
All control students[b]	31.6	19	47.8	46	42.9	37	51.9	53	51.6	53

Note. Spring 1999 scores are not available for all schools, and so this column is omitted. Only third graders (no retained students) included in Spring 2000 mean scores. BCP = Baltimore Curriculum Project; CTBS–4 = Comprehensive Test of Basic Skills–Fourth Edition; CTBS–5 = Comprehensive Test of Basic Skills–Fifth Edition.

[a]n = 171. [b]n = 104.

TABLE 3
Mean Normal Curve Equivalent Scores for Original Grade 2 Cohort at Baltimore Curriculum
Project and Control Schools Spring 1997–Spring 2000

| | Spring 1997 CTBS–4 Reading | | Spring 1998 CTBS–Reading | | | | Spring 2000 CTBS–5 Reading | | | |
| | Comprehension | | Vocabulary | | Comprehension | | Vocabulary | | Comprehension | |
	M	%	M	%	M	%	M	%	M	%
All BCP students[a]	39.1	30	39.5	31	42.9	37	48.5	47	44.9	40
All control students[b]	38.1	29	43.8	38	43.2	37	45.7	42	45.7	42

Note. Only fifth graders (no retained students) included in spring 2000 mean scores. BCP = Baltimore Curriculum Project; CTBS–4 = Comprehensive Test of Basic Skills–Fourth Edition; CTBS–5 = Comprehensive Test of Basic Skills–Fifth Edition.
[a]n = 182. [b]n = 132.

"on track" students). These tables offer a related picture of the regression analyses presented in Table 1.[15]

As regression analysis and these tables demonstrate, DI produced results in reading that were roughly equivalent, but not significantly better, than instruction in the control schools for a relatively nonmobile group of students.

Because sample sizes were so greatly reduced over the 4-year period of the study, we also analyzed test score results for the full group of third and fifth graders at DI and control schools in 1999–2000, many of whom had not been at the school for the full 4-year period. We conducted regression analyses, controlling for previous year's reading scores, demographic variables (race, gender, free or re-duced-price lunch status), attendance, and mobility (whether student was at the same school as the previous year). Although such an analysis is able to detect only a 1-year effect of DI on reading achievement, it provides useful information for ur-ban school districts with particularly mobile student populations. As Table 8 indi-cates, the effect of 1 year of DI on reading vocabulary scores was significant at the fifth-grade level, $F(1, 489) = 10.1$, $p = .002$, effect size = +0.24. DI did not, how-ever, have a positive 1-year effect on reading comprehension scores at the fifth-grade level, and had no 1-year effect on either vocabulary or comprehension scores at the third-grade level.

---

[15]Scale score conversions to measure achievement growth from spring 1997 Comprehensive Test of Basic Skills–Fourth Edition to spring 2000 Comprehensive Test of Basic Skills–Fifth Edition are not available.

TABLE 4
Mean Comprehensive Test of Basic Skills Scale Scores in Reading Comprehension for
1996–1997 Kindergarten Students at Same School in Spring 2000

School	M	SD	Mᵃ	Students
BCP School 1	647.9	44.1	631.3	39
Control School 1	630.1	41.9	641.3	31
BCP School 2	610.4	26.4	623.3	40
Control School 2	620.8	42.7	630.7	24
BCP School 3	616.3	40.3	601.2	37
Control School 3	607.5	49.1	592.9	34
BCP School 4	616.1	29.2	614.7	14
Control School 4	621.7	57.6	610.6	10
BCP School 5	629.9	46.5	633.3	26
Control School 5	628.6	36.2	638.4	14
BCP School 6	614.4	25.8	634.3	27
Control School 6	595.1	46.8	609.5	24
All BCP schools	623.4	39.1	622.7	183
All control schools	616.0	46.5	616.9	137

Note. Only students (both on track and retained) with kindergarten Peabody Picture Vocabulary Test (PPVT) scores and spring 2000 Comprehensive Test of Basic Skills (CTBS) scores are included, because adjusted means control for differences in PPVT scores as well as demographic factors (gender, race, free lunch status). A scale score of 627 is at the 50th percentile for Grade 3; a scale score of 616 is at approximately the 39th percentile. BCP = Baltimore Curriculum Project.
ᵃScale score (adjusted).

Tables 9 and 10 show the sizes of the NCE gains over the year (not controlled for demographic differences or preexisting achievement differences). Taken together with the multivariate regression analysis that does control for these differences, the results suggest that both DI and control schools are making positive progress in raising student reading achievement. Average achievement appears to be moving closer to grade level (50th percentile) at both sets of schools, although it has not yet reached this point.

The Effect of DI Reading on Mobile Students

Because mobility in urban districts has been identified as a pressing issue that affects achievement (Kerbow, 1996), and because previous research has suggested a particularly positive impact of DI on mobile students (Brent & DiObilda, 1993), we also sought to determine whether DI had a particularly useful impact on mobile students in this study. In a more preliminary report on this study (Mac Iver, Kemper, & Stringfield, 2000), we found a significant effect of DI instruction on 1-year gains in reading comprehension for fourth graders new to a study school (mobile transfer students). Those fourth graders new to DI schools ($n = 29$) gained an average of 6.4

TABLE 5

Mean Comprehensive Test of Basic Skills Scale Scores in Reading Vocabulary for
1996–1997 Kindergarten Students Still at the Same School in Spring 2000

School	M	SD	M^a	Students
BCP School 1	630.7	49.8	615.1	39
Control School 1	619.2	49.4	617.5	30
BCP School 2	590.4	43.7	601.5	40
Control School 2	607.3	68.6	615.6	24
BCP School 3	606.8	37.7	591.2	26
Control School 3	588.9	53.3	576.1	34
BCP School 4	597.6	52.1	597.6	16
Control School 4	606.5	50.1	594.6	14
BCP School 5	609.4	54.1	611.7	26
Control School 5	642.0	54.2	651.3	19
BCP School 6	591.4	28.8	609.9	29
Control School 6	593.4	32.4	605.8	29
All BCP schools	605.6	46.8	604.9	176
All control schools	606.5	54.1	607.3	150

Note. Only students (both on track and retained) with kindergarten Peabody Picture Vocabulary Test (PPVT) scores and spring 2000 Comprehensive Test of Basic Skills scores are included, because adjusted means control for differences in PPVT scores as well as demographic factors (gender, race, free lunch status). A scale score of 605 is at approximately the 37th percentile for Grade 3. BCP = Baltimore Curriculum Project.
[a]Scale score (adjusted).

TABLE 6

Mean Comprehensive Test of Basic Skills Scale Scores in Reading Comprehension for
1996–1997 Grade 2 Students Still at Same School in Spring 2000

School	M	SD	M^a	Students
BCP School 1	668.6	37.2	650.8	35
Control School 1	645.1	34.4	644.6	43
BCP School 2	607.6	52.9	618.9	24
Control School 2	636.7	43.4	647.4	26
BCP School 3	644.9	39.5	631.7	54
Control School 3	617.3	54.3	607.9	26
BCP School 4	607.9	55.3	616.6	16
Control School 4	634.7	39.4	628.0	14
BCP School 5	639.4	27.7	642.5	26
Control School 5	657.4	23.8	663.5	19
BCP School 6	639.7	36.8	650.6	29
Control School 6	630.5	32.5	647.5	29
All BCP schools	639.7	44.9	637.5	184
All control schools	637.0	40.3	639.6	157

Note. Only students (both on track and retained with scores in spring 1997 and spring 2000 are included because adjusted means control for differences in spring 1997 scores as well as demographic factors (gender, race, free lunch status). A scale score of 654 is at the 50th percentile for Grade 5; a scale score of 639 is at approximately the 35th percentile for Grade 5.
[a]Scale score (adjusted).

TABLE 7
Mean Comprehensive Test of Basic Skills Scale Scores in Reading Vocabulary for
1996–1997 Grade 2 Students Still at Same School in Spring 2000

School	M	SD	M^a	Students
BCP School 1	675.0	31.8	659.3	35
Control School 1	642.2	38.6	642.4	43
BCP School 2	614.8	33.5	623.6	22
Control School 2	626.8	30.4	635.7	25
BCP School 3	640.9	40.5	628.7	50
Control School 3	631.8	32.3	621.8	26
BCP School 4	629.6	31.1	635.3	16
Control School 4	629.3	31.7	622.8	14
BCP School 5	638.0	35.4	641.5	26
Control School 5	650.1	21.2	657.5	19
BCP School 6	644.3	30.9	654.8	29
Control School 6	618.9	42.0	634.6	29
All BCP schools	643.5	38.9	641.1	178
All Control schools	633.5	35.7	636.2	156

Note. Only students (both on track and retained) with scores in spring 1997 and spring 2000 are included, because adjusted means control for differences in spring 1997 scores as well as demographic factors (gender, race, free lunch status). A scale score of 644 is at approximately the 46th percentile for Grade 5. BCP = Baltimore Curriculum Project.
[a]Scale score (adjusted).

TABLE 8
Effect Sizes of One Year of Direct Instruction on Spring 2000 CTBS–5 Scores, Controlling
for Previous Year's Score and Demographic Variables

	B	SD^a	Effect Size
Grade 3			
Reading comprehension	−.33	19.3	−.02 ($p = .782$) 6 pairs
	−.61	19.2	−.03 ($p = .678$) 4 pairs
Reading vocabulary	−.65	21.3	−.03 ($p = .607$) 6 pairs
	−1.19	20.6	−.06 ($p = .440$) 4 pairs
Grade 5			
Reading comprehension	−1.91	19.1	−.10 ($p = .096$) 6 pairs
	−2.27	19.4	−.12 ($p = .139$) 4 pairs
Reading vocabulary	4.21	17.8	.24 ($p = .002$) 6 pairs
	5.02	17.3	.29 ($p = .004$) 4 pairs

Note. CTBS–5 = Comprehensive Test of Basic Skills–Fifth Edition.
[a]Control group.

TABLE 9

Mean CTBS NCE Scores and Gain Scores in Reading Comprehension and Vocabulary for Grade-3 Students at BCP and Control Schools, Spring 2000 (Not Necessarily at Same School in Spring 1999 and Spring 2000)

School	Spring 1999 Grade 2				Spring 2000 Grade 3				Comprehension Gain		Vocabulary Gain		n
	Comprehension		Vocabulary		Comprehension		Vocabulary						
	M	SD	M	SD	M	SD	M	SD	M	SD	M	SD	
All BCP schools[a]	40.8	18.6	42.7	21.6	47.7	21.7	45.2	20.9	6.9	14.4	2.5	15.3	289
All control schools	38.9	16.6	41.7	20.6	45.1	19.8	44.9	20.2	6.2	14.2	3.2	16.3	242

Note. BCP = Baltimore Curriculum Project; CTBS = Comprehensive Test of Basic Skills; NCE = Normal Curve Equivalent.
[a]This refers to the number of students who took both comprehension texts; fewer took both vocabulary tests.

TABLE 10

Mean CTBS NCE Scores and Gain Scores in Reading Comprehension and Vocabulary for Grade 5 Students at BCP and Control Schools, Spring 2000 (Not Necessarily at Same School in Spring 1999 and Spring 2000)

| | Spring 1999 Grade 4 | | Spring 2000 Grade 5 | | | | Comprehension Gain | | Vocabulary Gain | | |
| | Comprehension | | Comprehension | | Vocabulary | | | | | | |
School	M	SD	M	SD	M	SD	M	SD	M	SD	n
All BCP schools[a]	45.5	17.8	40.6	21.2	44.1	19.4	46.8	19.9	−1.4	11.3	6.2	15.5	287
All control schools	39.7	17.8	36.8	20.6	41.2	19.3	40.2	18.1	1.5	14.3	3.4	17.9	199

Note. BCP = Baltimore Curriculum Project; CTBS = Comprehensive Test of Basic Skills; NCE = Normal Curve Equivalent.
[a]This refers to the number of students who took both comprehension texts; fewer took both vocabulary tests.

TABLE 11

Mean CTBS NCE Scores and Gain Scores in Reading Comprehension and Vocabulary for New Grade 5 Students at BCP and Control Schools, Spring 2000 (Not at Same School in Spring 1999 and Spring 2000)

	Spring 1999 Grade 4				Spring 2000 Grade 5				Comprehension Gain		Vocabulary Gain		
	Comprehension		Vocabulary		Comprehension		Vocabulary						
School	M	SD	M	SD	M	SD	M	SD	M	SD	M	SD	n
All BCP schools[a]	38.9	18.9	37.0	21.2	41.9	19.4	42.6	21.7	3.0	9.0	5.6	15.5	22
All control schools	29.3	14.0	22.0	20.6	29.7	19.3	28.8	12.7	0.4	12.1	6.8	12.1	23

Note.   BCP = Baltimore Curriculum Project; CTBS = Comprehensive Test of Basic Skills; NCE = Normal Curve Equivalent.
[a]This refers to the number of students who took both comprehension texts; fewer took both vocabulary tests.

NCE points in 1 year (from 31.8 to 38.2), compared with a gain of just 0.4 NCE points (from 35.4 to 35.8) for control students (n = 46).

Seeking to determine whether such an effect on new students could be replicated, we examined students new to the study schools in 1999–2000 (those who had transferred from another city school and who had a test score from the previous year). Table 11 presents the NCE gains for those students who had 1 year of DI in third grade; Table 12 presents the NCE gains for those students who had 1 year of DI in fifth grade.

New students at DI schools did have higher gains than students at control schools, but these differences were not significant.[16] It is also important to note that new fifth-grade students came into DI schools with significantly higher reading achievement scores than the new students coming into control schools, whereas new third graders coming into DI schools were slightly below new third graders coming into control schools.

Effects of DI on Measures of Oral Reading Fluency

Because some have argued for considering the results of more curriculum-based testing or individualized testing of student reading ability (Deno, 1985; Fuchs & Deno, 1992; Hall & Tindal, 1989; Hasbrouck & Tindal, 1991), we also conducted individualized tests of oral reading fluency in the second and third years of the study. Tests were conducted using passages from grade-level appropriate passages from RM as well as from other reading series that were similar to, but not the same as, the control school curricula. These tests, designed primarily by a NIFDI consultant for the BCP and conducted by independent researchers, measured only oral reading fluency (words read correctly in 1 min), with no measure of reading comprehension. Regression results using the independent (non-RM) individualized reading inventory spring 1999 test scores as the dependent measure of student achievement (controlling for 1998 CTBS–4 reading comprehension score, demographic variables, 1998–1999 attendance, and whether student was at the same school as previous year) indicated that DI had a significantly positive effect on oral reading fluency at both the second grade, $F(1, 473) = 5.13$, $p = .024$, effect size = +0.15; and fourth grade, $F(1, 415) = 12.96$, $p < .0005$, effect size = +0.26 levels. This was a 1-year effect of DI for all second and fourth graders in the study schools (including newly transferred students, not just those who had DI for 3 years). When analyses were restricted to students who had been in the same school for 3 years, effect sizes remained similar, but the effect was no longer significant at the second-grade level.

---

[16]This could be due to the relatively small sizes of these groups of new students. At the fourth-grade level, the control group has higher gains than DI students.

TABLE 12

Mean CTBS NCE Scores and Gain Scores in Reading Comprehension and Vocabulary for New Grade 3 Students at BCP and Control Schools, Spring 2000 (Not at Same School in Spring 1999 and Spring 2000)

| | Spring 1999 Grade 2 | | | | Spring 2000 Grade 3 | | | | | | | | |
| | Comprehension | | Vocabulary | | Comprehension | | Vocabulary | | Comprehension Gain | | Vocabulary Gain | | |
School	M	SD	M	SD	M	SD	M	SD	M	SD	M	SD	n
All BCP schools[a]	32.4	20.3	35.0	22.6	41.4	19.6	42.5	22.7	9.0	18.1	7.5	14.4	19
All control schools	35.9	16.2	36.7	19.2	41.7	18.2	41.5	20.0	5.8	12.0	4.8	18.4	40

Note. BCP = Baltimore Curriculum Project; CTBS = Comprehensive Test of Basic Skills; NCE = Normal Curve Equivalent.
[a]This refers to the number of students who took both comprehension texts; fewer took both vocabulary tests.

Effects of DI on Retention in Grade and Special Education Placement

DI schools had a much lower retention in grade rate than their control schools. Tables 13 and 14 summarize outcomes for the original kindergarten and second-grade cohorts by school.

Of the original kindergarten cohort, 2.4% of students at BCP schools (9 students) were in second rather than third grade in 1999–2000, compared with 9.6% at control schools (32 students), $\chi^2(1, N = 361) = 22.87, p < .0005$.[17] Among the original second-grade cohort, 1.4% of students at BCP schools (5 students) were in fourth rather than fifth grade, compared with 8.9% (31 students) at control schools, $\chi^2(1, N = 396) = 26.76, p < .0005$. Table 15 presents trend data on 4-year retention in grade rates at the BCP and control schools, using data available for the fall 1993 cohorts.

Due to limitations in the data available, it is difficult to ascertain how similar BCP and control schools were in their retention policies prior to the introduction of the reform. Because there was considerable variation in the earlier data at BCP and control schools, we cannot conclude with certainty that DI is responsible for a lower retention in grade rate. However, it is likely that the reform helps to account for the differential retention rate for the original cohorts, because the structural characteristics of DI allow for regrouping of students for reading instruction so that students may receive instruction at a lower grade level without being formally retained.

Differences between DI and control schools in assignment of students to special education were not as pronounced. Among the original kindergarten cohort, 5% of DI students were assigned to special education in 1999–2000, compared with 6% in control schools. Among the original second-grade cohort, 14% of DI students had special education status, compared to 10% in control schools.[18]

DISCUSSION

The evidence presented regarding the impact of DI on student outcomes in several elementary schools in an urban school district appears mixed. Perhaps most striking is the difference in rates of retention in grade between DI cohorts and control cohorts. There is also evidence of a positive impact on reading vocabulary test scores

---

[17]Percentages are calculated using the total number of original cohort in the denominator. When transfer students are eliminated from the denominator, the percentages of retained students are roughly doubled.

[18]Given the changes in how special education data were reported over the time period of the study, we do not attempt to present trend tables for special education.

TABLE 13
1996–1997 Kindergarten Students Sample Outcomes, Spring 2000

School	Number of Students F96	Number of Students on Track Same School S00	Number of Students Retained Same School S00	Students With Both Test Scores
BCP School 1	71	43	1	39
Control School 1	67	28	8	31
BCP School 2	65	38	2	40
Control School 2	60	21	6	24
BCP School 3	88	42	4	37
Control School 3	75	29	9	34
BCP School 4	31	15	1	14
Control School 4	31	11	1	10
BCP School 5	55	30	1	26
Control School 5	37	10	4	14
BCP School 6	69	28	0	27
Control School 6	63	25	4	24
All BCP Schools	379	196	9	183
All control Schools	333	124	32	137

Note. The difference between the number in the first column and the sum of the next two columns yields the number of students who transferred out of the original School over the course of the study. BCP = Baltimore Curriculum Project. F96 = fall 1996; S00 = spring 2000.

TABLE 14
1996–1997 Grade 2 Students Sample Outcomes, Spring 2000

School	Number of Students F96	Number of Students on Track Same School S00	Number of Students Retained Same School S00	Students With Both Test Scores
BCP School 1	57	42	1	35
Control School 1	87	42	7	43
BCP School 2	53	24	3	24
Control School 2	51	23	6	26
BCP School 3	103	65	0	54
Control School 3	78	30	4	26
BCP School 4	27	19	0	16
Control School 4	31	13	1	14
BCP School 5	62	32	0	26
Control School 5	35	17	6	19
BCP School 6	57	30	1	29
Control School 6	65	23	7	29
All BCP schools	359	212	5	184
All control schools	347	148	31	157

Note. BCP = Baltimore Curriculum Project. F96 = fall 1996; S00 = spring 2000.

TABLE 15
Four-Year Retention Rates for Kindergarten and Grade 2 Cohorts, Fall 1993–Spring 1997
and Fall 1996–Spring 2000

	% Retained at Least Once During 4-Year Period			
School	*1993–1994* *K Cohort*	*1996–1997* *K Cohort*	*1993–1994* *Grade 2 Cohort*	*1996–1997* *Grade 2 Cohort*
BCP School 1	—	1.4	—	1.8
Control School 1	10.0	11.9	0.0	8.0
BCP School 2	9.3	3.1	1.7	5.7
Control School 2	2.9	10.8	1.7	11.8
BCP School 3	13.9	4.5	6.7	0.0
Control School 3	13.5	12.0	4.2	5.1
BCP School 4	8.5	3.2	2.4	0.0
Control School 4	—	3.2	—	3.2
BCP School 5	0.0	1.8	0.0	0.0
Control School 5	1.6	10.8	2.0	17.1
BCP School 6	1.0	0.0	4.1	1.8
Control School 6	7.1	6.3	8.7	10.8

Note. Dash signals data not available. Percentages based on total number of students retained some time during the 4-year period, with the total number of students in the cohort in fall of the first year as the denominator. On average, one half or more have transferred out of the original school over the 4-year period, and outcomes for this large group are not determined. BCP = Baltimore Curriculum Project; K = kindergarten.

and measures of oral reading fluency, but no compelling evidence as to a significant effect of DI on reading comprehension (the primary dependent variable specified in the original evaluation plan). Although growth in reading comprehension achievement has occurred for students receiving DI, it does not appear to be significantly greater than for students receiving other reading instruction. This finding echoes previous findings regarding the impact of DI on reading comprehension.

Those who have emphasized the detrimental effects of retention in grade (e.g., Natriello, 1998; Owings & Magliaro, 1998) would applaud the low retention rate achieved at DI schools compared with their control school counterparts. At first glance, the low retention rates at DI schools are impressive. On the other hand, there is no evidence that DI students are achieving significantly higher in reading comprehension than their control counterparts, and lower achievers who are not retained in grade at DI schools are often reading from stories at a lower grade level; they may also be placed in reading groups with children at a lower grade level. Although these DI children do not endure the negative social consequences of formal retention, they still experience some of the effects of retention (grouping with younger children, learning opportunities pitched at the lower grade level). Only further longitudinal analyses will determine whether there is a long-term advantage to the form of social promotion practiced in DI schools. There may indeed be a cost savings if DI students finish school without the cost of an additional (retention) year.

The mixed achievement results described earlier suggest the need for a more nuanced evaluation of the effects of DI on reading achievement than provided by recent studies (e.g., Herman et al., 1999). Evaluations of DI must pay particular attention not only to the broad division between regular education and special education, but also to issues of particular measures of achievement, grade level, and characteristics of particular reading programs used by control groups.

Findings in this study differed somewhat depending on the particular measure of reading achievement used as an outcome variable. Although it was possible to find an "educationally significant" effect size (.25 or greater) using measures of oral reading fluency or CTBS reading vocabulary as outcome variables, the study did not uncover an educationally significant effect size of DI on reading comprehension, the original dependent variable proposed for the study during its design phase. Whether reading comprehension is the most important outcome variable to study will certainly remain an area of debate among educational researchers. We would argue, however, that it is important for practitioners to distinguish among particular areas of reading achievement as they weigh the evidence.

Although students receiving DI in reading have shown gains in their achievement over time, the question of whether DI produces significantly better achievement results than other programs may well depend on what type of reading program is implemented at the comparison school. If comparison schools have implemented a reading program that systematically presents phonetic instruction, albeit differently than does DI, it would be reasonable to expect that DI would be hard-pressed to show significantly better results than comparison schools (i.e., students showing increased reading achievement). DI is likely to fare much better when students at comparison schools have not received systematic phonetic instruction or the opportunity in upper elementary classes to work on decoding skills they may not have mastered earlier.

The control schools used a variety of basal readers during the first 2 years of this study. The extent of phonetic instruction varied from school to school and from classroom to classroom. In the fall of 1998 (the third year of this study), the school system shifted to the "Open Court" reading series (another highly prescriptive, highly phonetically based early reading program) for Grades K–2. Control members of the original kindergarten cohort therefore received instruction using Open Court during their second-grade year[19] at five of the six control schools.[20] It is possible that the lack of a significant difference in reading achievement between these control students and DI students at the end of third grade (1999–2000) could be

---

[19]Retained control students received both first- and second-grade instruction using open court.

[20]Control School 3 was part of a small group of students in the district that continued to use Houghton Mifflin in the primary grades.

due, at least in part, to the phonetically based instruction received by control students (for the duration of at least 1 year).

On the other hand, the school system adopted the Houghton Mifflin reading series for Grades 3 through 5, and control students in the original second-grade cohort (who were generally fifth graders in 1999–2000) had neither a strong phonetically based reading program in the earlier grades or a reading program that necessarily provided opportunities for them to acquire phonetic training or word attack skills in later grades. Deficits in the reading instruction received by these control students may help to account for the significant effects of DI on fifth grade-reading vocabulary scores in spring 2000 (as well as fourth-grade reading comprehension scores in a preliminary study; Mac Iver et al., 2000).

Although students receiving 4 years of DI in this study have made notable reading achievement gains, they did not perform significantly better than comparison students on measures of reading achievement, even when instruction began in kindergarten. It is possible that early implementation problems may have suppressed potential effects in their original cohorts, and that significant effects may emerge in later cohorts that experience a more mature implementation of the reform.

Although individual-level data are not yet available for the spring 2001 CTBS–5 administration, the preliminary report of aggregate level data indicates that the median percentile for first graders at each of the six original BCP schools is 54 or higher, and all BCP schools have equal or higher median percentiles in the first grade, compared to their control schools. These first-grade results reflect positively on DI as a reform effort, but the same pattern of results does not hold for other grade levels in the 2001 aggregate data. At those grade levels, DI schools are outperformed as frequently as they outperform their control schools. Plans are underway to continue longitudinal analyses of a cohort pretested during their first month of kindergarten in the fall of 1999, and we will report on those outcomes over the coming years. Although it is indeed possible that future research in these original schools may yield more striking evidence of DI's impact on achievement, the findings of this study suggest that DI is a viable option for raising urban student reading achievement, but that it is not necessarily more effective than other systematic programs that emphasize phonetic instruction.

REFERENCES

Berkeley, M. (2002/this issue). The importance and difficulty of disciplined adherence to the educational reform model. *Journal of Education for Students Placed At Risk, 7,* 221–239.

Brent, G., & DiObilda, N. (1993). Effects of curriculum alignment versus direct instruction on urban children. *Journal of Educational Research, 86,* 333–338.

Core Knowledge Foundation. (1995). *Core knowledge sequence.* Charlottesville, VA: Author.

CTB. (1991). *CTBS/4 technical report.* Monterey, CA: Macmillan/McGraw-Hill.

CTB/McGraw-Hill. (1997). *TerraNova technical bulletin 1.* Monterey, CA: Author.

Daneman, M. (1991). Individual differences in reading skills. In R. Barr, M. Kamil, P. Mosenthal, & P. D. Pearson (Eds.), *Handbook of reading research* (Vol. 2, pp. 512–538). New York: Longman.

Davis, G. (1999, October 27). Transcripts of nonpublished interview transcript conducted by Martha Mac Iver and Elizabeth Kemper on October 27, 1999 in Baltimore, MD as part of the qualitative research underlying this article.

Deno, S. (1985). Curriculum-based measurement: The emerging alternative. *Exceptional Children, 52,* 219–232.

Dunn, L., & Dunn, L. (1981). *Peabody Picture Vocabulary Test–Revised.* Circle Pines, MN: American Guidance Service.

Fuchs, D., & Deno, S. (1992). Effects of curriculum within curriculum-based measurement. *Exceptional Children, 58,* 232–243.

Engelmann, S. (1969). *Preventing failure in the primary grades.* Chicago: Science Research Associates.

Engelmann, S., & Carnine, D. W. (1982). *Theory of instruction: Principles and applications.* New York: Irvington.

Engelmann, S., & Engelmann, T. (1966). *Give your child a superior mind.* New York: Simon & Schuster.

Hall, T. E., & Tindal, G. (1989). Using curriculum-based measures to group students in reading. In G. Tindal, K. Essick, C. Skeen, N. George, & M. George (Eds.), *The Oregon Conference Monograph, 1989* (pp. 10–12). Eugene: University of Oregon, College of Education.

Hasbrouck, J., & Tindal, G. (1991). Curriculum-based oral reading fluency norms for students Grades 2 through 5. *TEACHING Exceptional Children, 24*(3), 41–44.

Herman, R., Aladjem, D., McMahon, P., Massem, E., Mulligan, I., O'Malley, A., et al. (1999). *An educator's guide to schoolwide reform.* Washington, DC: American Institutes for Research.

Hirsch, E. D., Jr. (1996). *The schools we need.* New York: Doubleday.

Kerbow, D. (1996). Patterns of urban student mobility and local school reform. *Journal of Education for Students Placed At Risk, 1,* 149–172.

Mac Iver, M., Kemper, E., & Stringfield, S. (2000). *The Baltimore Curriculum Project: Third year report.* Baltimore: Center for Social Organization of Schools.

Natriello, G. (1998). Failing grades for retention. *School Administrator, 55*(7), 14–17.

Owings, W. A., & Magliaro, S. (1998). Grade retention: A history of failure. *Educational Leadership, 56*(1), 86–88.

Schaffer, E., & Nesselrodt, P. (1993). *Special strategies observation system.* Charlotte: University of North Carolina, College of Education.

Slavin, R. E. (1987). A theory of school and classroom organization. *Educational Psychologist, 22,* 89–108.

Slavin, R. E., & Fashola, O. (1998). *Show me the evidence!* Thousand Oaks, CA: Corwin.

Stallings, J. A. (1980). Allocated academic learning time revisited, or beyond time on task. *Educational Researcher, 9*(11), 11–16.

Stanovich, K. (1991). Word recognition: Changing perspectives. In R. Barr, M. Kamil, P. Mosenthal, & P. D. Pearson (Eds.), *Handbook of reading research* (Vol. 2, pp. 418–452). New York: Longman.

Stringfield, S., Millsap, M., Winfield, L., Brigham, N., Yoder, N., Moss, M., et al. (1997). *Urban and suburban/rural special strategies for educating disadvantaged children: Second year report.* Washington, DC: U.S. Department of Education.

Thrift, G. (2000, August 2). Transcripts of nonpublished interview transcript conducted by Martha Mac Iver and Elizabeth Kemper on August 2, 2000 in Baltimore, MD as part of the qualitative research underlying this article.

JOURNAL OF EDUCATION FOR STUDENTS PLACED AT RISK, 7(2), 221–239

CASE STUDIES

The Importance and Difficulty of Disciplined Adherence to the Educational Reform Model

Muriel Berkeley

Baltimore Curriculum Project

Educational research has identified effective methods of raising student achievement, but has not yet established how to put these methods into consistent practice. Whereas several instructional models have proven effective in significantly improving student performance in low-performing schools, large-scale implementations of these models have produced inconsistent results. One reason for this may be that local and state education officials overburden schools by insisting that they implement too many initiatives concurrently (Hatch, 2001). Despite their support for one or more reform models, their actions may actually make implementation more difficult.

The Baltimore Curriculum Project (BCP), funded by the Abell Foundation, brought Direct Instruction (DI) and core knowledge (Core) to six Baltimore city public schools in 1996. Twelve other schools took on DI and Core subsequently. Evidence from the implementation of DI and Core in Baltimore city schools has indicated that the potential effectiveness of this curricular intervention has been diluted by the intervention of local and state education officials. However, some of these schools have been more successful than others. At City Springs Elementary, for example, test scores have risen consistently since the combined implementation of DI and Core. We believe that academic achievement (as measured by the Comprehensive Test of Basic Skills and the Maryland School Performance Assessment) has increased at City Springs because (a) the school has focused strictly on a high-fidelity implementation of the reform model, and (b) DI focuses on systematically accelerating the progress of every child. In this article, we describe im-

Requests for reprints should be sent to Muriel Berkeley, The Baltimore Curriculum Project, Suite 301, 711 West 40th Street, Baltimore, MD 21211. E-mail: mberkele@ix.netcom.com

plementation of DI and Core at City Springs, as well as the distractions that interfered or threatened to interfere with implementation.

CITY SPRINGS BEFORE DI AND CORE

In the spring of 1996, City Springs Elementary was a place of failure for both students and teachers. Many children could not read, and test scores were abysmal. No remnant of a one-time implementation of "Success for All" remained. Children listened to teachers only when they felt like it, roamed the halls, and left the building. The faculty, spinning like tops, reacted to one crisis after another. When DI was implemented the following fall, the primary focus was behavior management, as the faculty had to establish order before they could teach children to read and write. A Maryland State Department of Education (MSDE) report written in the fall of 1996 described City Springs as a "phoenix rising from the ashes" (Maryland State Department of Education [MSDE], 1997–1998).

THE REFORM MODEL: DI AND CORE

BCP was created by the Abell Foundation in 1996 to develop a challenging, structured curriculum with daily lesson plans available to any public school that wanted to use it. With the curriculum used at Baltimore's Calvert School and Home Instruction Department (now Calvert Educational Services) as its model, BCP decided between the available alternatives on the basis of research done on each program's effectiveness. BCP relied on the Educational Resources Information Center database as its primary source of research.

All of human knowledge is available for teaching, but writing realistic lesson plans for the elementary and middle school grades requires paring down all human knowledge—a daunting task. Therefore, the first decision BCP made was to use the curricular scope and sequence of the Core Knowledge Foundation as a guide for what to teach. Because the Core Knowledge Foundation had already devoted considerable resources to paring down "the whole realm of knowledge," BCP chose to use the fruits of their work.

The next question that BCP tackled was how to teach the basics: reading, writing, and mathematics. BCP's research on the effectiveness of existing programs uncovered two possible reading programs: DI and Success for All. At that time Success for All was only a reading program, whereas DI programs existed for teaching mathematics and writing as well. Emulating the Calvert model, BCP wanted to put together a complete curriculum that would be as internally consistent as possible, rather than functioning out of an amalgam of multiple programs, requiring different approaches at different times of the day. BCP reasoned that it would be more practical to train teachers to use a curriculum that stressed consistent teaching techniques. BCP also thought that children would be more successful if they could focus on skills and content, rather than adapting to different teaching approaches throughout the day. In addition, the DI programs included all the phonics, phonemic awareness, grammar, and mathematics recommended by the Core Knowledge Foundation. The DI reading and writing programs also included some of the geography, history, literature, and science recommended by Core. After BCP began implementation, a study commissioned by the Core Knowledge Foundation recommended DI's "Connecting Math Concepts" and "saxon math" as the two math programs that were most closely aligned to Core.

There were two other features of DI as a school reform model that attracted the attention of BCP: (a) behavior management, and (b) a system to frequently monitor student progress and performance. DI teachers are taught to ignore children who misbehave based on the idea that many children are so starved for adult attention that they will do anything, including misbehave, to get it. Teachers learn to positively reinforce the behavior they want while ignoring the behavior they do not want. Teachers learn to elicit attention to task and successful completion of tasks. DI's student progress and performance monitoring system allows teachers to catch academic problems before a child falls behind, or to accelerate the academic achievement of those students ready to move ahead. BCP decided to use DI programs for reading, writing, and mathematics because the programs had been demonstrated to be effective, because they were aligned with Core, because they included programs to teach basic academic skills, and because they incorporated systems to manage student behavior and monitor student progress and performance.

BCP's choices of DI and Core were validated by *An Educators' Guide To Schoolwide Reform* (American Institutes for Research, 1999). This guide listed just two elementary school reform models backed by solid research that extolled their effectiveness: DI and Success for All. There has not been as much research on Core (a newer reform), but the guide did list Core as "promising" (American Institutes for Research, 1999, p. 4).

After the BCP staff decided to use DI programs for reading, writing, and mathematics, they were left with the task of writing lessons for the geography, history, literature, science, music, and visual arts content in Core. BCP wrote lessons for Grades K–2 in 1996 and 1997, Grades 3 through 5 in 1997 and 1998, Grade 6 in 1998 and 1999, and Grade 7 in 1999 and 2000. Eighth-grade lessons are expected to be completed in 2001. BCP revised its lessons for Grades K–5 in 1999 and 2000, and is continuing to revise them. As written, the lessons have proved too time consuming, given the basic academic needs of most Baltimore city children.

Between 1996 and 2001, 18 Baltimore city public elementary schools have worked to implement DI and Core. BCP recommends the use of DI programs to teach children to read, write, compute, and reason; it recommends Core for teaching children critical information in geography, history, science, literature, music, and visual arts.

DI

Three key principles in DI schools are the following:

1. Every child will learn.
2. If the child has not learned the teacher has not taught.
3. The teacher must not assume what the child knows.

Teachers can meet such a high standard only if they have effective tools, if they are given effective training in how to use these tools, and if they are allowed to concentrate fully on the task at hand. DI principals know how to analyze lesson and test data, how to identify and solve classroom problems, and how to identify and solve instructional problems.

DI is an effective tool for teachers to use with any student, but is particularly effective with children struggling to master basic academic skills. Jonathan Mooney and David Cole were students not fortunate enough to have been enrolled in schools that used DI. Describing the agony of school for children who do not learn easily, they wrote, "we explored our histories and our wounds from growing up in a cruel educational system that told us at an early age we were lazy, stupid, and crazy" (Mooney & Cole, 2000, p. 20). In contrast, learners do not get frustrated when their teachers are using DI correctly because the authors of DI programs teach every prerequisite for a skill before the student is asked to perform it. When students do not master a particular skill, teachers do not blame the child, but rather analyze their own teaching to see what went wrong and how to fix the problem. DI teachers are trained to check how well students are learning each step, giving them the necessary help to succeed. Students are grouped homogeneously for instruction, allowing those who learn more quickly to progress as rapidly as they are able, and other students the time they need for success.

A leading obstacle to the academic achievement of disadvantaged children has been that they often have inadequate vocabularies for academic pursuits (Biemiller, 2001; Hart & Risley, 1995). Unaware of this, teachers might interchange one word for its synonym, potentially leaving disadvantaged students in confusion. For example, a non-DI teacher may use *answer* in one sentence and *reply* in the next. Students who do not know that answer and reply are synonyms are lost. DI lessons are scripted to insure that teachers use consistent language when they teach. The DI teacher would not substitute reply for answer without explicitly teaching that the two words have essentially the same meaning.

Another barrier to the academic success of disadvantaged students is insufficient background knowledge (Hirsch, 1987). If one thinks of the brain as a room with strips of velcro hanging from the ceiling, then the velcro is like background knowledge; it is what provides the scaffolding to situate new knowledge. As new knowledge is introduced it moves through the room and sticks onto a piece of velcro (if one is available). Typically, disadvantaged students do not have the velcro, or background knowledge, for new knowledge to attach to, and so may not be interested and may not learn. Students who do have background knowledge more easily retain whatever new knowledge is introduced, thereby further building their base of background knowledge. Many educational programs fail to serve disadvantaged children well because they make assumptions about what children learn outside of school. Because DI authors and teachers do not make assumptions about what their students learn outside of school, DI programs systematically develop critical background knowledge before explicitly applying and linking it to new knowledge.

Because disadvantaged children may have less academic vocabulary and background knowledge, efficiency of instruction is essential. Disadvantaged students' school time is precious and must not be wasted. Students cannot afford to mislearn information, because relearning material that one has learned incorrectly is more time consuming than learning new material. DI curriculum designers anticipate student errors, and design materials to avoid those mistakes. Students are taught one piece of information and given extensive practice with that information before a potentially confusing concept is taught (e.g., d and b, longitude and latitude, metaphor and simile).

In DI schools, teachers are trained not only to make no assumptions about what academic background children bring to school, but also to make no assumptions about what behavior they might expect. Teachers are taught that any behavior a teacher expects, they must teach. DI teachers make clear all possible behavioral expectations, such as how to walk in the hall, how to work independently, how and when to move around the classroom, and how to sit.

In addition to teaching every necessary step for the acquisition of academic skills, DI teachers monitor their students' performance thoroughly. Students with low academic skills are monitored verbally. Once students are able to read and write, teachers monitor academic performance through their written work. Teachers learn to monitor in class while the students are working, so that they might catch errors before they become habits. Any work that is not checked in the classroom is checked before the next lesson, so that students can correct their errors as quickly as possible.

Core

Core encompasses a rich body of knowledge including literature, geography, history, science, music, and visual arts. Founded by E. D. Hirsch, the Core Knowledge Foundation recommends that these subjects be taught in grades Pre-K–8. Hirsch pointed out that without clear agreement on what should be taught at each grade level, children will encounter gaps in their schooling (Hirsch, 1987).

The Implementation Schedule

BCP's original implementation plans called for schools to first implement DI reading and language programs. Once faculty were familiar with those programs, DI mathematics and spelling programs were to be introduced. Finally, once faculty were comfortable with the DI programs, implementation of Core was to begin. DI programs were introduced first because of the necessity of reading and language skills to all other learning. BCP also anticipated that the techniques teachers learned through implementing DI would help them more effectively teach Core.

The initial schedule for the implementation of DI and Core specified a 3-year phase-in of the complete curriculum. The first year was to be dedicated to implementing the DI reading and language programs, the second year to DI mathematics and spelling, and the third year to Core. BCP underestimated how much teachers and principals would have to learn to implement DI effectively, and how much teacher turnover would slow the progress of implementation. By the third year of the implementation, faculty were still concentrating on becoming proficient with DI techniques and helping children reach grade level in reading. As a result, full implementation of Core was delayed.

Uneven Results

The results of whole-school reform efforts typically differ significantly from school to school. Educators have data about what makes schools effective, but little information about how to use that data consistently to make schools effective (Olson, 2001). Eighteen Baltimore schools have used DI and Core, but they have not all gotten the same results. The results at City Springs Elementary School have been among the most impressive. The remainder of this article presents information and reflection about what has made City Springs successful with DI and Core.

WITHIN-MODEL OBSTACLES TO DI REFORM

Some obstacles to the implementation of DI are inherent to the model itself. DI is capable of almost unbelievable results because of its intricate curricular design and teaching techniques (refined over more than 30 years). Understanding the design and learning the techniques, however, is difficult and takes time. The DI model allows schools to accelerate the learning of every child, but successful implementation requires consistency and concentration. Teachers and administrators must be able to focus on the DI implementation because each person has so much to relearn.

Teachers must practice new techniques and learn the specific curricular content. Because DI lessons are scripted, teachers do not write lessons. Nevertheless, they do need to develop familiarity with the wording to pay attention to student responses and correct errors promptly. Teachers must report weekly on how many lessons they have taught and how their students have performed.

Principals, in turn, learn how to interpret the data their teachers give to them weekly. They learn how to solve instructional problems, how to secure additional training for those teachers who need it, and how to regroup and reschedule to meet students' changing instructional needs. Instead of helping teachers improve their lesson plans, principals help teachers use DI scripts correctly; complete an adequate number of lessons; correct children quickly and thoroughly; and maintain ratios of at least three specific praises to each criticism, three teacher initiated interactions to each student initiated interaction, and three correct academic responses to each incorrect one. Principals must also learn how to stretch all available staff, including assistants and secretaries where appropriate, to cover all instructional groups, and how to schedule the school day to ensure that students get the instructional time they need to succeed. With DI, paradigms shift and roles change.

WITHIN-SCHOOL OBSTACLES TO DI REFORM

Schools that commit to implementing DI and Core face many obstacles in addition to the inherent difficulty of implementing the reform. Some of the obstacles come from within the school and others come from outside it. Obstacles imposed from outside the school are the most damaging to the reform. The obstacles coming from within are largely a byproduct of human nature, that is, fear of and resistance to change. Fortunately, these obstacles disappear as people see children learn, and as they become accustomed to new ways. Every year since implementation began in Baltimore, BCP has surveyed teachers asking them what they think about using DI. Teachers' support for DI has increased the longer they have used the program, and they have consistently reported that DI programs are effective and increase student achievement.

Faculty who are committed to implementing DI and Core are committed to working hard at something their colleagues are not doing, that their supervisors do not like, that faculty of schools of education have told them is wrong, and that professional development activities discourage. The mindset of many people trained in departments of education is that children can learn almost effortlessly by discovering knowledge, and that drilling them with phonics or math facts is harmful. Comments such as, "DI is uncreative," "DI is bad for children," and "DI will not prepare students for the Maryland School Performance Assessment Program (MSPAP)," are omnipresent.

Many educators told BCP that teachers would refuse to use DI. However, at the 18 schools where DI was implemented, at least 80% of the teachers voted to bring the program into their schools. After the decision was made, any teacher who did not want to implement DI was allowed to transfer to another school. Not one teacher chose this option. However, after the first year of DI implementation, one teacher did leave City Springs Elementary School for reasons related to the program (a number of others left for other reasons), and we suspect that there have been a few teachers at other DI-implementing schools who left because of the decision to adopt DI. Teacher mobility data indicates that there are no more teachers leaving DI schools than leaving other Baltimore City schools. The teacher who cited DI as her reason for leaving City Springs has since sought out and returned to a DI school. Nonetheless, the anti-DI sentiment in the education profession is a constant distraction. Instead of concentrating on learning DI programs and techniques thoroughly (a multiyear challenge) teachers must often use their energy to learn and utilize non-DI activities that are viewed as good preparation for the MSPAP, although these activities may dilute the effects of DI on student achievement.

Other obstacles to effective DI implementation are those that hinder academic achievement in all urban schools: inadequate resources and student and teacher mobility. Only a few urban schools are fortunate enough to patch together sufficient resources (through special grants) to address the needs of children affected by neglect and abuse. The characteristically high student mobility in urban schools interferes with a school's efforts to provide all students with the necessary academic skills. Even if a school is providing its students with an effective education, children often transfer into the school with inadequate skills. Therefore, the faculty must cope with trying to remediate transfer students without impeding the momentum of those students who have been in the school longer.

High teacher mobility in urban schools is caused in part by the difficulty teachers experience in managing disadvantaged urban school students. For example, one highly trained and motivated DI teacher came to City Springs because she wanted to teach urban children using the tools DI provides. Although she was successful, she left after 2 years to get away from the stress of managing children who needed constant reinforcement to stay on task. At City Springs, during our first several years of implementation, teacher mobility increased because we had to move some teachers out who were not committed to working as hard as a full implementation of DI requires.

Despite barriers to change, whether a professional environment hostile to DI, inadequate resources, or student or teacher mobility, DI has invigorated every school that has adopted it. The learning of the children, the joy they take in their learning, and the success of the program eventually silences the doubts that inevitably accompany early phases of implementation. The difficulty of effectively implementing DI programs does not go away, however. Continuity of implementation is therefore essential.

OBSTACLES TO DI REFORM FROM OUTSIDE THE SCHOOL

The single biggest obstacle to the effective implementation of DI and Core is the channeling of school staff's concentration and energy into other initiatives, imposed on the school from outside. Over the last 5 years in Baltimore, pressure on principals to raise MSPAP scores, combined with MSPAP experts' assertions that DI will not prepare students to do well on MSPAP (despite the fact that they know little about DI) has been the primary obstacle to effective implementation of DI and Core. The pressure to raise MSPAP scores comes from Baltimore City Public School System (BCPSS) supervisors and from threats (backed up with action) from the MSDE that principals will be publicly shamed and lose their jobs if MSPAP scores do not increase.

The supervisors of Baltimore city public school principals are called area executive officers. During the first 2 years of DI implementation, the DI principals did not all report to the same area executive officer. Their executive officers were busy with schools that were not using DI and left implementation of DI to the schools. A single area executive officer was given responsibility for the DI schools beginning with the 1998–1999 school year. During the first 2 years of implementation, principals of DI schools worked collaboratively with BCP to solve common problems, such as how to show DI academic gains on the BCPSS report card, or how to get dispensation to avoid giving student assessments based on the city curriculum that DI schools were not using. The BCP DI–Core principal collaborative did not dictate to its members. Members discussed common problems and suggested a variety of solutions; principals were free to choose the solution that they thought would be most appropriate for their school community. The area executive officers were generally flexible and cooperative about listening to the BCP–DI principal collaborative. However, different principals responded to the ubiquitous MSPAP pressure differently. For example, during the first year of implementation, BCPSS administered citywide assessments every quarter that mimicked MSPAP and were based on the BCPSS curriculum. The BCP–DI principal collaborative successfully received dispensation from these assessments, which required a total of 3 weeks of instructional time, plus countless hours of teacher time for grading. One DI principal, however, did choose to interrupt DI instruction for 1 week in the fall to give the assessment. The area executive officer of that principal interceded and ordered the principal to stop giving the current assessment, as well as assessments in the second and third quarters. The principals differed on how much professional development time and instructional time they devoted to MSPAP preparation, but none focused all instructional time and professional development time on DI.

The DI–Core Area

At the end of the second year of implementation, BCPSS created a DI–Core area and put all the DI–Core schools under one area executive officer, who was a strong proponent of DI. This was a step toward institutionalizing DI–Core within BCPSS, leading in many ways to stronger program implementation. Five of the 6 schools that began implementation under his leadership got off to a faster start than any of the previous 11 schools had. After the creation of the DI–Core area, BCP staff did not have to run between area executive officers to get dispensations of one type or another.

On the other hand, the DI–Core area executive officer has not been inclined to give dispensations from area mandates; the mandates come from the DI–Core area staff. The staff at the DI–Core area office has less experience utilizing the DI and Core programs than many of the school-based staff. People who are not experienced with DI often underestimate the difficulty of learning and implementing DI. Because of this, too many other demands are placed on the schools; these other demands distract principals from fully implementing DI. No longer can principals choose the approach they think best for their school communities—every school has to use the same approach to each issue.

The DI–Core area mandates different goals for the DI–Core schools than the goals of the BCP DI–Core reform. The first goal of the DI–Core reform is accelerated progress through the DI programs, and the second is learning the Core material. The DI–Core area requires the schools to report quarterly on two milestones that do not support a focus on rapid progress through DI programs: (a) Each teacher must teach three DI lessons per week in each DI subject, and (b) each student must be given Core quarterly assessments that have been created by the DI–Core area.

The expectation that each teacher teach three lessons per week in each DI subject has had unintended but predictable consequences. Attempting to standardize how many lessons groups will complete in 1 week has proved impossible. Some instructional groups, depending on the material being taught, the learning rate of the students, and the instructional skill of the teacher, are able to complete many more than three lessons per week, whereas others cannot complete even three per week. The artificial standard of three lessons per week encourages teachers to push struggling students too quickly, while discouraging them from moving proficient students through programs as quickly as they could. Furthermore, the completion of a certain number of lessons per week does not necessarily reflect real progress. Inexperienced teachers sometimes move their students too quickly, and when they realize that the students have not achieved mastery, they are forced to move them back to repeat lessons. When the DI–Core area established the completion of three lessons per week as a quarterly milestone, they directed teachers' attention away from two crucial areas: (a) ensuring that students master the content of each lesson and (b) encouraging proficient students by accelerating lesson progress beyond three lessons per week.

The second milestone mandated by the DI area is student performance on area-created Core quarterly assessments. The DI–Core area pushed the implementation of Core more quickly than BCP had by mandating these quarterly assessments. BCP maintains that reading and language are fundamental to learning and must be emphasized until students are performing on grade level. The DI–Core area requires schools to give a quarterly Core assessment regardless of how quickly students are mastering reading and language. Teachers, many of whom are already overworked, must find the time and energy not only to teach

Core, but also to give and grade the assessments. The result of this mandate is that there are fewer resources available to bring students to proficiency with reading and language and teachers to proficiency with DI. When the teachers have reached proficiency with DI, they will be more effective at teaching Core because they will be able to use what they learn about curriculum design and instructional techniques from DI.

The DI area office has also required other activities that have distracted school-based personnel from thoroughly implementing DI. During the first year of the DI–Core area, the question of how to accurately reflect children's instructional levels on their report cards became a problem. In the first years of DI implementation, the BCP DI–Core principal collaborative worked out solutions to this problem. The report card must explicitly state the child's grade level; academic grades are also to reflect that level. DI brings a more precise and higher standard for grade level than schools typically have before implementing DI. In the early years of implementation, therefore, students' grade levels and grades drop because of the new more precise measurement and higher standard. The drop in grade level and grades upsets students and their parents. The BCP DI–Core principal collaborative devised a scale for interpreting the correlation between DI levels and grade levels that was more forgiving during the early years of implementation, and more accurate as the implementation continued and students reached higher levels of DI programs. The DI–Core area, however, decided to require schools to use a strict interpretation of DI levels and grade levels. There was a strong and negative reaction from parents when the first quarter grades came out. As a result, the DI–Core area changed its position. Considerable teacher and principal learning time was lost due to the debate and its aftermath.

Another DI–Core area action that set back implementation of DI was the transferral of principals from one school to another. One summer, eight DI–Core schools received new principals. In all but one case, the new principals came from other DI schools and were already familiar with DI. Nevertheless, in addition to continuing to learn about DI, the principals had to familiarize themselves with new communities, faculties, and student bodies. Principals of DI schools have to learn many things to become effective DI managers. For example, they have to learn exactly what each DI program teaches, when to use which program, and how to interpret and manage DI data. Transferring them to new schools only slows their acquisition of these important areas of knowledge.

Although the DI–Core area has never stressed the importance of implementing DI correctly, it has sent the message to DI–Core schools that effective implementation of DI and Core is the primary priority. The principals are held accountable for raising MSPAP scores with the strategies identified by the area office, and for turning in paperwork by announced deadlines. Clear focus on doable priorities is necessary for success.

MSPAP: The Test

MSPAP is a performance-based assessment given to all public school third, fifth, and eighth graders each May. The test is designed to assign scores to schools rather than to individual students. The school scores are based on the performance of students in reading, writing, language usage, mathematics, science, and social studies. Students are tested for half a day for 5 days in a row.

All the students in the same grade do not take the same test. The state assigns students to testing groups. Some testing groups perform scientific experiments, whereas others perform historical, geographic, or economic analyses based on data given in the test. Some testing groups use mathematical skills to design rooms or tracks, whereas others analyze or write poems and stories. Each group engages in different kinds of activities in the course of the week. Groups are assigned scientific, literary, or mathematic work; others perform data analyses.

All items ask for written answers of varying length; there are no multiple-choice items. Maryland teachers are hired each summer to score the tests. To insure that all scorers use the same standard, teachers are trained to use detailed scoring rubrics.

Although the schools get a reading score, the test does not assess reading directly. On some forms of MSPAP, students are asked to read a passage and then answer some analytical questions. On other forms, they perform a task based on written instructions, and answer questions based on the task. In either case, a student might read and understand the passage or instructions, but use a format in answering the question that the rubric does not allow. Students might have a problem not with reading but with how they interpreted the question or framed their answer.

MSPAP Fear

MSPAP is feared by teachers, principals, and other administrators because MSDE uses MSPAP scores to decide which schools to label "reconstitution (takeover) eligible." Out of these, they decide which schools to reconstitute. The label of reconstitution eligible shames a school's faculty while threatening careers.

MSPAP Pressure

Pressure to raise MSPAP scores comes from both BCPSS and MSDE. The schools follow every suggestion they are given about how to raise MSPAP scores, but because MSPAP experts offer differing advice, their efforts do not provide a coherent educational program. One pervasive recommendation is that classroom teaching should look like MSPAP testing, for example, that children should be seated at desks arranged in groups of four or five, rather than in rows. In contrast, whereas DI programs do include group work, in most DI classrooms, desks are arranged in rows.

MSPAP instruction requires that students problem solve in groups, and then write answers individually. MSPAP preparation does not focus on the acquisition of necessary skills before assignment of related tasks. DI lessons, on the other hand, introduce necessary skills and repeat them until the entire class is at mastery. Once students have mastered the skills taught they are often assigned to group activities based on newly acquired skills. The MSDE has said that one of the purposes of MSPAP is to change classroom practice. Perhaps they want classroom practice to "look like" MSPAP. However, research has suggested that DI is more effective than MSPAP-directed classroom teaching (Adams & Engelmann, 1996; Gersten, Woodward, & Darch, 1986). However, the importance of raising MSPAP scores is of primary importance in Maryland. Officials of both MSDE and the BCPSS are very clear that raising MSPAP scores is a top priority. Although both MSDE and BCPSS officials have endorsed the implementation of DI and Core, they have also made clear that raising MSPAP scores is more important than implementing DI or Core.

MSDE auditors visit DI–Core schools that are reconstitution eligible, which includes City Springs and most of the DI–Core schools (these schools became reconstitution eligible based on test scores prior to implementing DI). In the fall of 2000, the MSDE auditors gave the DI–Core schools high marks for positive school climates, focused students, explicit teaching, positive reinforcement, students on task, and effective student management. They criticized the schools for the lack of a number of elements theoretically linked to success on MSPAP. They said that the schools do not use MSPAP-like rubrics. Although DI instruction does teach students to use rubrics to evaluate their own work, these rubrics do not resemble those used on MSPAP. The MSDE auditors also criticized the schools for not using performance-based instruction. By performance-based instruction, they were specifically referring to teaching children by giving them problems to solve or other tasks to perform. DI programs do give children problems to solve and tasks to perform, but only after children have been explicitly taught the requisite skills and have demonstrated that these skills have been mastered.

The MSDE auditors also criticized the DI schools for not differentiating instruction, that is, providing appropriate instruction to different children. Differentiation of instruction in DI schools happens largely by reorganizing instructional groups to accommodate student needs, and by providing as much or as little practice as the individual requires. The MSDE auditors thought that the DI schools did not provide adequate higher order questions. DI programs actually explicitly teach students to think through higher order questions (Carnine, 1991). Finally, the MSDE auditors questioned the connection between DI programs and the Maryland Learning Outcomes (MLOs), on which MSPAP is based. Elaborate alignments have been done that have shown where the MLOs are met in DI programs.

The DI–Core schools might have been better served if the auditors' comments had focused on the considerable positives they found in the schools. Positive school climate, focused students, students on task, and effective student management are not easy to achieve, but the auditors' reports placed pressure on the schools to change their priorities and foci. However, if the schools were to change their priorities and their DI techniques to more closely resemble MSPAP, they might lose what they have achieved. Schools that responded to the auditors comments by using professional development and instructional time to address these comments took away from professional development time that could have been spent helping teachers become more proficient in DI techniques, and instructional time that could have helped children get further ahead in DI programs.

Baltimore schools are being pushed to show immediate results. When schools in Baltimore take on the challenge of implementing DI–Core, they may not even be given the 5 years that is generally thought to be minimum for a reform to become institutionalized. In fact, test scores often go down in the early years of implementing any school reform. Gilmor Elementary School was in its second year of implementing DI when MSDE handed over management to Edison Schools, based on its test scores from its first year of using DI and several years prior. When test scores were announced for Gilmor's second year of DI implementation, both MSPAP and Comprehensive Test of Basic Skills (CTBS) scores had risen, but by then MSDE had taken DI–Core out of the school. MSDE announced that it was taking over Westport Elementary/Middle School after the school had been implementing DI for 3 and a half years, although Westport's eighth-grade MSPAP scores had risen more than the eighth-grade scores of any other city school, and overall, the middle school had the highest composite index of MSPAP scores in its history. MSDE felt that the MSPAP scores were not high enough.

MSDE's emphasis on raising MSPAP scores as quickly as possible is so strong that a MSDE official told City Springs that they should decrease their efforts with low-performing students and focus instead on teaching higher performing students, because the higher performing students would be able pull up the school's MSPAP scores. Inherent to any DI implementation is the focus on teaching every child effectively. It is not possible for a school to implement DI well and simultaneously ignore or shortchange low-performing students.

THE FOCUS AT CITY SPRINGS ELEMENTARY SCHOOL

The focus at City Springs Elementary School from Day 1 of implementation has been on using DI and Core as they are intended to be implemented, as defined by the BCP and the National Institute for Direct Instruction. During the first and second years of the implementation, years when the priorities were to be DI reading, writing, spelling and mathematics programs, the principal devoted her time and energy to learning about the design and techniques of DI, and she held her teachers accountable for the same. The principal's message to teachers about the importance of handling behavior consistently and effectively and of implementing DI as it was designed to be used was unambiguous. The principal noticed when teachers let their praises fall below their corrections, when their lesson progress fell below what was possible, and when students' written work showed lack of mastery or was not checked. In addition, when the prinicipal noticed a lapse in implementation she informed the teacher in question. Several teachers left the school because of the relentless pressure to perform. The principal did not distract herself or her teachers from the implementation of DI with initiatives recommended by MSPAP experts. She knew that the faculty had chosen DI as the tool to best teach students critical academic skills, and that the students would be unable to perform on MSPAP until they had mastered reading, writing, and mathematics skills.

During the first year of implementation, City Springs and BCP applied to be partners in the New Schools Initiative (NSI). NSI is a BCPSS venture to allow nonprofit organizations to work with Baltimore city public schools that are exempt from some systemic directives. The original purpose of the NSI was to see if flexibility from systemic operations can allow schools to come up with effective educational programs to meet the needs of all students, including those considered to be "special education." City Springs and BCP have been able to use their NSI partnership to protect City Springs from some BCPSS systemic initiatives that they felt would interfere with the effectiveness of the DI programs.

City Springs, with the support of its NSI partner (BCP), does not use the milestones that the DI–Core area prescribes. For its quarterly milestones, City Springs predicts the percentages of students at each grade that will work in the appropriate DI program for that grade. This focuses the school on progress through programs. The City Springs faculty uses DI programs all day with students who are below grade level in academic skills. They use Core lessons with students who are performing at or above grade level.

When City Springs and BCP planned for the third year of implementation, the year when BCP had originally planned to introduce Core, they decided that they needed to focus on basic academic skills for another year. Teacher turnover had interfered with the development of a faculty proficient in DI techniques, which in turn had interfered with student progress. A significant portion of the student body were still below grade level. During the third year of implementation, therefore, City Springs continued with a full day of DI programs, including a second reading period.

City Springs began the fourth year of implementation with an introduction of Core customized for City Springs by its own faculty. Progress in basic academic skills during the first quarter was disappointing, however, and the faculty decided to replace the Core instructional period with a second reading period for those students whose progress indicated that they would not stay on or above grade level.

City Springs opened its fifth year of implementation (2000–2001) with a full day of DI programs, including two reading periods. The faculty asked to do this for the first month of school because a full day of DI programs sets a tone of productive academic work for students, and the design of the programs helps new teachers get a rhythm of instruction characterized by effective corrections, adequate repetition, and students achieving mastery. Later in the fall, teachers began to introduce Core to students who were on or above grade level. The Core lessons allow teachers to extend the skills emphasized in DI writing lessons. With the Core lessons and the writing activities, the teachers work to incorporate all that they have learned from DI lessons about effective teaching: modeling, leading, testing, and correcting, until the children's work shows that they have mastered the material.

Throughout the 5 years of implementation, professional development for City Springs faculty has focused on clear faculty needs with regard to behavior management and DI techniques. The principal has resisted pressure from both MSDE and BCPSS officials to teach faculty about various aspects of MSPAP preparation. Similarly, she has resisted pressure to alter the school's curriculum to include MSPAP preparation.

If the implementation of DI and Core is allowed to continue at City Springs, the use of Core will increase with students who are performing on or above grade level. Faculty are fine tuning Core lessons in preparation for increased use, as an increasing number of students are on or above grade level in reading. Extended writing activities will be part of the Core lessons, as will the effective teaching techniques that teachers have learned from their DI experience.

RESULTS OF DI–CORE AT CITY SPRINGS
ELEMENTARY SCHOOL

City Springs' test scores prior to the implementation of DI and Core were very low. City Springs had the reputation of being one of the worst performing schools in the city. Baltimore city public schools are judged primarily by their MSPAP scores (third and fifth grades only), and secondarily by their scores on the CTBS, a norm referenced test, at all grade levels.

Although City Springs' MSPAP scores are still well below the state standard of 70% of students reaching proficiency in reading, writing, language usage, mathematics, science, and social studies, its composite index of MSPAP scores has increased every year since the implementation of DI and Core in 1996. This is highlighted in Table 1.

CTBS scores have been increasing at City Springs, particularly in the early grades, as shown in Table 2.

The median percentiles of City Springs 2001 CTBS reading scores at first (82nd percentile), second (63rd percentile), and fifth (67th percentile) grades were higher than the median of the rest of the DI–Core schools as a whole and higher than the city-wide median. The median percentiles of City Springs 2001 CTBS math scores at first (61st percentile), second (65th percentile), third (60th percentile), and fifth grades

TABLE 1
Percentage of City Springs Third and Fifth Graders Scoring Satisfactory on the Maryland
School Performance Assessment Program

Grade and Subject	1994 (Before DI–Core)	1997	1998	1999	2000
Grade 3 reading	1.3	3.4	6.5	10.1	9.3
Grade 3 writing	6.5	11.8	9.4	18.3	23.6
Grade 3 language usage	0.0	13.6	15.6	15.7	27.3
Grade 3 mathematics	0.0	1.7	11.5	5.9	5.7
Grade 3 science	6.5	0.0	7.8	11.3	12.7
Grade 3 social studies	0.0	2.9	7.8	11.3	12.7
Grade 5 reading	2.0	9.3	10.2	11.8	10.9
Grade 5 writing	5.9	7.0	27.0	23.5	20.0
Grade 5 language usage	0.0	14.3	34.4	20.6	36.4
Grade 5 mathematics	0.0	8.8	4.8	0.0	16.4
Grade 5 science	0.0	1.8	4.8	8.8	30.9
Grade 5 social studies	2.0	3.5	4.8	11.8	20.0

Note.   DI–Core = direct instruction–core knowledge.

TABLE 2
City Springs Comprehensive Test of Basic Skills Medians 1998–2000

Grade	1997–1998		1998–1999		1999–2000		2000–2001	
	Reading	Math	Reading	Math	Reading	Math	Reading	Math
1	28	8	43	18	65	71	82	61
2	26	14	30	14	39	18	63	65
3	28	18	28	12	31	16	50	60
4	20	9	30	9	14	21	32	38
5	14	9	12	13	22	47	67	50

(50th percentile) were higher than the medians for the DI–Core schools as a whole and higher than the citywide median, as shown in Table 3.

City Springs' CTBS scores in the early grades have been increasing for several years, reflecting the growing effectiveness of instruction in kindergarten in recent years. DI's success at moving children to higher grade levels is dependent on teaching children to read in kindergarten. The increase of scores at the upper grade levels may have been possible in 2001 because effective teaching in kindergarten and first grade allowed school leaders to turn their attention to the upper grades.

Test scores cannot tell the whole story of a school. City Springs has not always provided a quiet, orderly environment for learning, but it does today. Students perform in reading celebrations and compete in math rumbles (math fact competitions

TABLE 3
2001 Comprehensive Test of Basic Skills Medians: City Springs, DI–Core, BCPSS

	City Springs		DI–Core Area		BCPSS	
Grade	Reading	Math	Reading	Math	Reading	Math
1	82	61	65	54	54	51
2	63	65	43	43	39	41
3	50	60	40	39	42	41
4	32	38	33	30	33	33
5	67	50	44	31	41	34

Note. BCPSS = Baltimore City Public School System; DI–Core = direct instruction–Core knowledge.

similar to spelling bees), as well as spelling bees. Fifth graders are studying a seventh-grade U.S. history program. In 2000, five City Springs fifth graders' CTBS scores earned them places in the advanced academic program at Roland Park Middle School, Baltimore's premier middle school. No one at City Springs remembers such success previously. In the spring of 2001, fourth and fifth graders who were studying U.S. history visited Monticello, where they told their guide about Thomas Jefferson's accomplishments as our nation's third president, explained the significance of the Declaration of Independence, and discussed the Lousiana Purchase and the Lewis and Clark expedition. They visited the U.S. Courthouse for the District of Maryland, where they asked Judge Andre Davis about the implications of the first 10 amendments to the U.S. Constitution on teachers' right to search student' lockers, on the Ku Klux Klan, controversial rap lyrics, and Timothy McVeigh's execution.

CONCLUSION: FOCUS ON TEACHING EVERY CHILD

If our public schools are to reform themselves to teach every child effectively, they need dedicated principals and teachers trained in effective instructional tools. Principals and teachers need freedom from distractions so that they can focus on teaching. It should be no surprise that educational programs like DI have been shown to be ineffective if they are not used as they were designed to be used. The pressure on Baltimore city public schools to raise MSPAP scores immediately is so great, and the consequences of not raising scores so painful, that there are serious disincentives to trying any research-based school reform. Schools feel safer following whatever the latest MSPAP wisdom is. Most Maryland schools are using MSPAP preparation activities. It would be interesting to see what effect research-based reform efforts could have on MSPAP scores if they were fully implemented, rather than being diluted by MSPAP preparation.

Results at City Springs suggest that effective implementation of DI with some Core can raise test scores. If City Springs continues to have the flexibility to continue with the DI–Core reform, we expect scores to continue to rise as we teach more Core and continue to refine our DI expertise. Even City Springs, however, has not been entirely sheltered from systemic distractions. What might happen to test scores if a school or group of schools were told by MSDE and BCPSS that they would be held accountable not for MSPAP scores, but for 5 years of faithful implementation of a research-supported reform?

REFERENCES

Adams, G. L., & Engelmann, S. (1996). *Research on direct instruction: 25 years beyond DISTAR*. Seattle, WA: Educational Achievement Systems.

American Institutes for Research. (1999). *An educator's guide to schoolwide reform*. Arlington, VA: Educational Research Service.

Biemiller, A. (2000). Vocabulary: The missing link between phonics and comprehension. *Perspectives, 26*, 26–30.

Carnine, D. (1991). Curricular interventions for teaching higher order thinking to all students. *Journal of Learning Disabilities, 24*, 261–269.

Gersten, R., Woodward, J., & Darch, C. (1986). Direct instruction: A research-based approach to curricular design and teaching. *Exceptional Children, 53*, 17–31.

Hart, B., & Risley, T. (1995). *Meaningful differences in the everyday experience of young American children*. Baltimore: Brookes.

Hatch, T. (2001, February 14). It takes capacity to build capacity: Why the biggest threat to reform may be system overload. *Education Week, 19*(1), 44, 47.

Hirsch, E. D., Jr. (1987). *Cultural literacy: What every American needs to know*. New York: Houghton Mifflin.

Maryland State Department of Education (MSDE). (1997–1998). *Challenge grant report to the Maryland General Assembly*. Baltimore: Division of Student and School Support Services, Maryland State Department of Education.

Mooney, J., & Cole, D. (2000). *Learning outside the lines*. New York: Simon & Schuster.

Olson, L. (2001, February 14). Low-performing schools lack help, study says. *Editorial Projects in Education, 20*(22), 28, 34.

JOURNAL OF EDUCATION FOR STUDENTS PLACED AT RISK, 7(2), 241–263

The BIG Accommodation Model: The Direct Instruction Model for Secondary Schools

Bonita J. Grossen

University of Oregon

Research during the last 2 decades has found the BIG Accommodation Model to be successful in helping students with disabilities achieve rigorous academic standards in mainstream classrooms at the secondary level. This research project tested the effects of the BIG Accommodation Model in accelerating the learning of highly at-risk students in low-achieving secondary schools. The project began with 1 highly problematic middle school in Sacramento, CA and resulted in record gains for all ethnic groups, for English language learners, and for students performing at all levels in the areas of both language arts and mathematics. The project further established a professional development model that allowed for replication of success in other middle schools. Successful replication depends on the presence of three components: the curricular materials designed around "big ideas," electronic progress monitoring, and in-class coaching. The initial training model provides a particularly cost-efficient means for achieving high-quality implementations.

During the last 2 decades, research and development efforts in education have focused on the goal of closing the achievement gap between students with disabilities and general education students. The Direct Instruction (DI) model has emerged as one of the most successful models for accomplishing this goal. Table 1 highlights the findings of recent research studies evaluating whether students with disabilities are able to achieve rigorous standards in general education classes.

The remarkable successes documented in Table 1 were achieved primarily through unique engineering of the BIG Accommodation curricular materials. Table 2 contrasts traditional teacher-directed instruction with the six major instructional engineering principles used in "The BIG Accommodation" (Carnine, 1994), designed to accommodate diverse learning needs. These principles of instructional design are described in more detail in Kameenui and Carnine (2001).

Requests for reprints should be sent to Bonnie Grossen, 292 West 12th Street, Eugene, OR 97401. E-mail: bgrossen@oregon.uoregon.edu

TABLE 1
Research on the Effects of Instruction With Accommodations in Closing the Achievement
Gap Between Special Education and General Education Students

Area	Description
Reasoning	1. On a variety of measures of argument construction and critique, high school students with learning disabilities scored as high as high school students in an honors English class and higher than college students enrolled in a teacher certification program (Grossen & Carnine, 1990) 2. In constructing arguments, high school students with disabilities scored significantly higher than college students enrolled in a teacher certification program and scored at the same level as a group of college students enrolled in a logic class (Collins & Carnine, 1988).
Science	3. On a test of problem solving to achieve better health, high school students with disabilities scored significantly higher than nondisabled students who had completed a traditional high school health class (Woodward, Carnine, & Gersten, 1988). 4. On a test of problem solving that required applying theoretical knowledge and predicting results based on given information, mainstreamed middle school students with disabilities scored higher than a class of general education students taught in a school-centered treatment (Grossen, Carnine, & Lee, 1996). 5. On a test of misconceptions in earth science, mainstreamed middle school students with learning disabilities showed better conceptual understanding than Harvard graduates interviewed in the film, *A Private Universe* (Schneps, 1987). 6. On a test of earth science problem solving, mainstreamed middle school students with learning disabilities scored significantly higher than nondisabled students who received traditional science instruction (Woodward & Noell, 1992).

(continued)

242

TABLE 1 (*Continued*)

Area	Description
	7. On a test of problem solving involving earth science content, most of a group of mainstreamed middle school students with learning disabilities scored higher than the mean score of the nondisabled control students (Niedelman, 1992).
	8. On an advanced chemistry test, high school students with disabilities and remedial students scored higher than a group of high-performing students in an advanced placement chemistry class on the subscale covering chemical equilibrium. The students matched the performance of the advanced placement students on subscales requiring application of concepts of chemical bonding, atomic structure, organic compounds, and energy of activation (Hofmeister, Engelmann, Carnine, 1989).
Mathematics	9. On a test of problem solving requiring the use of ratios and proportions, mainstreamed high school students with disabilities scored as well as nondisabled high school students who received traditional math instruction (Moore & Carnine, 1989).
	10. On a test requiring the application of fractions, decimals, and percents, age-grouped fifth and sixth grade low-achieving students scored significantly higher than high-achieving students learning in a constructivist treatment (Grossen & Ewing, 1996).
History	11. On a history test that required analyzing primary source documents, the scores that mainstreamed high school students with learning disabilities attained on the use of principles and facts in writing did not differ significantly from nondisabled control students (Carnine, Caros, Crawford, Hollenbeck, & Harniss, 1996).
	12. Middle-school urban children of poverty and some with limited English increased their history vocabulary proficiency at a rate five times that of suburban middle-school students (Carnine et al., 1996).

TABLE 2
The Contrast Between Instruction With Accommodations for Diverse Learners and
Traditional Instruction

Principles of Accommodation for Diverse Learners	Traditional Instruction
Presentation of big ideas, concepts, and principles that facilitate the most efficient and broad acquisition of knowledge across a range of examples. Big ideas make it possible for students to learn the most and to learn it as efficiently as possible, because "small" ideas can often be best understood in relation to larger, "umbrella concepts."	Presentation of a barrage of unrelated facts and details. The links between concepts are obscured.
Teaching of conspicuous strategies made up of specific steps that lead to solving complex problems.	Strategies are seldom taught.
Background knowledge is pretaught.	Important prerequisite learning is often neither evaluated nor taught.
Mediated scaffolding provides personal guidance, assistance, and support that gradually fades as students become more proficient and independent.	Little direction or provision for scaffolding the progression of learning toward greater independence is provided.
Judicious review requires students to draw on and apply previously learned knowledge over time.	Review is often minimal.
Strategic integration blends new knowledge with old knowledge to build big ideas.	Spiraling of topics does not carefully integrate units.

BIG IDEAS: GETTING MORE ACHIEVEMENT FROM LESS LEARNING

Big Ideas in Remedial DI Programs

All the BIG Accommodation programs are new generation DI programs organized around "big ideas." Big ideas yield more power from less learning time and are the key to accelerated learning. The older generation DI programs for remediating skill deficits of secondary students provide simpler examples of big ideas. For example, the big idea in *Corrective Reading* (Engelmann et al., 1999) is the relation between sounds and letters in words. Through learning 57 sound–symbol relations (the big idea), students learn to read all the words in the language. The 57 sound–symbol relations have been carefully thought out to maximize generalizability. For example, the sound taught for the letter y is "yee," which works both at the beginning and end of words: yellow (yee-ellow), puppy (pupp-yee). And, it works in the middle of words: gym (g-yee-m). Students who are taught using *Corrective Reading* (Engelmann et al.) grow in reading at two or three times the normal rate, making it possible for many students to catch up in 1 year of instruction (for a review of the research, see Grossen, 1998).

Another remedial program, *Spelling Through Morphographs* (Dixon & Engelmann, 1999), teaches 600 morphemes and three rules for connecting them, enabling students to spell 12,000 words. The following are examples of four sets of morphemes, which combine to form four words. All four words have the morpheme "ion" in common:

1. In fect ion.
2. In flate ion (drop the final "e" when the next morpheme begins with a vowel).
3. In tent ion.
4. Pro fess ion.

Notice how the confusion in deciding whether to use "sion" or "tion" is eliminated with this analysis. If the speller considers the root meaning, the spelling is clear.

Big Ideas in Teaching Cognitively Complex Content

The new generation DI programs in the BIG Accommodation model teach cognitively complex content using the big idea analysis. Some examples follow.

Reasoning and writing. A big idea in the reasoning and writing (Engelmann & Grossen, 2001a, 2001b) program is a ruling-out process for constructing knowledge. This ruling-out process is the essence of the scientific method. Figure 1 illustrates one of the early tasks. Students must figure out what is in the mystery box and write a paragraph describing their thinking process. The outline diagram provides a template for their paragraphs. The icons graphically represent the type of thinking involved. The trapezoid prompts a summary statement, or topic sentence. The boxes illustrate the stepwise nature of the ruling-out process used in constructing knowledge. And finally, another upside-down trapezoid indicates a concluding sentence. To figure out the mystery object, students read the first clue, "The object is red," and then review the possibilities. Following the outline diagram, they write, "Clue A rules out the banana. That object is not red," and so on.

This thinking strategy has wide applications. Figure 2 illustrates the application of the ruling-out process to shopping. Henry needs a jacket and has several requirements. In this scenario there is a jacket that meets his requirements. In other activities, the students also encounter scenarios where no option meets all the requirements; they must weigh the alternatives and choose the best option. Students use this same ruling-out process for many other kinds of applications. For example, they use it to select the best plan for accomplishing a goal.

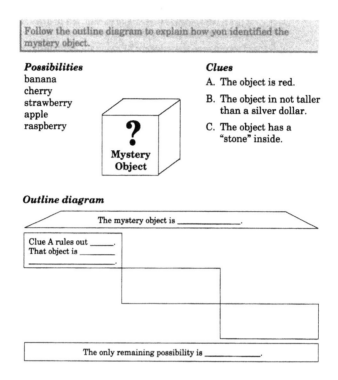

FIGURE 1   The mystery box.

This ruling-out process also represents the fundamental thinking involved in setting up and interpreting the outcomes of scientific experiments. Figure 3 illustrates a problem requiring an experiment before a conclusion can be made. Not all the possible explanations for an observation have been ruled out. The students describe a short experiment and then describe how to interpret the data, depending on how the experiment turns out. This experiment will rule out remaining possible explanations for the observation.

The outline diagrams provided in Figures 1 through 3 provide students with a clear model of the wording and thinking processes involved. Later, these prompts are faded, after students have internalized the thinking patterns and are able to work successfully without the prompts.

Earth science.   The central big idea of the earth science videodisc program (Systems Impact Incorporated, 1987) is convection. Most textbooks describe convection with only one paragraph, so students never learn that convection is the basis for making predictions in earth science. For example, meteorologists predict the weather based in large part on their knowledge of convection. Woodward (1994) compared the videodisc program organized around the big idea of convection with

Part A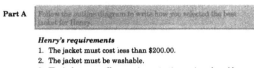

Henry's requirements
1. The jacket must cost less than $200.00.
2. The jacket must be washable.
3. The jacket must offer superior protection against the cold.
4. The jacket must weigh no more than 4 pounds.

Facts

Jacket	Stormbuster	Windblaster	Leader	King Kold	Wilderness
Price	$179.00	$187.99	$156.00	$206.00	$187.00
Weight	4 lb.	3 lb. 2 oz.	2 lb. 8 oz.	3 lb. 7 oz.	4 lb. 3 oz.
Protection against cold	superior	superior	good	superior	superior
Cleaning	washable	dry clean only	washable	washable	washable

Outline diagram

The only jacket that meets all Henry's requirements is _____ .

Requirement __ rules out _____ . That jacket _____ .

The only remaining jacket is _____ .

FIGURE 2   Henry's shopping problem.

a videodisc program with a standard unit organization; he found that organization around the big idea resulted in better learning, both qualitatively and quantitatively.

Understanding U.S. history. The text, *Understanding U.S. History* (Carnine, Crawford, Harniss, & Hollenbeck, 1998), uses the problem–solution–effect big idea to organize the events of history. Students learn that history is built around attempts to solve problems among groups of people. Every solution to a problem generally leads to a new problem. For example, the automobile solved a transportation problem, but created a new problem: pollution. History, therefore, can be characterized as a chain of problems. By studying the ways humans have solved problems in the past, and the effects of those solutions, students seem better able to identify solutions for the future, while attempting to avoid the mistakes of the past.

Bigger ideas integrate across content areas. The programs and practices in the BIG Accommodation provide for transfer across subject areas, thus maximizing instructional efficiency. Students learn important skills for processing, critiquing, and researching information, that they apply in all subject areas. They learn, for example, that opinions must be based on evidence, that the evidence must

Follow the outline diagram to write about the problem with
Sam's test.

Sam's test

Sam did an experiment with maple seeds. He planted 600 seeds
at a depth of one-half inch below the surface of the dirt. He
controlled the temperature of the soil so it was above 60 degrees
Fahrenheit. Nearly all the seeds sprouted.

He planted another batch of seeds two inches deep. He put
them in a place that had a temperature that was less than
60 degrees. Almost none of those seeds sprouted.

Sam's conclusion

A temperature above 60 degrees causes the seeds to sprout.

Outline diagram

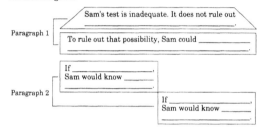

FIGURE 3   Sam's experiment.

logically support the opinion, and that the evidence must be accurate according to a
reliable source. They learn to look for contradictions and inconsistencies, to look at
all possible explanations for a set of facts, and then look for more information to
rule out some of the explanations.

THE PROBLEM: AT-RISK SECONDARY SCHOOLS

Because the BIG Accommodation model improved the performance of students
with disabilities on higher level cognitive tasks, we hypothesized that it would
also work to accelerate the learning of large numbers of at-risk secondary students. Implementing the BIG Accommodation model in schools serving
high-poverty neighborhoods would certainly present new problems that we had
not yet encountered in our work with students with disabilities in middle class
schools. Low achievement has been correlated with high poverty (Hodgkinson,
1992), English as a second language, and disability. These problems are difficult
to resolve; breaking the cycle of low performance at the middle school level in
high-poverty neighborhoods would indeed be challenging.

THE STRATEGY: BUILD A BIG BEACON

My approach was to work with a middle school that faced as many problems as possible to see what it would take to turn performance around. If performance could be turned around, then that site could be used as a training and demonstration center (a BIG Beacon) to teach and guide personnel from other schools with similar problems.

The school that fit those criteria was Charles M. Goethe Middle School in Sacramento, CA, the lowest performing middle school in one of the lowest performing districts in northern California at the time of our study. Goethe Middle School had a long-standing reputation of ineffectiveness. Of the elementary schools that fed into Goethe Middle School, most promoted a majority of students with mean percentile scores in the single digits. Ninety-five percent of the students received free or reduced-price lunches, 56% lived with families that received Aid for Dependent Children, approximately 40% were English language learners (ELL) from diverse language backgrounds, and 91% were comprised of various minorities.

GOETHE: THE MIDDLE SCHOOL THAT COULD

The transformation in the spirit of Goethe Middle School in the first year of the BIG Accommodation implementation was documented in a film (Palfremen, 1997) available from the Middle School Division of the Sacramento County Office of Education. The film includes testimonials and scenes describing the transformation of Goethe Middle School.

Quantitative evaluation of growth for low-performing middle school students has been problematic. Norm-referenced summaries of performance, such as the Stanford Achievement Test–Ninth Edition (SAT9), used for school accountability in California, are not sensitive to the growth of students at the low end of the distribution. To understand this lack of sensitivity, imagine a student performing at each percentile as a runner in a race of 100 competitors. The longer the race, the larger the gap: The main bunch of runners progress further down the road while stragglers spread out further behind. To pass 10 runners (or to gain 10 percentile points) requires 1 runner at the tail end of the pack to cover much more distance than 1 in the middle of the pack. Similarly, norm-referenced tests require more learning to gain points at the ends of the distribution than they require for students near the 50th percentile, or for groups who started later (younger students).

An example using real data from the Multilevel Academic Survey Test (MAST; Howell, Zucker, & Morehead, 1985), which has norms for groups in Grades 2 through 8, shows that the same amount of gain in raw score produces very different values for a student in Grade 3 versus one in Grade 8. For the same raw score gain from pretest (12) to posttest (28), a student in Grade 3 would show 48 percentile points gain (28 points on a normal curve equivalent [NCE] scale), whereas a student in Grade 8 would show only 4 percentile points gain (14 points on an NCE scale). This phenomenon occurs on any non-referenced test.

The MAST can be used to compare the performance of every student with that of norm groups from a wide range of age levels. For example, the raw score of 12 equaled the mean score of the second-grade group; the raw score of 28 equaled the mean score of the fourth-grade group. Both the Grade 3 and Grade 8 students in the example moved from working at a Grade-2 to a Grade-4 level. Both students made gains of 2 years in 1 year of academic work. This type of analysis represents the growth more fairly.

According to the MAST, the median-score student at Goethe increased two grade levels during the first year both in reading comprehension and in mathematics. The median score in reading improved from the fourth- to the sixth-grade level, and the median score in math improved from the fifth- to the seventh-grade level. In the analyses of the MAST scores from Goethe Middle school, no differences were found between seventh- and eighth-grade students; therefore, scores across both grades were aggregated for the analysis. Figure 4 shows how students at Goethe improved in grade-level equivalent scores in reading; Figure 5 shows how students improved in mathematics. The performance levels of the Grade-7 and Grade-8 students at Goethe Middle School shifted substantially from the lower to the higher grade-level ranges.

ELL

To determine the effect of the BIG Accommodation model on the performance of ELL, I analyzed pre and posttest scores of the MAST using the same cut scores. Figures 6 and 7 display the analyses for ELL. As the figures indicate, the shift from low to higher performance was stronger for ELL students in reading than for the group as a whole. The number of students reading at approximately grade level (Grade 7 and above) increased by more than 350%.

Results by Ethnic Group

Schoolwide data from the MAST were disaggregated by ethnic group. The results of this analysis for Year 1 for reading are displayed in Table 3. In reading, all ethnic groups made substantial progress. The mathematics instruction had more differential effects by ethnic group. Perhaps the different grouping arrangements used for math and reading can explain these differences. For reading instruction, students were mixed ethnically and grouped according to specific reading needs. For mathematics instruction, students were grouped according to their English language level, with native speakers grouped separately from ELL, who were taught in

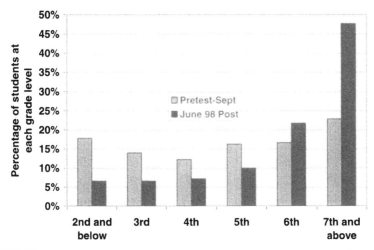

FIGURE 4   Year 1 change in reading performance (students performing at each grade level) on the Multilevel Academic Survey Test, September 1997 to June 1998 ($n = 518$).

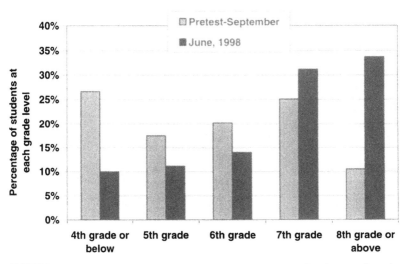

FIGURE 5   Year 1 change in mathematics performance (students performing at each grade level) on the Multilevel Academic Survey Test, September 1997 to June 1998 ($n = 518$).

smaller groups (20). In effect, this meant that large numbers of African Americans and very few White English-speaking students were taught in groups of 30 to 35. (In Year 2, students were grouped for math instruction according to their skill needs, regardless of their language level or disability. Consequently, results were consistent in mathematics across all ethnic groups.)

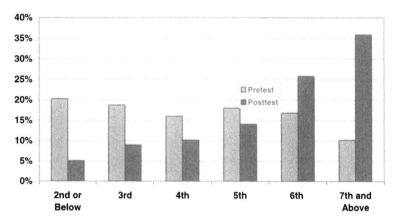

FIGURE 6   Year 1 change in reading performance (students performing at each grade level) for English language learners on the Multilevel Academic Survey Test, September 1997 to June 1998 (*n* = 256).

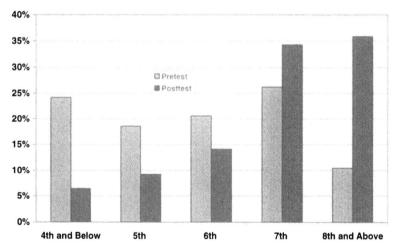

FIGURE 7   Year 1 change in mathematics performance (students performing at each grade level) for English language learners on the Multilevel Academic Survey Test, September 1997 to June 1998 (*n* = 256).

Gifted Students

Gifted students were also placed in the high-level reading program (*Reasoning and Writing: Level F,* Engelmann & Grossen, 2001b). Table 4 shows the percentile gains made by the Grade-7 and Grade-8 gifted groups on the MAST.

TABLE 3
Grade Equivalent Gains on MAST in Reading, by Ethnic Group

Ethnicity	No.	Grade-Level Equivalent		Change
		Pre	Post	
Asian	210	4.6	5.9	+1.3
Black	142	4.6	5.8	+1.2
Latino	120	3.9	5.5	+1.6
White	48	5.2	7.3	+2.1
Native American	4	3.2	4.9	+1.7

Reduced Behavior Problems

During the first year of implementation, the last period of the school day was the only period in which students in all classrooms were being taught using DI. During the other periods of the day, the instruction was mixed; some groups were learning with DI, others were not. The vice principal reported that during the last period of the day, there were rarely any referrals for behavior. During each of the earlier periods of the day, there was an average of 8 to 10 referrals per class period. The success students were experiencing in learning seemed to be reflected in their behavior.

YEAR 2: GOETHE MIDDLE SCHOOL BECOMES A BIG BEACON

California's statewide assessment using the SAT9 began in spring 1998. Because performance on the SAT9 has been the focus for accountability and evaluation, I used primarily the SAT9 for Year 2 of the DI implementation at Goethe Middle School. Being a statewide measure, the SAT9 also allowed comparisons with other schools. Concurrently, I continued to use the MAST for subgroup analyses. The subgroup analyses for Year 2 with the MAST were similar to the Year 1 reports, so they are not reported here. The correlation of the MAST raw scores with the SAT9 percentile scores was quite high (Pearson $r = .76$).

Longitudinal Comparisons

The state of California publishes percentile equivalents for mean raw scores for all grade levels at all schools in California. The published mean scores in percentiles for the same cohort for reading were, for Grade 7 (1998), $M = 21$st percentile; for Grade 8 (1999), $M = 35$th percentile. According to the MAST the progress during Year 1 for the same cohort in reading was a change from a median percentile of 9 to a median percentile of 25. Although 35th percentile at the

TABLE 4
Percentile Gains in Multilevel Academic Survey Test Reading for Gifted
Students

Grade	Percentile for the Mean Pretest Score	Percentile for the Mean Posttest Score
7	35	86
8	36	85

end of Year 2 is still well below the mean, the extent of the improvement after implementing DI seems substantial.

For mathematics, the same cohort scored as follows on the SAT9: For Grade 7 (1998), 27 = mean percentile; for Grade 8 (1999), 35 = mean percentile.

Comparisons

The SAT9 also allowed comparisons with other schools. A comparison school was selected in the same district. The comparison school had very similar demographic statistics, the same pretest score on the SAT9, and was also implementing a new research-based reading program (although, not the BIG Accommodation model). The scores for the same cohort at the comparison school were as follows: In Grade 7 (1998), the score was 21; in Grade 8 (1999), the score was 29.

Officials in the California Department of Education reviewed all the middle schools in the state and found that the gains that Goethe showed in reading for the same cohort ranked fifth highest in the state. The schools making greater gains than Goethe Middle School were all schools with higher initial pretest performance. No low-achieving school made gains comparable to those made at Goethe. Generally, it has been difficult to turn around low-achieving middle schools.

By Level

Raw scores on the MAST at the low end of the distribution had a lower correlation with the SAT9 percentile scores than MAST raw scores at the high end of the distribution. This finding corroborated a theory that the MAST raw scores were more sensitive to gains for very low-achieving students, whereas the SAT9 was more sensitive to the learning gains of higher performing students.

On the MAST, students at all instructional levels made 2 years gain for 1 year of instruction. The SAT9, however, seemed to show little gain for the lower instructional levels and higher gain for the higher levels.

To see which reading program levels in the DI model contributed most to the SAT9 gains, I used a "net shift analysis" (Lindman, 1968). Although about as dated as *t* tests, the net shift analysis provided a means for weighting the low- and high-end scores of the distribution to compensate for the problems in percentile comparisons described earlier. With the net shift analysis, individual percentile score distributions can be used to evaluate growth, on a relative scale, by comparing distributions of test scores made by groups of pupils on standard tests with distributions made by other groups of students on the same tests.

By identifying the percentage of student scores that must be shifted to an adjacent cell (interval) to make the two distributions equivalent, the net shift analysis technique reveals changes in score distributions that may occur when different teaching methods are used. The technique also offers a more complete comparison between the distribution of scores made by a selected group of pupils and a norm group. Table 5 displays the net shift analysis values for each of the program levels used for reading at Goethe, including both the weighting to adjust low scores and the weighting to adjust high scores.

Regardless of whether the low- or the high-end scores are weighted using the net shift analysis, the higher levels of the programs show greater SAT9 gains than the low-end programs. The content of the higher level programs aligns better with the content of the SAT9 and with the grade-level standards. However, the lower level programs build the necessary foundation for students to be successful in the higher level programs. Clearly, it is necessary to implement the higher level programs to achieve significant gains on the SAT9.

YEAR 3: RESOURCE-EFFICIENT DISSEMINATION

Because of the improvement in performance at Goethe, and the growing awareness in all of California of the extent of illiteracy in secondary schools, both middle and high schools were eager to implement the decoding program used in the BIG Accommodation, the Corrective Reading program (Engelmann et al., 1999). Consequently, we turned our attention to developing an efficient model for training and replication.

Early Intensive Coaching

Designing lessons that are successful with diverse learners (because they incorporate the six principles of accommodation) is significantly more time consuming than actually delivering the lessons. Teachers simply do not have the time to design the lessons themselves. Consequently, DI models give the teachers the core lesson plans for teaching the big ideas. By having ready-made lesson plans, training can proceed more efficiently.

TABLE 5
Net Shift Analysis for Each Reading Program Level at Goethe Middle School

Net Shift	Corrective reading, Decoding, Level B1	Corrective reading, Decoding, Level B2	Corrective reading, Decoding, Level C	Corrective reading, Comprehension, Level C	Reasoning and writing, Level E	Reasoning and writing, Level F
n	22	47	33	42	149	124
Weighted low scores	8%	10%	36%	34%	34%	52%
Weighted high scores	9%	11%	42%	45%	45%	72%

No matter how efficient the training might be, it seems that in-class coaching remains a necessity. Joyce and Showers (1995) documented the extent to which different types of teacher training resulted in teachers applying what they learn in the classroom. They found that professional development that includes demonstration and simulated practice transfers to the classroom with 10% to 15% fidelity. With the addition of coaching, the rate of transfer increases to between 80% and 90%.

Because the DI procedures are so specific, workshop training often leaves teachers with the impression that a good implementation merely follows these procedures in a rather "robot-like" fashion. This is not the case. A teacher who implements well is constantly responding to nuances in the students' performance. Learning this kind of responsiveness in simulated practice conditions with adults is almost impossible, because when proficient persons role-play naive learners they have a great deal of difficulty responding the same way naive learners do.

The skills involved in bringing the low performers to criterion, while keeping the lessons challenging for the most proficient, seem best taught to teacher trainees in the context of watching a model with real students in the classroom, while having an opportunity to copy the model. In the resource-efficient training system I developed for replicating the knowledge gained at Goethe, model schools host training sessions where teachers in training actually practice the presentation techniques with master teachers in the model school with the master teachers' students. The master teacher first models the techniques, then team-teaches with the trainee, and finally monitors and gives feedback to the teacher who by that stage should have become quite proficient in the strategies. With this training model, teachers are far more likely to use the programs in a manner that maximizes gains in their respective classrooms.

Even after teachers return to their classrooms, follow-up visits by an expert guest coach are still necessary, but do not seem to be required nearly to the extent that they are required when only workshop training is provided. Exper guest coaches work with teachers in their classrooms until the teachers and their instructional groups achieve the following four criteria:

1. Students respond correctly to new items that incorporate previously taught concepts 90% of the time.
2. Students are 100% on task 100% of the time.
3. Teachers give feedback to students in a ratio of three statements of specific praise for each corrective statement.
4. Students display pride and joy in their work.

Coaches are trained in specific techniques for helping teachers achieve the aforementioned goals and provide this coaching support for teachers in an in-class format. In-class coaching results in faster acquisition of new teaching behaviors than after-class feedback (Coulter, 1997). In this model, the coach identifies a specific teacher behavior aimed at improving student performance, models this behavior while the trainee is leading the teaching, observes the teacher incorporating the modeled behavior, and checks if the change in teaching behavior is yielding the expected change in student performance. (For more information about the specific coaching and training model, see Grossen & Scott, 2000.)

Electronic Progress Monitoring

In addition to the use of the BIG Accommodation curricula ("B") and in-class coaching ("I"), a third important factor of success is great expectations ("G"). Schools achieve great expectations with the assistance of an electronic system of continuous progress monitoring (Caros, 2001). The statewide accountability tests that occur at the end of the year come too late for anybody to identify problems and solve them. The progress monitoring system provides a formative evaluation process, which works much like a physicians' stethoscope, monitoring the health of the implementation on an ongoing basis. Teachers routinely enter their student mastery test results for each instructional group into a standard data entry form. Every 4 weeks, data showing the percentage of student at mastery in each instructional group and the rate of progress through the lessons are summarized and reported.

One report provides information about the rate of progress of all the instructional groups through the lessons as well as the percentage of students who are at mastery. A second report provides a list of the students who are not at mastery along with a possible reason, identified by the teacher. These reports serve as an efficient means for preventing eventual failure by guiding the focus for immediate coaching on the specific groups and individual students needing help, and also serve as a powerful means of motivating students and teachers by routinely recognizing their achievement and progress.

The goal of BIG Accommodation is for all students to be successful on all parts of the mastery tests at all times. Students who are proficient every step of the way are more likely to be proficient on statewide assessments. The coordinated efforts of all support personnel are required to support this goal.

SWAT teams (teams for providing extra support to the "students who wannabe achievers too") are organized to respond to the information in these reports. For example, one replication site scheduled a first-period schoolwide reading block. In the early progress reports, teachers identified attendance and tardiness problems as the primary reason for students who had not achieved mastery. The SWAT team involved the parent council in seeking a solution to the problem. The parent council provided funds to purchase incentives for students present at the first minute of school. Subsequent progress reports allowed the parent council to assess whether the investment was worthwhile. It was; mastery increased substantially.

Figure 8 illustrates how the data are used in the schoolwide system of support for teachers, which is also initially supported by external coaches who work with both the teachers and the support staff in providing research-based solutions to problems. The focus of all personnel is on enhancing the instructional interaction between teachers and students.

Results of the Replication Efforts of the Reading Component of the BIG Accommodation Model

In Year 3, I established two more training centers, one at Apple Valley Middle School in San Bernadino County and one at Raymond Cree Middle School in Riverside County. Subsequently, both schools more than doubled their target growth rate for the year and were placed on the list to receive the largest monetary awards from the state of California, Certificated Staff Performance Incentives, set originally at up to $25,000 per teacher.

Other training centers were established in northern California through the Sacramento County Office of Education at the following locations: Starr King Middle School, LeRoy Greene Middle School in Sacramento County, and at South Lake Tahoe Middle School. Over 800 teachers in over 50 schools in more than 30 districts were trained in the remedial reading programs. Fewer schools implemented the higher level reading programs.

Of these schools, several used the MAST to evaluate the performance of students placed in the decoding levels of the Corrective Reading program (Engelmann et al., 1999). Table 6 displays a summary of these results for all 11 schools. Instructional methods that are less accommodating of diversity did not raise the performance of students in the lowest ranges of performance, as seen in

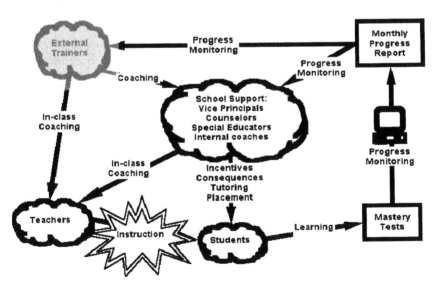

TABLE 6
Change in Literacy Levels of Students Placed in Corrective Reading—Decoding for 11
Schools in California

Schools	No.	Percentage Scoring Below 2nd-Grade Level			Percentage Scoring Above 5th-Grade Level		
		Pre	Post	Change	Pre	Post	Change
Control school	59	56	53	−3	5	14	+9
S1[a]	245	55	31	−24	9	24	+15
S2[b]	59	44	25	−19	10	37	+27
S3[a]	129	44	18	−26	13	33	+20
S4[b]	150	41	15	−26	16	38	+22
S5[a]	282	34	14	−20	20	53	+33
S6[b]	338	34	14	−20	22	55	+33
S7[a]	183	27	13	−14	6	21	+15
S8[b]	82	24	13	−11	20	43	+23
S9[b,c]	110	23	6	−17	20	49	+29
S10[b,c]	558	17	9	−8	42	56	+14
S11[b]	455	14	5	−9	44	61	+17

[a]The period between pre and posttest for these schools is 4 months. [b]The period between pre and posttest for these schools is 8 months. [c]These schools are in their second year of implementation.

the control school in Table 6. Only 3% of the students in the control sample moved out of the second-grade-and-below performance level, where 56% of the sample performed. Schools implementing Corrective Reading (Engelmann et al.), an instructional model designed specifically to raise the performance of all students, were able to move substantial numbers of students out of the lowest performance ranges. Even schools beginning implementation only in the second semester made substantial progress with the students in the lowest performance ranges by the end of the year. Schools in the second year of implementation reduced the percentage of students performing in the lowest range to less than 10% of the sample. These two schools, one of them Goethe Middle School, were both schools with demographic profiles representative of the most troubled schools in America.[1]

External coaches identified schools that implemented components of the BIG Accommodation with fidelity, using an implementation fidelity rubric. These schools were categorized according to whether they implemented only the low-level programs for decoding, or whether they also included an implementation of the higher level reading programs. Table 7 displays these categories in

[1]Color pie charts displaying the results reported in Table 6 in greater detail can be found at www.higherscores.org.

TABLE 7

Summary of SAT9 Performance for BIG Schools, Compared to California Eighth Graders

Grade 8 SAT9 Scores	Number of Schools	Mean SAT9 Percentile[a]: Pre (1999)	Mean SAT9 Percentile[a]: Post (2000)	Change in Mean	Percentage of Schools in Quartile 1: Pre (1999)	Percentage of Schools in Quartile 1: Post (2000)	Percentage up to Quartile 2
Full BIG[b]	1	21	35	14	58	39	19
Schoolwide BIG reading[c]	7	32	40	8	47	37	10
Partial BIG[d]	21	49	55	6	27	20	7
California eighth graders[e]		43	47	4	33	27	6

Note. SAT9 = Stanford Achievement test–Ninth Edition.

[a]Percentiles of the mean raw scores provided on the California Department of Education web site for each school. [b]Full BIG: All programs implemented, including *Understanding U.S. History* (Carnine, Crawford, Harniss, & Hollenbeck, 1998) and *Expressive Writing 2* (Engelmann & Silbert, 1983). [c]Schoolwide BIG Reading: Schools tested all students for placement in a reading program, Corrective Reading, (Engelmann et al., 1999); "decoding" and "comprehension" and Reasoning and Writing (Engelmann & Grossen, 2001a, 2001b), as in the Goethe Project. [d]Partial BIG: Schools selected students scoring below the 25th or 35th percentile in reading, and placed only those students in corrective reading (Engelmann et al., 1999; "decoding"), the remedial component of BIG. [e]California: Percentiles for the mean raw scores of all the Grade-8 students in California (www.cde.ca.gov).

the left column. For each of these categories of schools, the percentages of students performing in each quartile of the SAT9 were collected from the California state Web page (www.cde.ca.gov). Table 7 displays the changes in mean scores and the movement out of the bottom quartile for these schools.

No schools have replicated the entire BIG Accommodation model. The bigger gain in performance for schools implementing the higher level reading programs in addition to the lower level programs was consistent with the earlier analysis that the higher level programs contribute more to gains on standardized test scores, although learning gains for the lower level programs are important and significant.

DISCUSSION: THE WORK CONTINUES

Two significant achievements of the Goethe Research Project were the development of a training model that results in consistently high levels of success across implementations, and evidence that the newer generation DI programs have been very effective in significantly raising the performance of students performing at or near grade level.

Implementing the BIG Accommodation with fidelity in low-achieving schools is a challenging task. The concept of building a BIG Beacon school, which provides a model of a high-quality implementation and serves as a training site, seems clearly the most resource-efficient way to expand. I am working to develop BIG Beacons in Florida, Kansas, and Hawaii. The work continues in California as well.[2]

REFERENCES

Carnine, D. (1994). The BIG Accommodation program. *Educational Leadership 51*(6), 87–88.

Carnine, D., Caros, J., Crawford, D., Hollenbeck, K., & Harniss, M. (1996). Designing effective U.S. history curricula for all students. In J. Brophy (Ed.), *Sixth handbook on research on teaching: Vol. 6. Advances in research on teaching* (pp. 207–256). Greenwich, CT: JAI.

Carnine, D., Crawford, D., Harniss, M., & Hollenbeck, K. (1998). *Understanding U.S. history.* Eugene: University of Oregon.

Caros, J. (2001). *Emerald ice: Fourth-dimension database.* Vancouver, BC: Seira.

Collins, M., & Carnine, D. (1988). Evaluating the field test revision process by comparing two versions of a reasoning skills CAI program. *Journal of Learning Disabilities, 21,* 375–379.

Coulter, G. (1997). *An examination of the effectiveness of in-class instructive feedback and afterclass instructive feedback for teachers learning specific teaching behaviors.* Eugene: University of Oregon.

Dixon, R., & Engelmann, S. (1999). *Spelling through morphographs.* Blacklick, OH: Science Research Associates.

---

[2]Further information on the available trainings can be found at www.higherscores.org.

Engelmann, S., Carnine, L., Johnson, G., Hanner, S., Meyer, L., & Osborne, S. (1999). *Corrective reading.* Blacklick, OH: Science Research Associates.

Engelmann, S., & Grossen, B. (2001a). *Reasoning and writing: Level E.* Blacklick, OH: Science Research Associates.

Engelmann, S., & Grossen, B. (2001b). *Reasoning and writing: Level F.* Blacklick, OH: Science Research Associates.

Engelmann, S., & Silbert, J. (1983). *Expressive Writing 2.* Blacklick, OH: Science Research Associates.

Grossen, B. (1998). *The research base for corrective reading: SRA.* Blacklick, OH: Science Research Associates.

Grossen, B., & Carnine, D. (1990). Diagraming a logic strategy: Effects on more difficult problem types and transfer. *Learning Disability Quarterly, 13,* 168–182.

Grossen, B., Carnine, D., & Lee, C. (1996). *The effects of instruction designed for diverse learners and constructivist instruction on middle-school students' achievement and problem solving in earth science.* Unpublished manuscript, University of Oregon, Eugene.

Grossen, B., & Ewing, S. (1996). Raising mathematics problem-solving performance: Do the NCTM teaching standards help? (Final report). *Effective School Practices, 13*(2), 79–91.

Grossen, B., & Scott, C. (2000). *A case study of a professional development center model for disseminating direct instruction.* Unpublished manuscript, University of Oregon, Eugene.

Hodgkinson, H. L. (1992). *A demographic look at tomorrow.* Washington, DC: Institute for Educational Leadership, Center for Demographic Policy.

Hofmeister, A., Engelmann, S., & Carnine, D. (1989). Developing and validating science education videodisks. *Journal of Research in Science Teaching, 26,* 665–677.

Howell, K., Zucker, S., & Morehead, M. (1985). *MAST: Multilevel Academic Survey Test.* San Antonio, TX: Psychological Corporation.

Joyce, B., & Showers, B. (1995). *Student achievement through staff development: Fundamentals of school renewal.* New York: Longman.

Kameenui, E., & Carnine, D. (2001). *Effective teaching strategies that accommodate diverse learners.* Columbus, OH: Merrill.

Lindman, E. (1968). *Net-shift analysis for comparing distributions of test scores.* Los Angeles, CA: University of California, Center for the Study of Evaluation of Instructional Programs.

Moore, L., & Carnine, D. (1989). Evaluating curriculum design in the context of active teaching. *Remedial and Special Education, 10*(4), 28–37.

Niedelman, M. (1992). Problem solving and transfer. In D. Carnine & E. Kameenui (Eds.), *Higher order thinking: Designing curriculum for mainstreamed students* (pp. 137–156). Austin, TX: PRO-ED.

Palfremen, J. (1997). *Goethe: The middle school that could* [Videotape]. Boston: Palfremen Film Group.

Schneps, M. H. (Director/ Producer). (1987). *A private universe* [Motion picture]. Boston: Harvard University and Smithsonian Institute.

Systems Impact Incorporated. (1987). *Earth science.* St. Louis, MO: Phoenix Film.

Woodward, J. (1994). Effects of curriculum discourse style on eighth graders' recall and problem solving in earth science. *The Elementary School Journal, 94,* 299–314.

Woodward, J., Carnine, D., & Gersten, R. (1988). Teaching problem solving through computer simulations. *American Educational Research Journal, 25*(1), 72–86.

Woodward, J., & Noell, J. (1992). Science instruction at the secondary level: Implications for students with learning disabilities. In D. Carnine & E. Kameenui (Eds.), *Higher order thinking: Designing curriculum for mainstreamed students* (pp. 39–58). Austin, TX: PRO-ED.

JOURNAL OF EDUCATION FOR STUDENTS PLACED AT RISK, 7(2), 265–271

COMMENTARIES

Commentary

Jerry Silbert
University of Oregon

Two important questions are addressed in this issue. What is the potential of the Direct Instruction (DI) model to improve reading comprehension of children in high poverty schools, and under what conditions will the DI model produce maximum gains in reading comprehension?

Before beginning a discussion on the potential of the DI model to improve students' reading comprehension, it is important to first define what constitutes the DI model. Unlike some instructional models that are only implemented under the auspices of specific organizations, a number of schools and different organizations identify themselves as implementing DI. What these schools and organizations have in common is the use of DI curriculum materials authored by Siegfried Engelmann of the University of Oregon. Over the past 30 years, Engelmann has been the senior author of almost 50 instructional programs referred to as DI programs, including DISTAR Reading, Language and Math, Reading Mastery, Horizons, Corrective Reading, Spelling Mastery, Expressive Writing, Reasoning and Writing, and Connecting Math Concepts. The Berkeley article in this special issue explains the uniqueness of these DI curriculum materials in serving as an effective tool for those working with at-risk children.

The use of the DI curriculum materials constitutes only a part of what Engelmann had in mind when he developed the DI model, however. The DI model Engelmann (1988) created is a comprehensive implementation model that includes the following:

Requests for reprints should be sent to Jerry Silbert, University of Oregon, 805 Lincoln Street, Eugene, OR 97401. E-mail: jsilb24034@aol.com

1. Major emphasis on teaching language and vocabulary concepts beginning in kindergarten and continuing throughout the elementary grades.
2. Flexible grouping based on students' performance.
3. Prioritization of time to support acceleration of learning of basic literacy skills in lower grades.
4. Intensive ongoing professional development focused on classroom performance of teachers and students.
5. Data-driven management with frequent and systematic monitoring of student performance.
6. Performance-oriented management in which senior personnel monitor performance of all elements of implementations and respond with solutions whenever student learning give indications of not being at desired levels.

The DI model was developed as part of the federally sponsored Follow Through Project that was, and remains, the largest experimental study of the effectiveness of various philosophies in teaching low-income children in the primary grades. The University of Oregon DI model was one of 15 models in the Follow Through Project, which provided the opportunity for advocates of various philosophies to try out their ideas in the classrooms. The University of Oregon DI model produced the highest levels of performance in all academic areas and, to the surprise of many, the highest gains in several measures of self-concept.

Even though the DI model produced the highest reading comprehension scores among all the instructional models, Engelmann and his colleagues (Becker, 1977) were concerned that students were still not at the desired levels. A number of steps were proposed, including more systematic vocabulary instruction, more instruction on reasoning skills, and expanded comprehension instruction in the intermediate grades.

Unfortunately, the DI model developers were not given a chance to build on what they had achieved during the Follow Through Project. Despite the Follow Through Project's findings that more structured systematic instruction had produced higher levels of student achievement, education embraced the constructivist orientation of some of the other instructional models. New guidelines of curriculum organizations and state and district curriculum departments made it virtually impossible to systematically implement DI in a district. Just a handful of schools around the nation, usually led by maverick principals, continued intensive implementations of DI.[1]

After more than 1 decade, during which the use of DI decreased in regular education classes, several events in the 1990s prompted a rebirth of the use of DI. One such event in the early 1990s was the featuring of Wesley School in Houston on an

---

[1]See Carnine's (2000) article, "Why Education Experts Resist Effective Practices," available online at www.edexcellence.net/library/carnine.html

episode of ABC's *Prime Time Live*. Wesley School, which began using DI in the late 1970s, had continued to use DI despite district discouragement and continued to consistently produce impressive levels of achievement. Since the *Prime Time Live* show, a stream of visitors numbering in the thousands from around the country have visited Wesley. A number of these visits resulted in schools adopting DI. In addition, the publication of several reports in the late 1990s identifying the DI model as one of the few models with significant research evidence for improving student performance in high-poverty schools led to further use of DI.

Although the developers of the DI model were pleased at the renewed acceptance of DI, the last half of the 1990s was also a time of frustration. Many schools and districts that purchased the DI curriculum materials did not incorporate the other components of the DI model needed to maximize student achievement. For example, a number of schools purchased the DI reading programs, but did not implement the DI language programs that the developers see as a critical element of preparing students for more advanced comprehension in later grades. Most districts have provided only a fraction of the professional development that the DI developers had provided during the Follow Through Project. Few schools have incorporated the data-driven management system.

Still, there have been some very encouraging achievements. Berkeley's (2002/this issue) description of City Springs Elementary School in Baltimore presents strong evidence about the extent of gains that can be achieved with DI. As Berkeley pointed out in her article, the implementation of DI at City Springs was the most congruent of all the schools in the Baltimore DI project with the guidelines of the DI model. Improvement in test scores occurred each year. The improvements shown in the 2001 test scores for City Springs were especially significant. The fifth-grade class, which included the first group of fifth graders to have gone through 5 years of high-level implementation of the DI model as a whole, scored significantly above the national average. In addition, the test scores throughout all grades of the school have improved dramatically, raising City Springs from one of the lowest performing schools in the city 5 years ago to a school now in the top quartile of schools.

City Springs was one of the six schools included in the evaluation project reported on in this issue by Mac Iver and Kemper. Their report analyzes the achievement outcomes of the first 4 years on DI implemented in six Baltimore city public schools. In presenting the data on children who began DI in kindergarten in the six schools, Mac Iver and Kemper showed statistics that indicate children whose average performance in kindergarten at the beginning of the project was at the 19th percentile on the Peabody Picture Vocabulary Test, were by the end of third grade performing on average at the 49th percentile on the Comprehensive Test of Basic Skills–Fifth Edition reading comprehension test.

Mac Iver and Kemper (2002/this issue) pointed out that the control group, students from comparable schools who had been in the same school for 4 years, also produced similarly impressive gains. An interesting statistic is the difference in retention rates. The retention rate in the control schools (32 of 156 students, 20.5%) was much higher than the retention rate in the DI schools (9 of 205 students, 4.4%). Monitoring the gains made by children who were retained in the control schools and the performance of comparable students in the DI schools over the next years may provide important information on alternatives to retention.

The articles by Berkeley (2002/this issue) and Mac Iver and Kemper (2002/this issue) include discussions of what constitutes fidelity to implementing the DI model. Just like a relay team in a race, for the DI model to produce desired levels of student performance, all the components of the model must be well implemented. For example, in kindergarten, the expectation of the developers is to have a very high proportion of children complete and master the first level of the Reading Mastery program. For children who enter school with significant deficiencies in literacy skills, reaching the desired level will take both morning and afternoon reading periods. If this amount of time is not provided, even though many components are being well implemented, children will not reach desired benchmark levels. The Mac Iver and Kemper article tells of the number of years it took to get the kindergarten program fully in place, as many schools had only half-day kindergarten classes when the project began. By the fourth year of the project, virtually all schools had full-day kindergarten classes, and many were implementing both morning and afternoon reading periods. The benefits of this level of implementation can be seen in Baltimore City Public Schools reports on student performance for the 2000–2001 school year, the first year that children from fully implemented DI kindergarten classes were in first grade. Twelve of the 17 DI schools in the Baltimore City Public Schools DI area during the 2000–2001 school year had first-grade scores at or above the 65th percentile. Four of the 17 schools had median scores between the 48th and 60th percentile. Only 1 school scored significantly below grade level, on average. Seven of these schools improved over 20 points from the 1999–2000 school year.

Evidence about the relation between how well DI is implemented and student achievement gains is dramatically illustrated in City Springs. The relation between student achievement and fidelity of implementation is shown in the article about the RITE project (Carlson & Francis, 2002/this issue). RITE, an acronym for Rodeo Institute for Teacher Excellence, is supported by the Houston Livestock Show and Rodeo Foundation. The RITE project began with six schools during the 1997–1998 school year, and now supports the implementation of DI reading and language programs in Grades K–2 in 20 Houston Independent School District schools that serve high-minority populations. The project is led by Thaddeus Lott, former principal of Wesley School.

The RITE project implements many of the components of the DI model in a manner highly congruent with the system that Engelmann (1988) developed. RITE (a) places a focus on high-quality implementation in kindergarten; (b) provides a high quantity and quality of in-class coaching; (c) monitors students' performance systematically; (d) prioritizes the use of time for reading instruction in the lower grades; and (e) provides overall management in which all components of the implementation are monitored for effectiveness, and actions are implemented in a timely manner to deal with problems which are limiting students' progress.

Data from the RITE project for the 2000–2001 school year are very impressive. In examining the performance of children in second grade on the reading comprehension component of the Stanford Achievement Test–Ninth Edition (SAT9), we see very strong positive effects: Children with 3 years in the RITE DI program by the end of second grade (i.e., children beginning RITE in kindergarten and continuing through second grade) performed at average levels that exceeded those of their peers in comparison groups, as well as national norms. Significantly fewer children with 3 years in the RITE program scored below the 25th percentile, and significantly more performed above the 50th percentile on the SAT9 reading skills test. Specifically, only 12% of these children performed below the 25th percentile, whereas 66% of these children scored above the 50th percentile on the SAT9 reading comprehension test. In contrast, 32% of comparison school children scored below the 25th percentile, whereas only 39% scored above the 50th percentile.

The article on the RITE project goes on to present evidence of the relations among the provision of training services to teachers, the extent to which teachers implement procedures as specified, and the level of student performance (Carlson & Francis, 2002/this issue).

Analyses of teacher observation and intervention data indicated that the more intervention provided to a teacher, the more improvement there was in the observed teaching skills (behavior management and teacher corrections). Furthermore, successful implementation of the more advanced teaching techniques required by the RITE program was significantly related to students' performance. Teachers who showed higher levels of implementation all year or part of the year had students who were performing at significantly higher skill levels than teachers who showed low levels of implementation all year. These findings are important in that they close the trainer–teacher–student feedback loop by showing that teacher behavior relates to student performance.

The reports on the implementations in Broward County and Fort Worth present situations that are very different from those in Baltimore and Houston in regard to level of implementation of components of the DI model (Ligas, 2002/this issue; O'Brien & Ware, 2002/this issue).

Broward County was the first large district in the nation in the 1990s to systematically support the implementation of DI as the main reading program in multiple schools. When Broward County began implementation in 1994, there was still significant resistance to structured reading instruction in kindergarten. Therefore, the first years of the implementation did not include high levels of implementation of the DI model in kindergarten. As shown by data from Houston, a high level of implementation in kindergarten is critical to significantly improved test scores in later grades. Another factor to be considered in Broward is the allocation of more coaching resources and administrative focus to the upper elementary grades than to the lower elementary grades. The article by Ligas (2002/this issue) on Broward County pointed out that alliance coaches spent only 20% to 30% of their time in the primary grades. It is understandable that a district would provide more resources to the grades on which accountability provisions were forthcoming.

Fort Worth began implementing DI during the 1998–1999 school year. Prior to that time, most of the reading instruction in the district had been based on whole language. Because few of the persons assigned to provide support to schools had a background with DI, almost all of the coaching for teachers was provided by outside consultants during the first 2 years. Although the publisher and district officials worked hard to provide more than customary amounts of training, the level of coaching provided was less than one fifth of what DI developers recommend.

The article by Bonita Grossen (2002/this issue) dealt with the use of DI curriculum for children who did not learn sufficient literacy skills in the primary grades. In a number of middle schools serving low-income students, Grossen found over one half of the children reading at or below a fourth-grade level. Grossen presented some encouraging data on accelerated progress achieved with these children. She also reported on improved achievement for middle school students who began the school year performing near, at, or above grade level and who were placed in higher level DI programs. It is important, though, to keep in mind that the higher level reasoning and social studies programs that Grossen used in the model for middle school and which are resulting in increased achievement are also part of the elementary grade DI model being used at City Springs.

In summary, the articles in this issue provide us with evidence that the DI model does improve student reading comprehension when implemented with high fidelity. The question of the full potential of the DI model to improve student performance when children are in DI for their elementary career is not yet answered. The articles on the RITE project and City Springs provide an indication that the potential achievement gains may be very significant. What is clearer, though, is that these gains will not be achieved without high levels of implementation of the model.

REFERENCES

Becker, W. C. (1977). Teaching reading and language to the disadvantaged—What we have learned from field research. *Harvard Educational Review, 47*, 518–543.

Berkeley, M. (2002/this issue). The importance and difficulty of disciplined adherence to the educational reform model. *Journal of Education For Students Placed At Risk, 7*, 221–239.

Carlson, C. D., & Francis, D. J. (2002/this issue). Increasing the reading achievement of at-risk children through direct instruction: Evaluation of the Rodeo Institute for Teacher Excellence. *Journal of Education For Students Placed At Risk, 7,* 141–166.

Carnine, D. W. (2000). *Why education experts resist effective practices.* Retrieved from http://www.edexcellence.net/library/carnine.html

Englemann, S., Becker, W., Carnine, D., & Gersten, R. (1988). The Direct Instruction Follow Through model: Design and outcomes. *Education & Treatment of Children, 11*(4), 303–317.

Grossen, B. J. (2002/this issue). The BIG Accommodation model: The direct instruction model for secondary schools. *Journal of Education For Students Placed At Risk, 7,* 241–263.

Ligas, M. R. (2002/this issue). Evaluation of Broward County alliance of quality schools project. *Journal of Education For Students Placed At Risk, 7,* 117–139.

Mac Iver, M. A., & Kemper, E. (2002/this issue). The impact of direct instruction on elementary students' reading achievement in an urban school district. *Journal of Education For Students Placed At Risk, 7,* 197–220.

O'Brien, D. M., & Ware, A. M. (2002/this issue). Implementing research-based reading programs in the Fort Worth independent school district. *Journal of Education For Students Placed At Risk, 7,* 167–195.

Helping Students From Low-Income Homes Read at Grade Level

Barak Rosenshine

College of Education
University of Illinois, Urbana

Since 1963, a great deal of time, money, and effort has been devoted to closing the gap in reading scores and bringing children who are on free and reduced lunch (FRL) to grade level on standardized tests at Grades 3 and above. To date, we have not been very successful. There have only been a few schools with 70% or more of FRL students and where the students are reading at grade level, at the end of third grade, on a standardized test. A report by the Heritage Foundation (Carter, 2000) listed 15 successful neighborhood, low-income public schools that have reached this goal. A report by the Dana Foundation (The Charles A. Dana Center, 1999) listed another three. In preparation for this article, I asked the direct instruction (DI) personnel for the names of DI schools that met these criteria. Outside of the studies in this issue, the DI personnel were only able to supply the names of 8 schools.

There are two repeats on the aforementioned lists, leaving a total of about 25 schools. That is a large enough list to show that this goal can be achieved, but the small number of schools also shows that this goal is not reached very often.

Many of the schools on the lists developed their own programs by using and adapting existing materials and by adding additional components such as science fairs and extensive outside reading. The other approach is to adopt a program such as Reading Mastery (RM), Open Court (OC), Success for All, or Exemplary Centers for Reading Instruction. Some of the schools on the Heritage Foundation and Dana Foundation reports are DI and OC schools, but we do not know how many because these reports are skimpy on instructional details. To date, however, neither approach has been as successful as we would like in bringing FRL students to grade level in third and fourth grade.

Until now, the research on DI or OC has only occurred school by school. The reports here from Broward County, Baltimore City, Fort Worth, and the Texas Ro-

---

Requests for reprints should be sent to Barak Rosenshine, Department of Educational Psychology, College of Education, University of Illinois, Urbana, IL 61801. E-mail: rosenshi@staff.uiuc.edu.

deo Institute for Teacher Excellence (RITE) program represent something extraordinary. For the first time since Project Follow Through there are systematic studies of DI in several districts during the same approximate time period, with the number of involved schools ranging from 6 to more than 30 in a particular district. There was training of teachers, monitoring of teacher implementation, and monitoring of student progress in all the studies. After a time when we only read results for a single school, it is wonderful to see the results for 4 school districts in this issue. Working on the district level allows for much more study of implementation and more complete analysis of the results. Another advantage of the design of this research is that every case was a new start and this enables us to study issues of training, implementation, and teacher turnover.

As I discuss, the reports from the well-done studies of the Fort Worth and RITE programs are incomplete because they only present second-grade scores, and we need standardized test scores in third and fourth grade to assess the effects of any reading program. However, this research is continuing and hopefully, the *Journal of Education for Students Placed At Risk* will publish reports from these four sites as new scores become available.

The act of gathering and publishing such an important set of studies is itself a valuable contribution. The 4 multiyear studies of DI, combined with the 2 multiyear case studies provide an important addition to our knowledge. We owe a special thanks to Martha Mac Iver and Elizabeth Kemper for bringing together this unique set of studies. I had a number of questions as I worked on this article, and I thank Martha Mac Iver for her exceptional help in answering or finding answers to these questions.

THE EFFECTIVENESS OF DIRECT INSTRUCTION

If DI is well implemented, we ask, will children who are eligible for FRL and who stayed with the program since kindergarten be reading at grade level, on a standardized test, at the end of third or fourth grade?

Third or fourth grade is the important criteria because, in the past, investigators have found a drop-off in standardized test scores as FRL students moved from first grade to third and fourth grade. Jeanne Chall (1990) labeled this phenomena "the fourth-grade slump." Standardized tests in reading begin with a focus on decoding in first grade and shift to a focus on reading comprehension in third grade and higher. Therefore, success, for a program with students from poor families, must involve nothing less than helping students read at grade level, on standardized tests, at the end of third grade and higher.

RM is an extremely effective program for teaching decoding to all children. No one disputes this. However, the critical and unanswered question is the effectiveness of RM, or any reading program, for teaching reading comprehension to children from a low-income background.

Unfortunately, three of the four reports in this special issue cannot be used to answer this important question. The reports from the Fort Worth and RITE programs only report standardized test scores in reading for first and second grade. Broward County does have third-grade standardized test scores, but, as discussed later, the variations from school to school were so large that one cannot use the overall results as a test of DI.

The RITE study does present data on the percentage of third graders who passed the Texas Assessment of Academic Skills (TAAS) exam. However, passing the TAAS is not the same as reading at grade level on a standardized test because we do not know the grade-level equivalent, on a standardized test of reading comprehension, for a passing score on the TAAS.

The Baltimore city study is the only one of the four studies in which DI was well implemented and nationally normed student reading achievement scores at the end of third grade were presented. In their Table 2 (Mac Iver & Kemper, 2002/this issue), they show that the mean score for the 171 students, across six DI schools, who began the program in kindergarten and who remained in the program for 4 years is at the 49th percentile. I think this is a wonderful finding, but there were only six DI schools in the study and only four of these six schools were high-poverty schools.

Because of the lack of standardized test data for third grade from Fort Worth and RITE, and the variations in Broward County, we cannot use these reports to help answer this important question. However, these studies are ongoing, and we look forward to future reports from these districts.

Decreasing Scores

An example of the drop-off in reading scores appears in the Fort Worth study (O'Brien & Ware, 2002/this issue). In Table 4 of the Fort Worth report there were drops, from Grade 1 to Grade 2, for reading scores in the entire district. Table 6 shows that the percentage of students at grade level dropped, from Grade 1 to Grade 2, for both OC and RM. For RM, the drop was from 52% in first grade to 45% in second grade, and this figure would probably be lower if it included only FRL students.

The results are similar in the RITE study (Carlson & Francis, 2002/this issue). Table 5 in that article gives the percentage of students above the 50th percentile for first and second grade, for RITE students, by number of years in the program. An impressive 66% of second-grade students are above the 50th percentile, but this is down from 78% in first grade. Similarly, Carlson and Francis noted that there were no significant differences between RITE and comparison students in their achievement score gain in second grade, after controlling for second-grade performance.

Reporting results.   The authors of the RITE study (Carlson & Frances, 2002/this issue) and the authors of the Baltimore city study (Mac Iver & Kemper, 2002/this issue) reported separate results for students by the number of years they were in the DI program, beginning with kindergarten. This is an excellent and necessary practice because it enables us to see scores for students in the optimal setting—students who were with the program since kindergarten. I hope that in future years all studies will report standardized test scores for third- and fourth-grade students grouped by years in the program. We need this specific information to evaluate long-term programs.

Variations in DI

There are variations in the instructional activities that take place in schools that use RM. These variations took two forms: variation in the number of DI components that were used in the school, and variations in the number of non-DI reading activities.

Variations in the number of DI components.   In Baltimore city, as noted in Footnote 7, "Regular implementation of the direct instruction program generally includes 1 ½ hr of reading, 1 hr of language arts, 1 hr of mathematics, and about ½ hr of spelling and handwriting ... " (Mac Iver & Kemper, 2002/this issue). In addition, the DI personnel supervising the Baltimore schools asked them to add an additional 45 min of reading in the afternoon for students who were reading below grade level. This adds up to 3 hr in reading and language arts plus the additional 45 min.

In contrast, according to these reports, the only DI in the Fort Worth and the RITE schools was the 90 min of RM. Therefore, DI time on reading and language arts ranged from 90 min in Fort Worth and RITE to 3 hr or more in Baltimore city.

Non-DI components.   Another variation in DI occurs when schools add additional, but non-DI, reading components to their program. An example of this addition occurs in the Wesley School in Houston, which I have visited.

The Wesley School is rightly hailed as a very effective school for children from low-income families. For many years, mean scores for third-, fourth-, and fifth-grade students at Wesley have been above grade level on standardized tests. However, in addition to RM, the Wesley School has a second reading period where the OC series is used. Therefore, Wesley is an example of a school that added a component to DI, a component that we see has a potent effect by itself.

Broward County schools also added additional, but non-DI, components to their reading program. The Broward County report stated that

It was never intended to use reading mastery as the only instructional tool ... School staffs are encouraged to adapt ... the teaching ... process to students' needs. Schools have the ability to move into additional reading basals as the principal sees fit, based upon data. (Ligas, 2002/this issue, p. 120)

Therefore, as a result of this decision, some schools in Broward County combined RM–Third Edition with a Houghton Mifflin or a McGraw-Hill reader. In addition, all schools had teachers trained in the teaching of Junior Great Books—a program that focuses on inferential questions on authentic literature—and this program was used in many classrooms. Schools also had two computer-assisted reading instruction programs.

Although the studies of Fort Worth and RITE report that the schools used 90 min of RM and no other DI components, we were not told about additional reading activities during the school day. Are the reading and language arts activities in the RITE and Fort Worth schools limited to the 90 min of RM each day? Unfortunately, we do not know.

This use of additional reading components in nominally DI schools makes the interpretation of the DI literature very difficult. Schools with a high percentage of FRL students want to do all they can for their students. Many schools introduce history projects, book fairs, science fairs, and class discussion of novels and other additional reading and writing components. Such additions seem quite appropriate, but these additions make the problem of evaluating DI very difficult.

Because of these variations readers of DI reports do not know which schools are pure DI, which have added components, and what these added components are. When we read that DI is successful, the success might be due to the additional components or to the combinations. Reports on the Wesley School, for example, never mention the additional reading period with the OC reading series. Because of these additional reading activities in schools, it is very important that any research on DI describe all the reading activities that take place during the day.

Instructional Implementation

The RM program demands that teachers implement the program well, and the RITE report has shown an apparent correlation between level of implementation and student achievement on the TAAS. In the Fort Worth, RITE, and Baltimore city studies, there was extensive monitoring of each teacher's instructional procedures, and each study reported a high level of teacher implementation. Such information is essential for evaluating the effectiveness of RM or any instructional program.

The researchers evaluating the Fort Worth and RITE programs developed their own standards for measuring implementation, standards that focused on the correctness of student responses and on teacher responses to student errors. However, apparently researchers in each study had to develop their own implementation measurement tools. I am surprised that after all these years there is no official DI implementation form.

Both Mac Iver and Kemper (2002/this issue) in Baltimore city and O'Brien and Ware (2002/this issue) in Fort Worth attempted to use the number of units mastered as a measure of implementation. This is an excellent idea.

Therefore, there were two approaches to measuring implementation in these studies, a process approach and product approach. I hope to read more about both approaches in future reports.

Three Approaches to Improving Instruction

It appears that schools have used three approaches to attempt to raise student reading comprehension scores. The first, as shown in the Fort Worth, RITE, and Baltimore city programs, is to take a developer's program and ask the developers for guidance in implementing the program. A second approach, as shown by Wesley School in Houston, is to follow the developer's program but add additional components.

Local development.   The third approach is for individual schools to select materials and develop their own program. The Heritage Foundation (Carter, 2000) lists 15 nonselective public schools that serve a high FRL population and where students are reading at grade level in third grade and beyond. Two DI schools are on that list—Wesley School in Houston and Portland Elementary in Portland, Arkansas—but there are also 13 schools in that list that developed their own program. The schools use a variety of reading series. PS 161 in Brooklyn used OC as their reading series but have added many reading activities during the day. When I visited 2 of these schools I learned that the principal and faculty in each school developed their own program, based on existing programs and the school's modifications, and they are continuing to revise their programs.

There are two examples of local development in these reports. The control schools in Baltimore city developed their own programs and some of them had high reading comprehension scores at the end of third grade. In Broward County, the schools began with RM and then, in some schools, made local modifications.

However, local development did not work in the Broward County schools. Table 3 of the Broward County report (Ligas, 2002/this issue) showed that the mean score in reading comprehension at the third-grade level was at the 26th percentile. It is possible that students in 1 or 2 of the approximately 30 alliance schools are reading at grade level, but if that is so, then the scores for the remaining schools are even lower.

Therefore, local development sometimes works and sometimes does not work. It worked in the 13 successful schools identified by the Heritage Foundation. Local development worked in some of the control schools in Baltimore city. However, local development did not work in Broward County.

Ninety Min Versus 3 Hr

There is a fascinating contrast in these reports between the schools in the Fort Worth and RITE programs and the schools in Baltimore city. In all three sites there was extensive teacher training, extensive monitoring of the teachers' instruction, and additional training when necessary. Both studies reported very high levels of implementation.

However, in Fort Worth and RITE, apparently, there was 90 min of RM and no additional DI programs, and in Baltimore city there was more than 3 hr of DI reading, writing, and language arts plus an additional 45 min for students who needed extra time.

We look forward to the third- and fourth-grade standardized test scores for Fort Worth and RITE. Will the teaching of phonics in kindergarten followed by 3 years of only 90 min of RM be sufficient to bring these students to grade level? We eagerly await the results. I am also glad that the OC readers were included in Fort Worth because then we will also have data on the effects of 90 min of that program.

I would hope that the 90-min approach, beginning with a strong phonics program in kindergarten, would be successful because such a success would greatly diminish the burden on teachers and increase the change of helping FRL students everywhere.

The Problem of Outside Demands

The article by Berkeley (2002/this issue) has an important section on the influence of outside demands on practice at the City Springs Elementary School in Baltimore city. As she explained it, all third-, fifth-, and eighth-grade classes in Maryland have to take the criterion reference tests that are part of the Maryland School Performance Assessment Program (MSPAP). There is pressure to raise MSPAP scores because low scores can lead to a school being labeled "reconstitution (takeover) eligible." Because of this pressure, some principals in DI schools spent a week or more preparing students for the MSPAP.

Berkeley (2002/this issue) also pointed out "one of the purposes of the MSPAP is to change classroom practice" by promoting more group-based classroom activities. We do not know how many other states attempt to use the statewide tests to move students toward constructivist-type activities. That pressure does not happen in Texas or Illinois, but the possibility that some statewide tests are used to promote specific classroom practice is worth watching.

The Problem of Teacher Turnover

Berkeley (2002/this issue) and Mac Iver and Kemper (2002/this issue) noted that some teachers left the DI schools because they did not like the structured program. As Berkeley observed, professors of education have taught their students that children can learn almost effortlessly by discovering knowledge on their own, and DI or OC do not fit this romantic ideology.

Berkeley (2002/this issue) and Mac Iver and Kemper (2002/this issue) also noted that initially some teachers left the DI schools because they could not master or did not want to master the specific DI instructional procedures. RM has specific time allotments, prescribed activities, prescribed ways of teaching, and accountability for student mastery and student progress. Some teachers leave the program because they do not like these procedures. These issues are very well illustrated in these articles.

However, despite these problems, Berkeley (2002/this issue) noted that after a few years, teacher turnover in the DI schools in Baltimore was the same as teacher turnover in other Baltimore city schools. This is very good news.

Another reason for turnover in successful schools for FRL students has been the intensive time and energy demands on teachers. The time demands were not discussed in these articles, but the Heritage Foundation reported this problem in some of their 15 neighborhood successful high FRL schools.

Three reasons for teacher turnover, then, may be (a) unwillingness to teach in structured program, (b) the difficulty of learning a specific format, and (c) the amount of time and effort that is demanded. I think the third problem is the most difficult. It may not be possible to maintain a program at a high level if it demands extraordinary work by the teachers—which is why I wish more had been written about teacher turnover and the amount of work required in Fort Worth and RITE. If both RM and OC program can succeed on 90 min a day, then the demands will not be as great as those in the Baltimore schools and, if successful, this approach could more readily be used in other schools. However, this issue of teacher turnover due to intensive demands needs to be discussed further.

Phonics and Comprehension

In Baltimore city, Mac Iver and Kemper (2002/this issue) compared the reading achievement scores for third-grade RM students who had been in the program since kindergarten with the scores of students in similar schools who did not receive RM. Mac Iver and Kemper noted in their Table 2 that in spring 2000, the median reading score for the RM students was at the 49th percentile. In comparison, the students in the control schools were at the 53rd percentile.

Based on these results—where RM and the control schools did equally well—Mac Iver and Kemper (2002/this issue) wrote that if a comparison school had implemented a reading program that systematically presents phonics instruction, then DI "would be hard pressed" to show a significant effect.

I think Mac Iver and Kemper's (2002/this issue) focus on early instruction in phonics is very important. Without question, the first step in helping FRL students read at grade level is a well-designed phonics program in kindergarten and provisions for brining all children to mastery in that program. Systematic phonics should be part of all kindergarten programs for FRL students.

I like the Mac Iver and Kemper (2002/this issue) statement because it allows us to separate the phonics component and the comprehension component of a reading series. The question then becomes the following: If systematic phonics is taught well in kindergarten, then what reading instruction and activities are necessary to bring students to grade level in reading comprehension at the end of third and fourth grade?

Based on this distinction, one might reasonably ask whether the comprehension section of RM is superior in its effects to the comprehension section of OC, and whether either reading series is sufficient to bring these students to grade level in reading comprehension. Hopefully, we will have one answer from Fort Worth in 2 years or so. I like the Fort Worth approach of specifically comparing two reading series. I would hope that such comparisons between reading series could continue in other cities.

If all FRL students master decoding in kindergarten, then it is also possible that other seemingly well-designed reading comprehension programs might also achieve the same results. I have looked at the Houghton Mifflin and the MacMillan/McGraw-Hill series and I am also impressed with the focus on comprehension-monitoring activities and word-Web activities in those series. We wonder how well these series would do if all students were decoding fluently when they entered first grade.

Of course, none of these reading series have worked consistently in the past to bring FRL students to grade level. However, I think we might get clearer answers in the future if we ask how well RM, or OC, or other reading series would work when all the children enter first grade having mastered decoding.

Settings for Instruction

There are three settings for reading comprehension instruction in FRL schools: 90 min, all day, and extended day. I present and describe them in the hope that they will be considered in conducting and discussing future research in this area.

One possibility, as already noted, for teaching reading comprehension, is 90 min of systematic instruction in reading and reading comprehension using a program such as RM and OC. The Heritage Foundation report shows that there was much more work than a 90-min reading session in the successful schools they cite. However, maybe this approach will work when students have mastered decoding in kindergarten. Hopefully, we will have an answer to this question, from Fort Worth and RITE, in 2 years or so.

Another setting is full-day programs such as the DI programs and the control programs in Baltimore city. Many of the schools in the Heritage Foundation report had additional activities beyond the school day. These activities included Saturday School, after-school tutoring programs, additional tutoring during the school day, and summer school programs.

As one moves from 90 min a day to the extended day activities there is a chance to introduce more practice, more support, and more reading activities. Are there additional activities necessary or can strong results be obtained with daily 90 min sessions? We await further research.

Additional Approaches to Bringing FRL Students to Grade Level

Hirsch (2001) wrote about "the reading gap" between middle class and low-income students, a gap that widens as students move from first grade through third and fourth grade. Hirsch believes that this gap is really a "vocabulary deficit" and comes about because the lower class children do not have the broad range of knowledge and language that middle class students have.

One solution to this deficit is extensive reading. The students in the successful schools I visited engaged in a great deal of reading during school and after school. I would expect that similar programs took place in many of the schools in these studies. Unfortunately, these reports do not mention any reading outside of the specific times devoted to RM, OC, and the 3-hr DI program.

Perhaps these programs will succeed more often if the aforementioned elements are augmented with extensive additional reading of literature, science, and history. Perhaps these programs will succeed more often if they are augmented with the structured questioning procedures that are part of Junior Great Books, or augmented with extensive after-school activities. Perhaps there will be gains if schools focus directly on the format of the tests as is done in the test-preparation booklets that now flood schools.

It is wonderful to see these programs in four sites and to read this research. The extent and level of this research is far superior to what we have had in the past. These programs are ongoing, and we await the data from the next 3 years.

REFERENCES

Berkeley, M. (2002/this issue). The importance and difficulty of disciplined adherence to the educational reform model. *Journal of Education for Students Placed At Risk, 7,* 221–239.

Carlson, C. D., & Francis, D. J. (2002/this issue). Increasing the reading achievement of at-risk children through direct instruction: Evaluation of the Rodeo Institute for Teacher Excellence. *Journal of Education for Students Placed At Risk, 7,* 141–166.

Carter, S. C. (2000). *No excuses: Lessons from 21 high poverty schools.* Washington, DC: The Heritage Foundation.

Chall, J. (1990). *The reading crisis: Why poor children fall behind.* Cambridge, MA: Harvard University Press.

The Charles A. Dana Center. (1999). *Hope for urban education: A study of nine high-performing, high poverty, urban elementary schools.* Washington, DC: U.S. Department of Education, Planning and Evaluation Services.

Hirsch, E. D. (2001, May 2). The latest dismal NAEP scores. *Education Week, 20.* Retrieved from http://www.edweek.org/ew/ewstory.cfm?slug=33hirsch.h20&keywords=Hirsch

Ligas, M. R. (2002/this issue). Evaluation of Broward County alliance of quality schools project. *Journal of Education for Students Placed At Risk, 7,* 117–139.

Mac Iver, M. A., & Kemper, E. (2002/this issue). The impact of direct instruction on elementary students' reading achievement in an urban school district. *Journal of Education for Students Placed At Risk, 7,* 197–220.

O'Brien, D. M., & Ware, A. M. (2002/this issue). Implementing research-based reading programs in the Fort Worth independent school district. *Journal of Education for Students Placed At Risk, 7,* 167–195.

JOURNAL OF EDUCATION FOR STUDENTS PLACED AT RISK, 7(2), 285–286

NOTES ON CONTRIBUTORS

MURIEL BERKELEY, the president of the Baltimore Curriculum Project, has taught in elementary schools, middle schools, and universities throughout her career. She studied social science research at Johns Hopkins University, where she earned her doctorate.

COLEEN CARLSON is an assistant research professor of psychology at the Texas Institute for Measurement, Evaluation, and Statistics at the University of Houston. Her research interests include early literacy experiences, reading and language development, and measurement and statistics.

DAVID FRANCIS is a professor of psychology and the Director of the Texas Institute for Measurement, Evaluation, and Statistics at the University of Houston. Dr. Francis is interested in the application of random effects, latent variable, and item response models to problems in psychology, education, and health.

BONITA GROSSEN has researched effective models of instruction for students with disabilities and other low-achieving students, specializing in secondary level, higher-level thinking, and the achievement of rigorous standards.

ELIZABETH KEMPER is an assistant professor in the Department of Educational Research and Leadership at North Carolina State University.

MARIA LIGAS is research specialist with Title I, Research and Evaluation in the Broward County Public Schools, Broward County, Florida.

MARTHA ABELE MAC IVER is an associate research scientist at the Center for Social Organization of Schools at Johns Hopkins University. Her current research includes evaluations of whole school reform programs, school-to-work programs in high schools, and privatization of instructional delivery in urban public schools.

DAN O'BRIEN is associate director of the Texas Schools Project and assistant professor of economics at the University of Texas at Dallas. His research focuses on the determinants of cognitive growth and educational progress for Texas students.

BARAK ROSENSHINE is an emeritus professor of educational psychology at the University of Illinois at Urbana. His major interests are research on classroom instruction and research on cognitive strategies.

JERRY SILBERT used Direct Instruction (DI) programs as a classroom teacher. He is coauthor of two college texts on (DI) and has coauthored several DI programs with Engelmann. He has assisted in DI implementations in numerous schools throughout the country.

ANNE WARE is a senior evaluation specialist assigned to the Fort Worth Independent School District (FWISD) Reading Evaluation and Title I Evaluations.